El Paso del Norte

T

0 50 100 200
Miles

Chihuahua

Galveston

Monterey   Matamoros

M E X I C O

TAMAULIPAS

GULF OF MEXICO

Aguascalientes   St. Luis Potosi
Tampico

Guadalajara   Leon   Guanajuato

Querataro

San Lorenzo

Morelia   MEXICO CITY   Jalapa
Chapultepec
Cuernavaca   Puebla   Vera Cruz
Orizaba

Oaxaca

P A C I F I C   Acapulco
O C E A N

THE TWO MARSHALS

By the Same Author

History

    THE DUKE
    PALMERSTON
    MR. CHURCHILL
    THE SECOND EMPIRE
    THE HUNDRED DAYS
    THE HUNDRED YEARS
    THE HUNDREDTH YEAR

Essays

    IDYLLS OF THE QUEEN
    BONNET AND SHAWL
    THE MISSING MUSE
    THE LIBERATORS
    MEN OF LETTERS
    MEN OF AFFAIRS
    MEN OF WAR
    STILL LIFE

Correspondence

    THE QUEEN AND MR. GLADSTONE
    GLADSTONE AND PALMERSTON

Americana

    THE OTHER AMERICAS
    INDEPENDENCE DAY
    ARGENTINE TANGO
    CONQUISTADOR

A reproduction of the plaque by
F. J. Kormis, specially made for this book.

THE TWO MARSHALS

BAZAINE · PÉTAIN

BY PHILIP GUEDALLA

"Deux spectres ont évoqué le passé."
VERLAINE. *Colloque sentimental.*

NEW YORK · REYNAL & HITCHCOCK

PRINTED IN THE UNITED STATES OF AMERICA
BY THE CORNWALL PRESS, CORNWALL, N. Y.

À toutes les gloires
de la France

"L'ÉTERNEL.

"*Dis a cette pauvre France que je ne lui ai pas encore retiré son mandat, qui est d'étonner le monde par ses volte-face et ses relèvements; j'ai mis en elle le principe de résurrections sans fin. Ses défaillances pourraient être suivies d'étranges explosions d'énergie, et si alors un homme se rencontrait. . . .*"

RENAN. *Le Jour de L'An 1886*

CONTENTS

ILLUSTRATIONS

MAPS

THIS book is more than the story of two French soldiers, although that story is worth telling by reason of the strange inversion of their two careers. For one of them surrendered Metz in 1870 and was sentenced to death, while the other surrendered France in 1940 and was sentenced to become its ruler. The first Marshal was made a scapegoat by his defeated country; and when the second Marshal came to power, the scapegoat was France.

But as the first of them was born a year before the Grande Armée marched to Moscow, when Napoleon was at the zenith, their two careers follow the whole curve of French military power from the height of the First Empire to the depth of Vichy; and the two life-stories unite to form one unbroken picture of the French army for a hundred years.

Some traces of the subject can be found in "The Second Empire," which I have intended for many years to follow with a study of Bazaine. The task is far from simple, since his countrymen have been at pains to efface all traces of his career apart from his court-martial. But a good deal is revealed by patient excavation in unlikely quarters, and the nine volumes of "La Intervencion Francesa en Mexico segun el Archivo del Mariscal Bazaine" (Mexico City, 1907–10) are invaluable for that phase of his career. I have been fortunate enough to acquire a few of his unpublished letters as well as to visit the chief scenes of his activities in Algeria and Mexico.

Marshal Pétain is almost equally elusive, since the literature stimulated by the Vichy Government inevitably errs on the appreciative side. Objectivity is hardly to be looked for in M. Henry Bordeaux's "Images du Maréchal Pétain" (Paris, 1941), and still less in M. Vaucher's hagiography, "Quand le Maréchal Pétain prend son bâton de pélerin"; and General

Laure's massive "Pétain" (Paris, 1941) is not unduly critical. But I have endeavoured to correct this unhealthy tendency by a full study of the relevant material relating to his career in the last war and by such personal enquiries as I have been able to make of individuals familiar with his activities before and after 1918.

A number of small points relating to both Marshals, which could easily have been cleared up by a short trip across the Channel, still remain obscure. But any minor errors into which I may have been led by a temporary inability to make it will, I hope, be corrected at an early date.

P. G.

CHAPTER I

FOREIGN LEGION

Beau chevalier qui partez pour la guerre,
Qu'allez-vous faire
Si loin d'ici?

CHANSON DE BARBERINE.

I

IT WAS the thirteenth of the month. The year had opened on
a world almost at peace. For France was an Empire, and
in 1811 continental Europe lay securely in the strong grasp of
Napoleon. The war was nearly over now. The Emperor's writ
ran from the Baltic to the Adriatic. Lübeck was a French
city, Rome the capital of a French Department; and French
gunners lounged in Marmont's forts above Ragusa. Beyond
Napoleon's advancing frontiers, which had just effaced Dutch
independence by the deposition of his brother Louis, King of
Holland, and the annexation of his kingdom, his brother
Jerome was King of Westphalia, his sister Caroline Queen of
Naples, and his brother Joseph King of Spain. True, the British, with their customary inability to see when they had lost
a war, still maintained themselves precariously in front of
Lisbon; and, to tell the truth, Marshal Masséna seemed to have
some difficulty in penetrating their position in the Lines of
Torres Vedras. But their backs were to the sea; their expedi-
tions practically always ended in evacuations; and when once
they had been disposed of, the continent would be at peace.
This blessing, when it arrived, would be a French peace. For

it was tolerably plain in 1811 that France had conquered Europe. Prussia was a cowed subordinate; Austria, with the memory of Wagram less than two years old, was the dutiful and anxious parent of a young Empress of the French; Russia scarcely stirred behind the northern mists; and the French Empire was supreme in a respectful world.

With the war nearly over and the Emperor in Paris, France was in her pride. All Europe lay in the shadow of the French army, of the incomparable instrument that had struck down two empires at Austerlitz and broken a kingdom in six hours at Jena. Its guns had rumbled into every European capital this side of Moscow under the resentful eyes of Germans, Dutchmen, Spaniards, and Portuguese; and its officers had jingled spurs across the floor of every palace between Potsdam and Madrid. The shakoes of the Line and the tall bearskins of the Guard had marched to victory across the continent behind its undefeated eagles. An unending cavalcade of big Cuirassiers sat their mounts stiffly beneath great helmets with long horse-hair tails or elbowed elegant Hussars in gay sling-jackets furred and braided to distraction. Cuirasses gleamed, plumes nodded, pennons fluttered over Lancer *schapskas*, as the masters of the continent dangled their *sabretaches* or tilted an impressive variety of military headgear; and a subject world was suitably impressed.

The master of them all, a plainer figure in the green and white of the Chasseurs of his own Guard, was at the Tuileries; and when Napoleon was there, Paris was the capital of Europe. A continent's affairs passed through his office, hung for an instant sharply reflected in the bright steel mirror of his mind, and were dismissed with a few words of curt dictation or the scrawl that, increasingly illegible, did duty for an Imperial signature. As 1811 opened, he was concerned impartially with the reorganization of the *Grande Armée* in fifteen divisions, and the problem of diverting American sailors from confiscated ships in Baltic ports to man French vessels, and an enterprising private secretary who had been making money out of the citizens of Hamburg, and coast defences along the Adriatic, demolitions near the Louvre, a little trouble with the Pope, and gunnery experiments at Seville. January went out upon an interesting notion of despatching a French frigate to visit his latest colony of Java; and he was soon instructing the police to keep an eye on a new gaming-house in the Rue Richelieu and to stop its patrons wearing masks to gamble in, and ordering a coastal raid on Lissa, and buying muskets from the Austrians to arm the Poles in case he had to go to war with Russia, and instructing literary men (through the Ministry of Police) to write the history of France without prior payment.

February was a busy month, with an expedition concentrating at Toulon for Sicily, and Soult groping at the gates of Badajoz, and Masséna starving in a brown wilderness of empty villages in front of Lisbon. It was the thirteenth of the month, when Lord Wellington wrote acidly from his headquarters to Beresford about a general who seemed to find it disagreeable to be out in bad weather. Perfectly aware that he commanded the last army of England and that, if it was driven off the continent, the war would follow it to British soil and that he commanded it because (as he wrote) he was Lord Wellington, he rarely spared himself and calculated coolly that his continuance in the Peninsula must eventually transform Buonaparte's whole system and dispel his dream of Empire. That day the Emperor, sublimely unaware, was writing to the King of Spain about new powder-magazines in the park at Madrid and directing the Viceroy of Italy to occupy stray islands in the Adriatic, to say nothing of ordering troop movements in Provence and Brittany, a fresh divisional commander somewhere in the Pyrenees, the discharge of an insolvent tax-collector at Rome, and a new army corps in Central Europe. The last was highly secret, with orders for its ammunition-stores to be built up and a hint of bridging-train in

3

readiness at Danzig. For his mind was ranging eastward now towards the Russian border; and the Corps of Observation of the Elbe shifted its axis to become the Army of Germany, with fifty thousand foot tramping through German towns behind the tricolour and French drums rousing German echoes.

That winter morning in 1811 (it was a Wednesday), French trumpets sounded for the dawn across a sleepy continent. The Tuileries began to stir; curtains were drawn, candles lit, and floors polished, as the palace came to life. The Emperor would be dictating soon. Another day had dawned for Paris, and beyond the palace windows the busy murmur of the city rose again. But as the chilly dawn came through the trees beyond St. Cloud, another palace hardly stirred. The winter light crept silently across its floors, where dust gathered in the long galleries of Versailles. Dim mirrors gave back tarnished gilding; empty terraces watched idle gods recline by empty fountains; and a still perspective drove between the silent alleys of the park toward the colonnade of Trianon that February day in 1811. In the little town beyond the palace and the park a child was born by the name of François-Achille Bazaine. It was the thirteenth of the month.

2

His father, whom the birth certificate described incorrectly as chief engineer of the Department of Seine-et-Oise, had left some time before for Russia. A man of some attainments, Dominique Bazaine was a national prizewinner in mathematics. But a French career failed to attract him, although he had a wife and family in France; and he preferred to serve the Czar. The emigrant applied his engineering knowledge to some purpose, achieved distinction in the public service on the side of architecture and education, and was sometimes credited with designing the defences of Sebastopol, with which Achille was to have some acquaintance. But Dominique saw no more of his family, which he elected to leave in France, together with a slight doubt as to how far his younger son was strictly entitled to bear his father's surname.

The Bazaines came from Lorraine. Indeed, their village lay, by a strange fatality, between the spires of Metz and the bare upland of Gravelotte; and since opportunities at Scy were limited, the latest member of the family was quite correct in subsequent allusions to his humble origin. For in later years he wrote bitterly to his sister (and few men indulge in fiction on the subject of their family when writing to a sister): ". . . *mon origine toute plébéienne et c'est sans doute parce que je sors du rang du People et du Soldat que les jaloux s'acharnent après moi depuis surtout mon élévation à la dignité de Maréchal.*" His mother, Marie-Madeleine Vasseur, maintained the mathematical traditions of the family, since her sister's husband's achievements in this forbidding field positively raised him to the Institute. But there was a higher symmetry about this birth within a mile of the Grand Trianon into a family that came from Metz. For the child lived to see a siege of Metz and a court-martial at Trianon.

But in 1811 Metz was far behind the frontiers of the Empire, and Trianon had no more cares than whether the Emperor and his young Empress would be coming back to stay that summer. For they had spent three weeks there soon after their wedding in the year before. (Napoleon made one of Pompadour's rooms into his library and sat beneath its painted allegories to devise one more solution of the eternal problem of American neutrality.) The winter days slipped by; and February, 1811, passed into March over the small head of Achille Bazaine in his mother's house at Versailles. When he was five weeks old, the Paris guns were booming for another infant; and a happy father at the Tuileries wrote proudly to Vienna that the French Empire had an heir. Besides the Emperor of Austria, who was the baby's grandfather, two kings, a queen, a grand-duchess, and a princess were favoured with the same intelligence under his hand; and when a lonely woman who was once his wife wrote wistfully congratulating him, Napoleon replied to Josephine without affectation that the child had his father's eyes, mouth, and chest and would, it might be hoped, fulfil his destiny. The small Bazaine was just two months old when the Emperor decreed unlimited festivities in honour of the Imperial christening—a state ceremony at Notre Dame, a banquet at the Hôtel de Ville, fireworks, loyal deputations, and the *Te Deum* sung in every corner of the Empire. Then his round resumed; and orders rained once more upon alarmed subordinates about Dutch luggers and new forts and church discipline and a Prefect who had really gone too far in vaccinating nervous citizens, the rising price of salt in Alsace, troop movements in all directions, the theft of six dozen cannon-balls from Bergen-op-Zoom, deficiencies of army clothing (there were only ninety-eight pairs of breeches in one store), and arrangements for a raid by 30,000 men on Ireland in the autumn.

The infant at Versailles had splendid neighbours after midsummer, when the Court came to Trianon. The Emperor was thinking of rebuilding part of the Château, if he could only do as well as Louis XIV. The fountains played; they risked themselves in boats upon the ornamental water; and the King of Rome took airings, suitably escorted, in the grounds. Versailles was growing modish once again. One night there was a play in the small silken theatre where Marie Antoinette had acted to her little world; and afterwards they walked about the garden, which was all illuminated under the summer sky.

In 1811 the Empire rode on the crest. For a brief interval it seemed to hang motionless above the depths. But the tide drew it on. For the war failed to end that year. The British still fought on in Portugal and forced the gates of Spain; the thunder of the guns rolled eastward, as the Russians swept into the game once more, drew off, fought at the gates of

Moscow, and then came on again under the black winter skies of 1812. The war, the never-ending war that had been sending young Frenchmen out to die for twenty years in Germany, Spain, Portugal, Poland, and Russia, was nearer now. It crept towards them across Germany; it passed the Rhine; it gathered on the road to Paris, where Marmont showed them how a Marshal could betray. Then it fell silent, until the drums of 1815 came beating up the road from Elba, and the Emperor sent his last army roaring up a trampled slope in Belgium towards the waiting redcoats. After that the war was over; and before the small Bazaine had his fifth birthday, France returned to count her dead.

3

His mother vanished early from the story. But a kindly Baron Roger, who professed a vague paternal interest, saw to his schooling. Not that Achille's scholastic progress was particularly calculated to gratify a guardian, since after passing through the Pension Barbet-Massin (where he had a dark-eyed schoolfellow named Bourbaki) he failed to follow his elder brother into the École Polytechnique. This fatal entrance examination barred the front-door to a professional career; and the failure rankled all his life. Forty years later, in the stormy evening of his long career, he could still write resentfully of *"les officiers sortis des écoles spéciales."* But the back-door still remained. Nineteen and penniless, he tried his luck as a grocer's boy. Yet though it was the golden age of tradesmen, when *César Birotteau* rose like a rocket, and young *Popinot* married his master's daughter and purveyed a splendid range of hair-restorers to a nation which had just enthroned the very image of M. Joseph Prud'homme in the person of King Louis Philippe, grocery made little of Bazaine. So, with the École Polytechnique closed to him by the examiners and commerce failing to attract, he took the broad path of adventure and one spring day in 1831 enlisted as a private soldier.

The unheroic and exhausted years that followed Waterloo were over now, and French gallantry had found a new theatre. There could be no more rides across the continent behind a small, grey-coated figure, no more marches into conquered capitals with clanging bands and shining eagles. All that was buried in a lonely grave at St. Helena beneath the island willows. But if an armed and watchful world denied them European adventures, there were other scenes and bluer skies. Beyond the southern shores of France the brown bulk of Africa climbed slowly into view; and the July Monarchy surveyed with curiosity the last conquest of the Restoration. France had a foothold, where the white city of Algiers lifted from the sea and Bourmont's men had scrambled ashore with their muskets held high out of the water and a distressing tendency to sing rude songs about their general, because he had deserted to the enemy three days before Waterloo. An epoch of stray fighting followed, opening with impetuous advances and frequently concluding with uncomfortable rearguard actions. For Africa showed little sign of a desire for liberation under the tricolour; and it was clear that if King Louis Philippe wished to succeed the Dey of Algiers, his troops would have to fight for the succession.

That meant that there was something better for French soldiers to look forward to than uneventful days in provincial garrisons; and when Achille Bazaine enlisted, his regiment was on active service overseas. But it was back in France before the year was out, and the recruit began to learn his business on the barrack square. A private in the 37th of the Line, he shouldered a musket, wore the long blue greatcoat and tall shako on which the Citizen King had just replaced the eagle of the Empire with a more blameless fowl, and marched in the red-trousered ranks. In three months he was a corporal; a year later, in 1832, he rose to be a sergeant; and as young

8

Bazaine progressed sedately through the non-commissioned ranks, bells were tolling in Vienna for the pallid youth, whose early promenades had come so close to him under the trees at Versailles. But if the army seemed less difficult than the École Polytechnique, this decorous ascent was not enough. For his regiment was still stationed in France. There was another unit, though, to which the tedium of home service was denied by law. An enterprising youth without parents found it more attractive; and at twenty-one the young sergeant transferred to the Foreign Legion.

4

Romance has many children; but of all—Crusaders, highwaymen, explorers, airmen, duellists—perhaps she loves the Foreign Legion best. A regiment of waifs, a vow of silence on the past and active service in the future are strangely attractive. No questions asked, no quarter given enhance the charm, and it is hardly to be wondered at that novelists, screen-writers, and even poets invariably succumb.

> Our fathers they left us their blessing—
>   They taught us, and groomed us, and crammed;
> But we've shaken the Clubs and the Messes
>   To go and find out and be damned
>   (Dear boys!)
>   To go out and get shot and be damned.

Half exile and half pugilist, the *légionnaire* appeals alike by his weakness and his strength. His visible deficiencies—no home, no family, and (best of all) no name—are fascinating; and when he compensates for any lack of civic virtue by an excess of martial qualities, he is irresistible. The background of a doubtful past, the foreground of the desert rarely fail; and no audience can be expected to spoil its pleasure with the untimely thought that these interesting ne'er-do-wells must be incorporated in a *cadre* of respectable professionals or that it was more than a generation before they ever saw a desert.

The Foreign Legion, when Bazaine joined it in 1832, fell a trifle short of the high standards of its later romance. For one thing, the desert was still a long way off, since French expeditions rarely penetrated far into Africa beyond the coast. Besides, it had not yet occurred to anyone that the Legion was particularly romantic, as it had only just been raised by the most unromantic monarch in French history. When King Louis Philippe deftly substituted himself for the less progressive Bourbons of the elder branch in the swift transformation-scene of the July Revolution, he was confronted with the slight embarrassment of a Swiss Guard. This had been natural enough for the ageing brothers of King Louis XVI, who were his predecessors on the throne of France; but it would never do for their enlightened cousin. Such emblems of the past were out of place in the bourgeois paradise over which he now presided; and the new King of the French promptly disbanded his Swiss regiments. But there was something to be said for retaining these extremely useful fighting men in some less suggestive form. Besides, the latest revolution had attracted quite a number of hopeful foreigners to Paris, whose enthusiasm for the sound of breaking glass was not shared in official circles and could be more usefully employed elsewhere. So hurried legislation conveniently authorised the enlistment of a Foreign Legion for service outside France. That could only mean Algeria; and the small army of occupation was presently supplemented by a new unit consisting of the martial Swiss, together with a fair number of Poles, Germans, Spaniards, and Italians, to whom the French service was more congenial than their own unhappy politics.

This military babel, in the red trousers and blue greatcoat of France, was organised with perfect logic, but poor prospects of regimental discipline, according to its varied races. Each battalion spoke its own language, retained its national prejudices, and looked down accordingly on the remainder of the Legion. Unfriendly to *esprit de corps*, this system was scarcely improved by the inevitable circumstance that desertion from a foreign army had often been the due preliminary of enlistment in the Legion. That formed a poor initiation in obedience; and it was small wonder that commanders viewed these martial Ishmaels with some misgiving, although they were embodied in a strong, unbending *cadre* of French officers and sergeants, and their softer side appeared in an intermittent tendency to cultivate the land.

Their ranks received the addition of a broad young sergeant named Bazaine in 1832, although he saw no active service until the next year. His long musket and big red epaulettes cast a sharper shadow now in the dusty glare of Africa; and he had exchanged the heavy shako of home service, redolent of the Empire and strongly conducive to apoplexy in hot climates, for the tall red *képi* of the Legion. His colonel was a Napoleonic veteran named Bernelle with an explosive temper, which had produced a marked improvement in the Legion's discipline, and a wife who was a feature of its life. Once, it was said, a lady-in-waiting or (as some preferred to think) a humbler member of the household, the colonel's lady exercised a strong ascendancy over both her husband and the formidable unit of which he was in command. One unhappy *légionnaire*, detailed for duty in her garden at Algiers, received fifteen days' imprisonment for the misdemeanor of arriving while she was reposing on a garden-seat in light attire; another incurred penalties for looking irreverently in the direction of her balcony. For a lady could not be too careful with the Foreign Legion, although her predilections were believed in some quarters to account for the high proportion of good-looking officers upon her husband's staff. But though he was a sergeant-major now, such heights were far beyond Bazaine.

The Legion's avocations in 1833 were arduous and varied. The Spanish companies were at Oran, the Belgians in insanitary quarters up the coast at Bona; but the bulk of the regiment was stationed round Algiers, where they alternated between turns of duty in unhealthy outposts and their billets in some native houses on the sunny heights of Mustapha. One hot May morning the King's birthday was duly celebrated by a service in the open air, a brief allocution, and loyal cries of *"Vive le Roi!"* after which the Legion resumed its common round in the ring of fortified posts enclosing the small *hinterland* of Algiers. A fortnight later they were busy harvesting under armed protection. For agriculture out of sight of Algiers was palpably unsafe without a covering force of Zouaves, Chasseurs d'Afrique, and guns. But that year it passed off without accidents; a large native audience assembled to enjoy the unusual spectacle of men at work and hung about their camp to taste the novelties of European diet; and vast quantities of forage for the cavalry were safely carted to the coast and shipped to army stores. The tribes were restless; and a visiting commission, which risked itself as far afield as Blida, twenty-five miles inland, was slightly damped by the murder of a friendly Kaid and an encounter with three decapitated Europeans on its homeward journey. Elsewhere life for the Legion was no less crowded with pleasing incident. The dusty outskirts of Oran, the rocky coast, and lonely blockhouses saw them at work; and in November the young sergeant-major received another grade. For Bazaine was a *sous-lieutenant*. Now he had outflanked the École Polytechnique as, his musket laid aside, Achille became an officer at twenty-two. True, he had risen from the ranks; but that need not prevent him rising further, since there were always opportunities, and the Legion was perpetually on active service.

The next year opened for the Legion with a sweep in the Mitidja, in the course of which they gratified the friendly natives with the transfer of a good deal of their less obliging neighbours' property. A successful *razzia*, in which the

charms of cattle-lifting were combined with military operations, was apt to end in a wholesale redistribution of flocks
and herds, tents, carpets, and other portable possessions; and
the Legion were becoming skilled practitioners in this agreeable form of warfare. But more serious preoccupations were
accumulating round Oran. The situation in that area was
dictated by a handsome and resourceful Arab named Abd-
el-Kader. Son of an influential *marabout*, whose spiritual
authority invested operations with the sanctity of a holy war,
he exercised a growing influence in the western territories on
the confines of Morocco. From his capital at Mascara he
controlled Tlemcen and threatened the French settlements
along the coast; and an arrangement with the local French
commander at Oran seemed to ensure that he would not be
interrupted in the consolidation of a power that would soon
be strong enough to drive them out. After a few skirmishes
of limited success the French garrison was mainly passive.
The Foreign Legion at Oran had been affected by political
developments in Spain, where the prospect of a civil war at
home was more stimulating to Spanish *légionnaires* than an
interminable vista of discomfort under the French flag. A
wise administration having no wish to retain their services
against their will, the Spaniards were shipped home to fight
their fellow-subjects and replaced by Poles. But the newcomers found Oran unrestful, since a local mutiny in another
unit was followed by a bad outbreak of cholera; and in 1834
it seemed extremely doubtful how long Abd-el-Kader would
let them alone. For his ambitions were extending rapidly, and
the ministers of King Louis Philippe appeared to have some
difficulty in making up their minds how far they were
prepared to go in order to retain the conquests of King
Charles X.

Their doubts were hardly likely to be resolved by the new
Governor-General, since Count d'Erlon, who had been indecisive in his prime, was markedly opposed at seventy to pre-

cipitate solutions. Owing his new position to his country's chronic weakness for distinguished soldiers of advanced years, he found its problems no less formidable than those which had confronted him one fatal Friday in 1815, when his command had oscillated all day long between the battlefields of Quatre Bras and Ligny, arrived in time for neither, and thus ensured inadequate results at both. The situation in Algeria was far beyond this veteran. Faced with the growing power of Abd-el-Kader, he simultaneously challenged and conciliated the Emir, who received alternate gifts of French munitions and advice. But it was too late for half-measures, since a fresh victory over a native competitor confirmed Abd-el-Kader's control of the interior in 1835, regaling his delighted followers at Mascara with large quantities of loot and nine camel-loads of human heads. This thundercloud hung over the coast settlements; and when he proposed to victimise two friendly tribes outside Oran, the French commander decided on firm action and gave *sous-lieutenant* Bazaine his first opportunity of taking part in an important operation.

It was just after midsummer, when he marched out of Oran with the Poles and Italians of the Foreign Legion. The little column was two thousand strong, with four squadrons of Chasseurs d'Afrique, a few guns, and some more French infantry. It was a fairly hazardous proceeding, since the march of science had not yet given Europeans that marked superiority of armament which was to render savage warfare in the later Nineteenth Century one-sided and unchivalrous. But in 1835 an Arab with a flintlock was not unfairly matched against a Frenchman armed with a Napoleonic musket. Besides, injudicious presents of French arms and ammunition to Abd-el-Kader had done their best to remedy any inequality; numbers were overwhelmingly on his side; and a deserter from the Foreign Legion obligingly imparted European discipline to his infantry. So there was a strong element of risk, as Trézel's column turned its back on the blue sea beyond Oran and wound its way into the hills.

Abd-el-Kader was waiting for them with six thousand horse and thirteen hundred foot; and this opposition was distinctly formidable for four squadrons and four battalions, encumbered with far too many heavy vehicles. But the first encounter passed off moderately well. The column was attacked in a defile; the Poles were roughly handled; an excited trumpeter sounded the retreat; but the column rallied, and the Italians of the Legion did good service. The heavy transport was a serious embarrassment; but they brought off their wounded and reached the safety of the plain. The night and the next day were quiet. But Abd-el-Kader was watching from the hills; and when the French turned back towards the coast to evacuate their wounded and renew supplies for a fresh effort, he followed unobserved. They marched at dawn; and as the sun climbed in the sky, the little column moved on without incident. But they were shadowed by Abd-ed-Kader; and where their track passed between the foothills and the unpleasant green of a large marsh, they were trapped in the full glare of an African mid-day. The Legion scrambled into action. But the column was surprised. There was a wild stampede, with guns firing, a good deal of shouting, heavy waggons full of wounded bogged in the marsh whilst unheroic drivers cut the trace and galloped off to safety, and scared *légionnaires* bolting for the plain. The screams in rear told them that Abd-el-Kader's men had found the wounded; and three companies of the Line vanished, as someone said, like partridges. Trézel and a few brave men made desperate efforts to retain the semblance of an army. But the column melted into panic; yelling men went mad, stripped themselves naked in the intolerable heat, and went singing, dancing, stumbling through the glare away from the horror of the Macta. The survivors reached the coast that night. But more than a quarter of the little force's strength were killed or wounded; and though they had brought off their guns with one ignominious exception, two waggons now represented all their transport, large quantities of equipment were gone, and the expedition had ended in complete disaster. It was little wonder that Trézel's unhappy fight on the Macta stayed in French memories with the evil notoriety of Hicks Pasha's destruction at El Obeid or Baratieri's at Adowa.

This was a harsh initiation in the realities of war. Bazaine, who had been wounded in the right wrist at the first engagement, was not disabled by this injury from earning Trézel's warm commendation in his despatch for a display of courage and intelligence under trying circumstances—"*le jeune Bazaine a montré une rare bravoure et donne les plus belles espérances par sa capacité et toute sa conduite. Il a été blessé.*" Within a month they made him a lieutenant, and shortly afterwards he was decorated with the Legion of Honour. So a promising career had opened in the ill-omened marshes of the Macta.

5

His next scene of action was in Spain. The melancholy incapacity of Spaniards to settle major issues without killing other Spaniards has produced an intermittent civil war, which recurs at intervals in Spanish history. Its name may vary; but the issues are substantially the same, whether the insurrection is headed by Don Carlos or by General Franco. For the broad question, which still remains unsettled, is whether Spain should move with the times or stand upon the ancient ways; and where less spirited communities resort in such emergencies to the unmanly expedient of an election, the stronger temper of the Peninsula prefers a civil war. In 1835 this took the form of an extremely promising revolt of the northern provinces in favour of Don Carlos under the device of *Dios, Patria y Rey*. Taking the first two for granted, his claim to reign as king was founded on the alleged inability of his elder brother to transmit the crown to a small girl named Isabella; and his own perfect authenticity was attested by the high antiquity of his opinions no less than by the Bourbon-Hapsburg malformation of his lower jaw. Unhappily the throne was occupied by his niece, sustained by her mother, the Queen-Regent Maria Christina; and this lively lady, who relieved her royal widowhood with a secret marriage to a bald, but attractive, guardsman and a morganatic family of four, became the emblem of resistance to his claims. *Cristinos* confronted Carlists in defence of the young Queen against her unattractive uncle; and there was every prospect of a long and indecisive civil war.

But civil wars in Spain are often interesting to other people besides Spaniards. For they have a way of raising issues which concern the world at large; and Europe watched the Spanish controversy with a growing tendency to take a hand. If reaction triumphed with Don Carlos, the result could hardly fail to gratify reactionary politicians at Vienna and St. Petersburg; and Prince Metternich paid the small Queen the unusual compliment of writing that "Queen Isabella" (aged four) "is the Revolution incarnate in its most dangerous form, which Don Carlos stands for the principle of monarchy at grips with pure Revolution." If, on the other hand, the Queen retained her throne, it was quite evident across the Pyrenees that she would be a more congenial neighbour to King Louis Philippe than a strict Legitimist, who would be bound to view him with the disapproval due to a successful revolutionary. France's attitude was plain; and Great Britain's was the same, if not a trifle more so. For starting from the axiom that anything that Metternich might want was wrong, Lord Palmerston proceeded to the same conclusion that an independent Spain was a British interest of the first order. Lying at the western gate of England's seaways, it was highly undesirable that Spain should ever pass under hostile influence;

and that being so, the Spanish civil war had better end without Don Carlos on the winning side—and without leaving the Queen's adherents too grateful to the French. So Palmerston enunciated his belief that "there should be neither an Austrian Spain nor a French Spain, but a Spain which should be Spanish." A similar contingency in Portugal, in which another wicked uncle faced another youthful Queen, had just concluded satisfactorily after a good deal of fighting by British soldiers in unlikely uniforms of Portuguese design. The main thing was to show the right side how to win. True, it was someone else's war; and non-intervention was a sacred principle. But, as Talleyrand observed, non-intervention was "a metaphysical and political term meaning about the same as intervention."

That was how matters stood, when Palmerston deftly united "the constitutional states of the West" in a Quadruple Alliance designed to counterbalance the military monarchies of Central and Eastern Europe and to keep reaction out of Spain. Spanish efforts in this direction had not been conspicuously successful hitherto; and there was nothing for it but to supplement the Queen's resources. The British contribution was to consist of a good deal of moral guidance on the best way to humanise the war by mitigating its increasing savagery and a force recruited largely in his own constituency by Sir George De Lacy Evans. This veteran had served with some distinction in the Peninsula, at New Orleans, and on Picton's staff at Waterloo; and finding that the House of Commons afforded insufficient scope for his detestation of foreign tyrants, he raised a total of 10,000 men to serve the Queen of Spain. Drawn largely from his own political supporters, they were of uneven value for military purposes, because the gallant colonel sat for Westminster, and life in the Metropolis was a poor preparation for the discomforts of a Spanish civil war. Disabled from the start by an urban prejudice in favour of being fed, clothed, and even paid, the friends of progress were not at home in Spain; and the British Legion made no considerable contribution to *Cristino* victory. But the French made a wiser choice for this exacting role, offering the Queen a unit better calculated to stand the strain. For on the very day that Trézel's column reeled back from the panic on the Macta, a quiet room in Paris saw two diplomats sign a document by which France contributed the Foreign Legion.

The Legion, it was hoped, would find congenial employment in Spain. It was a French taunt that Africa begins south of the Pyrenees; and a unit formed in African campaigning might reasonably be expected to perform with credit in a Spanish civil war. Not that there was likely to be anything agreeable about the experience. The scene was picturesque beyond a doubt as Mr. Borrow, savouring its detail, noted in the intervals of leaving Testaments that year in most unlikely places on the orders of the British and Foreign Bible Society. "Hail," he exclaimed, "ye *aguadores* of Asturia! who, in your dress of coarse duffel and leathern skull-caps, are seen seated in hundreds by the fountain sides, upon your empty water-casks, or staggering with them filled to the topmost stories of lofty houses. Hail, ye *caleseros* of Valencia! who, lolling lazily against your vehicles, rasp tobacco for your paper cigars whilst waiting for a fare. Hail to you, beggars of La Mancha! men and women, who, wrapped in coarse blankets, demand charity indifferently at the gate of the palace or the prison. Hail to you, valets from the mountains, *mayordomos* and secretaries from Biscay and Guipuzcoa, *toreros* from Andalusia, *reposteros* from Galicia, shopkeepers from Catalonia! Hail to ye, Castilians, Estremenians, and Aragonese of whatever calling! And lastly, genuine sons of the capital, rabble of Madrid, ye twenty thousand *manolos*, whose terrible knives, on the second morning of May, worked such grim havoc amongst the legions of Murat!"

His invocation might delight the intending traveller. But

soldiers in the Carlist War were likely to learn rather more about the knives than about the picturesque diversity of provincial costumes. Local colour was all very well for English missionaries; but it was highly doubtful how much leisure the Foreign Legion would enjoy for the *mantilla* and the comb. For there was nothing particularly picturesque about a Spanish civil war for the participants. Both sides were developing a disagreeable tendency to kill their prisoners; and the next development was far from reassuring. For when it was rumoured that one faithful Carlist preferred to do so lingeringly with the bayonet in order (it was said) to habituate his troops, untrained presumably by bull-fights, to the sight of blood, an indignant Government devised a simple repartee and shot his mother, to which his filial response was to execute four women. There is a dismal gusto about Spanish civil wars, which foreign intervention rarely mitigates. Indeed, victory is generally found to rest with whichever side commands the largest measure of foreign aid.

French policy in 1835 was plain; and the Foreign Legion was unceremoniously transferred to the Queen-Regent's service. The foreigners were left no option; but French officers were allowed to choose between half-pay and active service in the Carlist War. They were fairly evenly divided on the choice, and there was a little trouble at Algiers. But the Legion sailed for Majorca, followed by the contingent from Oran. Bazaine was with the latter; and in case they were overcome by second thoughts before the transports left for Spain, nobody was allowed to go ashore at Algiers. Then the white houses slipped into the mist behind them, and they headed for the open sea. Blue August skies above, blue sea below, Bazaine at twenty-four was sailing for a country he had never seen to serve a cause in which he was not greatly interested. But he was still on active service with the Legion; and the young sergeant who had come from France was a lieutenant now.

The whole flotilla met at Palma and sailed on to Spain. Soon Tarragona stood up from the sea, and they saw the little houses huddled inside the great walls, Phœnician below and Roman above, beneath succeeding layers of Arab work and Christian architecture. Small figures on the quay were shouting *"Viva la libertad!"* On the next day they marched ashore, the Legion's band with consummate tact playing Riego's Hymn, the anthem of Spanish Liberalism. When they were challenged at the city gate, the guard turned out, as someone at the head of the column answered, "Spain: the Foreign Legion." Then they were marching up a narrow street with everybody cheering; and as the Legion swung four thousand strong into Tarragona, the crowd roared, *"Vivan los Extranjeros! Vivan los Argelinos!"* into the tanned faces of the men from Algiers. This was better than the back alleys of Oran or the marshes of the Macta.

They were still commanded by Bernelle, who was now a Spanish general. Madame Bernelle accompanied her husband to the seat of war; and his strong family feeling was attested by the presence on the Legion's strength of no less than five male relations bearing his name, including a veteran of Waterloo whose military value was impaired by chronic skin trouble as well as by excessive bulk. Harsh regimental critics might deplore this rush of Bernelles to the colours and the competition of so many relatives of their commanding officer for the limited supply of commissions and decorations. But the colonel had a shrewd sense of what the situation called for. Spaniards were impressed by a *caudillo;* and Bernelle did his best to look like one by means of an impressive staff and a highly decorative escort of bearded Pioneers. The Legion was reorganised on sounder lines than those provided by its existing division into one Italian, one Belgian, one Polish, and three German battalions. These were now fused in six mixed battalions with a hope that something might emerge which spoke one language and was more like a single unit. The experiment succeeded, and the Carlist War transformed the Foreign Legion.

This was more satisfactory employment than long fatigues under a baking sun in Africa. The population was a little scared of them at first, as Carlist clerics dwelt with eloquence on their depravity. But Spanish girls were bold, and there was a good deal to be said for Spanish wine. A common thirst united them, and a common feeling that the *légionnaires* were a band of exiles fighting against tyranny abroad for the eventual triumph of liberty at home. This sentiment found eloquent expression in their marching-song, composed by a literary sergeant-major. Its prosody was poor; but they knew the tune, and there have been worse anthems than the *Chant de la légion française en Espagne*:

> *Nobles proscrits, ennemis de tyrans,*
> *Réfugiés de tous les points du monde;*
> *La liberté vous ouvre d'autres champs,*
> *Où le canon d'un peuple libre gronde.*
> *Son bruit, par l'orage emporté,*
> *Ebranle la vieille Ibérie.*
> *Combattez pour la liberté,*
> *Vous reverrez votre patrie.*

Later verses dealt in some detail with the white eagle and the Virgin of the Poles, the rising hopes of Italy, and the prospects of freedom in the Rhineland; and as they sang it along dusty Spanish roads, the Legion found themselves. They were no longer a miscellany of aliens, but the soldiers of a cause:

> *Quand l'univers connaîtra tes soldats,*
> *Tu dois enfin cesser d'être étrangère;*
> *Tes fils auront droit de cité*
> *Sur une terre rajeunie;*
> *Tous les peuples en liberté*
> *Leur offriront une patrie.*

Bazaine eventually found himself with the local rank of captain commanding the *voltigeurs* of the 5th Battalion. Both his subalterns were French; but the battalion was commanded by a taciturn Italian, who was a survivor of the retreat from Moscow and may be presumed to have lost his native loquacity in that experience.

Their arrival on the scene was greeted by a harsh announcement from Don Carlos that his troops did not propose to give any foreigners the benefit of the Eliot Convention, by which the well-meaning efforts of British diplomacy had just induced both sides to conform, in theory at least, to the usages of civilised warfare. This was not reassuring; and when a Carlist column from the north made its way towards them across Aragon, they had their first taste of operations. Moving up-country into the bare hills that bar the road to Catalonia, they were scattered over a large area in small detachments. But the red-caps from Navarre were not quite so formidable as they looked; and Bazaine, with a single company, held out for some days in a little town on the Segre against three thousand of Guergué's Navarrese. Eventually he was relieved by two companies of the Legion commanded by a cheerful officer, who had once served in the Guard and left it (along with his Parisian creditors) for the Greek army. Bazaine's defence of Pons was mentioned in despatches by Bernelle; but this judicious officer, disliking the Spanish tendency to waste the Legion in small posts all over Catalonia, concentrated them and moved off towards the shadow of the Pyrenees. Now they were in Aragon; and as the days grew colder, columns of the Legion operated in the hills on the edge of Carlist country.

The first days of 1836 saw them marching through the winter weather to Vitoria, warmed by a rousing order of the day alluding eloquently to the Spanish constitution and the *Grande Armée*. They tramped through cheering villages, and shortly after their arrival they took a creditable part in a general attack on the Carlist positions. But though they crowned the heights in front of them, it was hardly possible to hold the ground that they had gained in driving snow; and, freezing and half-starved, they fell back to their starting-point, where the Spanish general resumed his acrimonious dispute with De Lacy Evans, and Bernelle quarrelled with his second-in-command because the latter could not get on with his wife. The rain fell steadily; and the Legion, after a long, uncomfortable march on freezing roads by way of Logroño, reached Pamplona to hold the gates of Navarre against Don Carlos. The Navarrese were unsympathetic. Carlists to a man, they conscientiously shot all their foreign prisoners and displayed some ingenuity in torture and mutilation. There were a number of minor actions, in which their marksmen concentrated on the Legion's officers and helpful voices could be heard directing their fire against the Frenchmen in the big red epaulettes—"*Muchachos, a las charreteras de la legion!*" The wind came singing down the pass from Roncesvalles, and the Legion spent a busy winter watching for the Carlists in their little caps.

As the days lengthened, the interminable war went on in shaggy Pyrenean valleys, and the British minister was still wringing hands over "this cannibal war, these two and a half years of *lèse-humanité*." For there is nothing hurried about civil wars in Spain; and the Legion spent the rest of 1836 in the same sanguinary discomfort. Bernelle's strict discipline irked them a little. But they found it harder to forgive his wife. For this indomitable lady was incurably addicted to their company, riding with them in male costume or driving in the centre of the marching column behind a team of mules with her maid and a personal escort of Pioneers. The Legion was not sensitive; but her commanding airs, unconcealed favouritism, and excessive stinginess were quite unpardonable. She might not be afraid of Carlist bullets. But discipline was not improved by a lady who rode with her husband's staff, especially when its good looks were an unblushing indication of her preferences. The ranks had a good deal to say, and said it audibly in five European languages. Trying but intrepid, she was known in their politer moments as the Princess of Navarre or Queen Isabella III; and her husband's prospects were not improved by this picturesque, but pervasive, Amazon who attained distinction as the only woman who ever shocked the Foreign Legion. Besides, he was as touchy about his own position as most men who listen too much to their womenfolk. He fought the Legion's battles with unsympathetic ministers at home; and when he had made himself a thorough nuisance upon grounds on which he was mostly right, he was replaced. The Legion gave him an emotional send-off, the Poles (whom he had helped to buy a splendid standard for their Lancer squadrons, that was never paid for and got no further than a tradesman's counter in Pamplona) conferring rather touchingly a decoration of their own.

His successor, who had risen from the ranks under the Empire, was less spectacular. A battered hat above a pair of downcast eyes, an ancient uniform, no epaulettes, and lamentable whiskers composed a figure which was not redeemed by a pair of long spurs and a big Turkish scimitar attached loosely to his person by a piece of cord. The Legion was not impressed; and neither was their new commander. A little shocked by the dimensions of Bernelle's staff, he reported acidly that he had never seen so many officers at Napoleon's headquarters as he found in Pamplona. Now the staff was not so large and, perhaps, not quite so handsome. Captain Bazaine, who had risen from the ranks as well, acted for some time as his chief of staff, emerging from the duties of a regimental officer to master the new problems of military administration. The situation was a shade involved, as Spanish civil wars are not so simple as they look. While Don Carlos still maintained the cause of pure reaction, the progressive side was slightly complicated in the summer by a military mutiny which sent a deputation of kneeling sergeants to the Queen-Regent at La Granja and imposed, with unfailing courtesy, a new constitution. This was followed by changes in the high command; and the unenterprising Cordova found a successor in Sarsfield, who was stone deaf, in uncertain health, and mostly sound asleep. It was now a problem of some delicacy to make head against the Carlists without undue concessions to the rising democratic tide. But the Legion's task was simplified by the return of an officer whom they all knew as second-in-command; and shortly afterwards he replaced the mournful veteran who was less familiar with their ways.

A cheery little man from Strasburg, Conrad was capable of easy pleasantries in five languages for the delectation of his mixed command. He had been wounded at Aspern-Essling, Fuentes de Oñoro, and Kulm, and captured at Leipzig. But what really endeared him to the Legion was his failure to get on with Madame Bernelle. Now they had got him back again with his cane and his little cap; and they would follow him anywhere on his white Arab, by which the Spaniards knew 'el bravo del caballo blanco.' He retained Bazaine as his chief of staff; and the fearless little man was the young captain's dream of what a soldier ought to be. Conrad might not know much about strategy, and he was far too good a soldier to question orders, however injudicious, emanating from superior authority. But when he saw the enemy in front of him, he charged. Bazaine had served with him since 1833 in Africa and in the early stages of the war in Spain. The younger man was utterly devoted to his senior; and in the four years that they had been together he came to regard himself as General Conrad's adopted son. Bazaine had never known a father; but if he had one, this was what he wished him to be like. Perhaps he might take after him one day.

The Legion went on fighting without much encouragement in the way of pay, food, or clothing from their Spanish friends. Habituated to discomfort, Spaniards share it ungrudgingly with their allies; and discipline began to suffer. Hungry *légionnaires* grew mutinous in the cold weather of 1837, and there were some desertions. But the dwindling force fought with some credit in the spring on mountain roads over which Wellington had fought before them; and in May Captain Bazaine was handling the staff-work entailed in moving three battalions, two squadrons, and a battery against the Carlists. They scored a small success outside the dull, but ancient, town of Huesca; and when the Legion charged into the smoke behind Conrad on his white horse, young Bazaine was with him. But the Spaniards on their flank were largely passive owing to their general's omission to give them any orders; and when Bazaine eventually found him, he was past giving them by reason of a fatal lance-thrust gallantly sustained while leading a charge of cavalry. True to the traditional ineptitude of the Spanish high command, Iribarren gave the young soldier a perfect lesson in how armies should not be led by disregarding a commander's duty in favour of exciting details and then falling bravely at a point where he should not have been. Returning to the hard-pressed Legion, who were dangerously isolated by their success, Bazaine helped to bring off a shattered remnant which had lost more than a quarter of its strength.

Now they were barely strong enough to make more than one battalion; and their next exploit was disastrous. For a Spanish general with a long record of defeat and a weakness for attacking fortified positions with bands playing launched them incautiously against the Carlists among some olive trees outside a little town in Aragon. Don Carlos was there himself with a considerable force, including his own Foreign Legion. Caught in flank by pure accident rather than design, the *Cristinos* wavered; and in the ensuing fight the two Foreign Legions met. They fought savagely under the trees, shouting to each other in their native French and German before resuming their cold butchery among the olives, Frenchmen and

Germans killing one another in a Spanish cause outside a little Spanish town with a big square church. Conrad was rallying his shaken men with a cap lifted on his cane, when he was shot through the head and dropped at Bazaine's side. The captain rescued his body with some difficulty, as the *légionnaires* streamed off in panic, got it on his horse, and left it safely in a carriage on the Saragossa road. Then he returned to rally the dissolving Legion, of which he took temporary command. Concealing Conrad's death from the disheartened *légionnaires*, Bazaine kept them together, ordered a retreat on Saragossa, worked out the march, arranged their rations, and then turned back to discharge the last duty to his general, handing over the command to a senior captain. He found a carriage for the body and rode beside it with a mounted escort across the strange red wilderness of stone through which the Ebro sweeps past Saragossa. The heat was blinding (it was June), as the dismal little cavalcade headed for the city; and they cast long shadows in the evening light, as they rode over the bridge into Saragossa between the gay, tiled cupolas of the Pilar and the great tower of the Seo. There was a hasty funeral. But the devoted chief of staff arranged a sumptuous memorial service crowded with respectful Spaniards; and a wounded sapper of the Legion undertook to supply a simple, but satisfying, monument.

What was Captain Bazaine to do now? The young man felt unutterably lonely, as Conrad was the only person he had ever cared for, and the general appeared to have adopted him. Now Conrad was dead; and in his bitterness Bazaine vowed that he would never fasten his affections upon any other man. There was little prospect for him in the Legion, since the grey olives of Barbastro had been fatal to both Foreign Legions. The Carlist Legion never fought again; and the French *légionnaires* were an unhappy remnant of eight hundred men on the edge of mutiny. Referring with some eloquence to his exertions, constant risks, and sleepless nights, he applied for a transfer to his "*chère patrie*," where the slight experience he had acquired in Spain might be employed. But a tactful colonel, who served as French commissioner at *Cristino* headquarters, assured the orphan that he was Conrad's noblest legacy. This stirred his pride; and when the discreet Senilhes asked the young man to take charge of his office at Pamplona whilst he went on leave, Bazaine accepted with alacrity. After all, he had his way to make; and this was more interesting than regimental duty. Soon Bazaine was writing him with eager regularity six times a week, and Senilhes was the recipient of that unlimited devotion which Conrad was no longer there to enjoy.

The situation at Pamplona was uncomfortable, with the Legion in dissolution and the *Cristinos* in a highly explosive state. An uninspiring colonel had replaced their fallen chief; mass desertion across the French frontier was on the increase (a rueful officer, succeeding to this sad inheritance, signed his official communications to the Minister of War, "*Le Lieutenant-Colonel commandant les débris de la légion*"); and when two battalions of Spanish infantry rebelled and took possession of the town, they were faced by the unusual spectacle of a civil war within a civil war. Spanish politics were always complicated; but this was almost too much for the Foreign Legion. While Colonel de Senilhes sipped his water at an adjacent health-resort on the French side of the Pyrenees and subsequently availed himself of the kindly offer of a lift as far as his own residence in Touraine, his youthful deputy in Spain observed developments. Bazaine, a careful student of local politics, reported on the situation with a shrewd appraisal of the strange workings of the Spanish mind. The situation at Pamplona was extremely delicate, and the main thing was to keep the few surviving fragments of the Legion out of trouble. It was plain that French officers would be well-advised to stay outside the stormy town. An order to this effect should, he felt, be put in writing, as this

would cover their new colonel, if anything unfortunate occurred. (Such caution did credit to an officer of twenty-six.)
Bazaine's foresight was grimly justified, when two French
subalterns were murdered in the street; and after this unhappy episode he reported freely on their latest colonel's
deficiencies to his new friend at headquarters.

The cruel war dragged on, and the disintegrating remnant
of the Legion remained a token of French hostility to Don
Carlos. Senilhes had got as far as Paris, saw the King, and
before returning to Pamplona moved the Foreign Minister to
ask the Minister of War to attach Captain Bazaine to his mission at *Cristino* headquarters. His enterprising deputy was
now transferred from the Foreign Legion to the 4th Light
Infantry and followed operations with the French mission.
Whilst a bare three hundred of the Legion passed the later
months of 1837 in dreary billets outside Jaca, he watched the
rise of Espartero, heard the gossip of headquarters, and studied
life among Spanish generals with strong political ambitions.
Since he lived nearer to the fountain of honour, he received a
Spanish decoration early in 1838. But this agreeable phase of
his education was nearly over, as he was warned in May that
he was soon to be recalled. Bazaine was happy where he was
and answered that he would not leave headquarters without
a formal order. If it came, he hoped respectfully (with a tentative allusion to his health) that it might be accompanied by
three months' leave, as he had not seen his country or his
family for six years The order came in June, and the Carlist
War went on for another eighteen months without Bazaine.

His four years in Spain had been most instructive. Campaigning with the Foreign Legion was a many-sided education; and the first lession imparted by it was the supreme need
of personal courage. They led a life of constant danger to an
almost permanent accompaniment of

> The flying bullet down the Pass,
> That whistles clear: 'All flesh is grass.'

Not that courage was enough without other qualities. Their failure to appreciate Madame Bernelle was ample evidence of that. But courage was the first requisite in an officer of the Legion. They would follow Conrad anywhere, because the little cap, the white horse, and the pointing cane went fearlessly before them into a storm of Carlist fire. Any officer who commended himself to Conrad was likely to be quite devoid of fear; and it is worthy of attention that, besides adopting the young man, he employed him as his chief of staff. This unusual compliment from the heroic colonel shows something of the captain's quality. For if Conrad was a man after Bazaine's heart, it seems to follow from their intimacy that Bazaine was all that Conrad felt a young officer should be. But the Alsatian colonel was a sound regimental officer into the bargain with an unusual degree of care for the men under his command, and his staff work was by no means a haphazard business. So Bazaine's apprenticeship comprised a course in military administration and the control of operations, though the force under his control never exceeded six battalions. This education was inspired by his intense devotion to the plucky little man; and Conrad's qualities became his *beau idéal*. The soldier of Bazaine's dreams would do just as he was told without regard to danger and would risk the lives of others as freely and, perhaps, unquestioningly as he had always been prepared to risk his own, if that was what the orders seemed to mean. Such blind obedience led the Legion up the deadly road to Huesca and among the fatal olives of Barbastro, as it subsequently took the Light Brigade to the muzzles of the Russian guns at Balaclava. But it was Conrad's way, and Conrad was his model.

Yet there was more for him to learn from this association than mere gallantry, since a man could hardly lead the Foreign Legion without a watchful eye on his command. Bazaine learned the art of war in a highly temperamental unit, where discipline was anything but automatic and a wise commander

continually kept his finger on the regimental pulse. How
could he be altogether certain of the mixed material under
his command? That uncertainty was something officers
would hardly learn to feel while serving with less flighty
units; and perhaps it never altogether left Bazaine. If the
Legion was to hold together, its solidity depended largely on
its officers, for whom Bazaine inherited from Conrad an exacting standard. This appears in a searching and largely
uncomplimentary report upon them compiled for official
purposes, and attributed to Bazaine. Dating from a period
subsequent to his transfer to the 4th Light Infantry, these
fiches are in his handwriting, and display a considerable turn
of phrase. A devastating candour is the normal idiom of such
documents, which are rarely charitable; but the interest of
this specimen lies in its revelation of Bazaine's dislikes. His
principal *bêtes noires* appear to have been gossips, gamblers,
and alcoholists. He was quick to note the failings of those
who had enjoyed a better education than his own; and a poor
opinion of the arts may be disclosed in his comment on one
subaltern, *"Né pour être artiste et non pour être militaire."*
The writer, who commended bravery ungrudgingly wherever he encountered it, could distinguish between mere
gallantry and real qualities of leadership. Intolerant of cow-
ardice, he put a proper value on the arts of management and
looked for them in vain in many of his former colleagues.
Writing for the information of the Ministry of War, he left
a somewhat discouraging impression of the Legion's present
officers, which the facts might justify, though it could, of
course, be remedied by the return of someone who was now
in the 4th Light Infantry. But there was no suggestion in his
paper of such possibilities, although they might suggest themselves to a discerning reader in the Ministry of War.

His service with the Foreign Legion imparted to Bazaine
its own peculiar lessons; but Spain taught him something
more. For one thing, he learned the language. Four years in

a country where no inhabitant speaks any language but his own is a long time; and it became as natural for Bazaine, writing to a French correspondent about the Legion in decline, to say that it *"se va accabando"* as to find the right French words. He was at home in Spanish company. Both the ladies whom he married afterwards were Spanish-speaking; and when the long adventure closed, he came back to end his days in Spain, dedicating his last word, *Épisodes de la Guerre de 1870 et le Blocus de Metz*, to the Queen whom he had served, when she was six and he was twenty-five, with the humble, the very humble duty of

FRANÇOIS ACHILLE BAZAINE

Ex-fusilier au 37e de ligne,
Ex-officier supérieur au service de l'Espagne,
Ex-Maréchal de France,
Réfugié en Espagne depuis 1874.

But that was in the mists and nearly forty years away, as a young officer began to learn his business in the Carlist War.

It is hardly an ideal training for the military character to graduate in civil war; and as Bazaine interrogated wooden-faced civilians in the foothills of the Pyrenees, he learned that no one can be trusted. For the first condition of survival was a watchful eye over the shoulder, and he was taught by stern experience not to be too impulsive. His situation after Conrad's death enforced the lesson. For young men left alone in a hard world learn to be wary. When the first storm of his grief was over, he had attached himself quite firmly to the French commissioner at Spanish headquarters; and as the attraction was mutual, his last ten months in Spain were passed in a still more instructive atmosphere than regimental life. He learned to study Spanish politics, since politics were indistinguishable from war in an age when democratic non-commissioned officers amended constitutions by the *sargen-tada* of La Granja and generals were apt to be less skilful in the art of war than in the management of a *pronunciamiento*. From this eminence he was a privileged spectator of the rise of General Espartero; and no one at the Queen's headquarters could fail to notice that war was not inseparable from politics. Above all, he learned that it was sometimes better to be cautious, that officers in awkward situations would do well to be covered by a written order. For the world is a hard place, especially for young officers without influence. He had his way to make; but after all that he had learnt in Spain it might be easier to make it.

6

Bazaine would soon be twenty-eight. On leaving Spain his local rank evaporated, and he reverted to the 4th Light Infantry as a lieutenant. But this eclipse was of brief duration; and by the next year he was back in the Foreign Legion with the rank of captain. (Perhaps someone at the Ministry of War had been intelligent enough to draw the obvious conclusion from his report upon its officers.) The Legion still flourished on its native soil in Africa. They had a Prussian colonel now, to say nothing of a captain named Saint-Arnaud with rather wolfish good looks and an unlimited determination to get on. The ranks were still a blend of every European nationality with the Germans in a majority, although the civil war in Spain began to flag and the Legion afforded disappointed Carlists an opportunity to go on fighting somebody.

The military situation remained obscure. For Abd-el-Kader's power was still unbroken in spite of Bugeaud's victory on the Sikkak and the fall of Constantine. But ten years of fighting in Algeria had begun to forge an instrument by which the country might eventually be conquered. A new army was developing in Africa with its own methods and its special aspect. There was a picturesque proliferation of local units, of short-coated Zouaves in their green turbans and

baggy Turkish trousers, of sky-blue Chasseurs d'Afrique
trotting through the dust on little Arab horses alongside the
fluttering burnous and bucket stirrups of the Spahis, and the
dark faces of the marching Turcos. In this new *décor* a
galaxy of rising talent soon replaced the hierarchy of Napoleonic veterans, known to their disrespectful juniors as
'*reliques de l'Empire*,' who were finding war in Africa a
shade bewildering. True, Bugeaud had learnt his methods
against Catalan *guerrillas* in the Peninsula. But the new reputations were Algerian—the dashing Lamoricière and his
Zouaves, the trim Changarnier whose elegance was unimpaired by a *toupet* and maintained by his invariable yellow
gloves, the Roman virtue of Cavaignac, and a younger constellation in which Canrobert, Le Bœuf, and Mac-Mahon
waited for their chance.

For Algeria was now the stage on which a rising officer
could make his way; and in 1840 Bazaine had a further opportunity. Miliana was an uncomfortable outpost in the hills,
from which Abd-el-Kader had just been driven after a sharp
engagement. The Emir left it in ruins and on fire; but the
French occupied the site and left a little garrison twelve
hundred strong consisting of the 3rd Light Infantry, Bazaine's
battalion of the Legion, and five guns. The outlook was
unprepossessing, as the place was far from healthy and isolated in the mountains among hostile tribes. But they were
expected to hold out until another column from Algiers
relieved them, if it managed to get through, at some uncertain
season later in the year. It was now the height of summer,
and their stores were insufficient from the start. The heat
began to tell upon them; and the whole garrison went down
with dysentery and fever, until they could rarely muster
more than a hundred men fit for duty on the walls against
the daily raids of Abd-el-Kader's waiting tribesmen. Men
went mad; a few deserted; the two battalions melted into
one; and in sixteen awful weeks nearly three-quarters of them

died in hospital. The walls were manned by anybody who could stand; they even had a sing-song twice a week. But their hopes gradually faded, until an Italian *légionnaire*, who had graduated in Abd-el-Kader's arsenal, slipped out of Miliana in native dress with a despairing note in cipher. He had seventy miles to cover before the news could reach Algiers. But five weeks later he was back again with word that Changarnier was on his way to their relief. They held on for another fortnight; and when the dapper general appeared with young Mac-Mahon riding behind him, the tricolour still fluttered over Miliana.

Captain Bazaine had survived the siege, and his service earned him a mention. But he had watched (as he was to watch again) an encircled garrison disintegrate and die behind the crumbling walls of Miliana. For Changarnier was only just in time. Almost three-quarters of the garrison were dead; twenty more of the survivors died that night; and out of twelve hundred men who had been left to hold the place no more than sixty were still alive at the year's end. Small wonder France was deeply shocked by the four months' ordeal of Miliana.

Bazaine's reward was a transfer to a new formation in the north of France. French policy in 1840 under M. Thiers was showing an increasing tendency towards bold, Napoleonic gestures. For the spirited historian, inspired by his own writings on the Consulate and Empire, inclined towards his great prototype so far as this was practicable for an elderly civilian in the service of Louis Philippe. This took the form of a bold foreign policy, which set nervous Germans singing *Die Wacht am Rhein* and de Musset retorting angrily,

> "*Nous l'avons eu, votre Rhin allemand!* . . .
> *Où le père a passé, passera bien l'enfant.*"

There was an increase of French armaments; and one symptom was the creation of a large training-camp at St. Omer for the formation of no less than ten battalions of *Chasseurs à pied*. Armed with Minié rifles and equipped with a dark uniform, these new formations attracted quite a galaxy of promising young officers. Young Canrobert was in the 6th, Bazaine was in the 8th, and the 10th was commanded by Mac-Mahon. Their training was severe; they drilled at the double; and as marksmanship, no less than dash, was to be their specialty, there was a shooting-match with prizes offered by the Duc d'Orléans himself. The royal heir was often at the camp with the reminiscent General Marbot in attendance; and when the officers shot for the prince's silver-mounted rifle, it was won by Bazaine. The captain had cut quite a figure in the streets of St. Omer with the Spanish decorations on his uniform. For his cross of Charles III, to say nothing of the military order of St. Ferdinand and the cross of Isabella the Catholic, was more striking than the Legion of Honour; and, of course, he had that too. But on the day he won the shooting-prize they chaired him round the range and drove him in triumph to the town in a decorated army waggon. At the gates of St. Omer a son of Marshal Ney crowned him with oakleaves, whilst everybody cheered. That afternoon the past united with the future, as Marbot's applause conferred the blessing of the Empire in the same uproar as Mac-Mahon, Forey, and Canrobert upon the broad young captain of the 8th Chasseurs.

When their training was complete in May, 1841, they marched to Paris; and as the crowded pavements heard the quickstep of their marching bugles and saw eight thousand waving plumes go by on eight thousand shakoes beneath a shimmer of fixed bayonets, Paris took them to its heart. One sunny day the King inspected them outside the Tuileries; his son and his dreary son-in-law from Brussels (recently enlivened by a small daughter named Charlotte) were with him; Marshal Soult presented colours to them with a few words in his Gascon accent; and afterwards the King received all the

officers inside the palace. A few days later they were at Vincennes to show off their paces to Soult and Grouchy; and the
survivors of the Empire saw what the young men could do.
Soon afterwards they left for Africa. The prospect of a European war had faded now. But when Bugeaud took the field
against Abd-el-Kader, there was work for the Chasseurs
to do.

Pock-marked, red-headed, and irascible, '*le père Bugeaud*'
had made a start towards a satisfactory decision in Algeria
by his successful operations on the Sikkak five years earlier;
and his return in 1841 as Governor-General was a final challenge to Abd-el-Kader. Now there were silver threads among
the red; and the army, startled by his appearance on a night
alarm in an enormous nightcap, had a strong tendency to sing
in affectionate derision:

> *L'as-tu vue,*
> *La casquette, la casquette,*
> *L'as-tu vue*
> *La casquette du père Bugeaud?*

Bazaine was now a captain in the 8th *Chasseurs à pied;* and
French flying columns took part in swift and effective operations, which kept Abd-el-Kader on the run. The days of
lumbering artillery and heavy transport were over now. For
Bugeaud made war on an elusive enemy by means of mobility
and surprise. His columns—three or four battalions, a few
mountain-guns on pack-mules, and two squadrons of Spahis
or Chasseurs d'Afrique—started from their base in the cool
darkness before dawn, marched through a blazing morning
with the native horsemen of the *goum* wheeling on their
flanks, and struck before the enemy was well aware that they
had started. It was a new technique, a form of military homœo-
pathy that rendered possible the conquest of Algeria. Early in
1842 the 8th *Chasseurs à pied* were operating in the hills beyond Oran. Abd-el-Kader had been hunted out of Tlemcen

and driven westward on Morocco. But he appeared at unexpected corners with a strong raiding force composed of his own followers and tribesmen of the Beni-Snassen from the hills across the border. French columns lunged successfully in his direction, until he turned to face them in a mountain pass, where the road winds up towards a crest that looks down on Nemours. When Abd-el-Kader stood to fight, he was attacked and routed by four French battalions. The Zouaves and Bazaine's battalion came in from one flank, while the other was assaulted by a Line regiment and Mac-Mahon's Chasseurs. The operation was successful; and the Emir fled southward down the long corridors among the empty hills.

7

While the interminable hunt for the elusive Abd-el-Kader went on, Captain Bazaine found something more absorbing than the round of regimental life. For he was appointed head of the *Bureau arabe* at Tlemcen. A large Moslem population, part Arab and part Berber with stray Turkish outcrops, was something that Napoleon had not foreseen; and in consequence his countrymen, who retained the administrative framework of the Empire through all their dynastic changes, had no certain guide as to how it should be administered. Left to their own resources, the new masters of Algeria had improvised a simple system under which native administration was entrusted to a military branch. A colonel at Algiers controlled a network of subordinates in local offices; and these administered their areas on lines that bore a strong resemblance to the old Turkish hierarchy. For under the *Bureau arabe* a nicely graduated scale of native dignitaries collected their own revenues and maintained what passed for order. All dealings with them were conducted by the new service of *Affaires arabes*, whose offices were now the centre of local government. Tribal politics, religious controversy, litigation, taxes, and police all fell within their province; and the local head of the *Bureau arabe* became the channel through which the French authorities imposed their will upon the population and the difficulties of unruly Kaids were transmitted to their masters. Interpreter, judge, tax-collector, and policeman, he administered extensive territories of which he spoke the language and explored the politics. His intelligence reports on local temper and affairs helped to form policy; his attitude to local worthies controlled their rise and fall; and his office became the focus of all native life, where anxious greybeards interviewed young officers fresh from St. Cyr with a profusion of grave, Arab courtesy, and the sun went down upon interminable arguments over innumerable brews of sweet, green tea.

These functionaries were mostly youthful; and at thirty-one Bazaine, a little older than the average, found himself in charge of the *Bureau arabe* at Tlemcen. The surrounding territory was a comparatively recent conquest; and with Abd-el-Kader still at large it was full of problems. The town, where square minarets lifted above crumbling walls and winding alleys, was a strange medley; and as Captain Bazaine went about his business in Tlemcen, he grew familiar with its sights —the gaunt walls of the citadel where Cavaignac and his Zouaves had stood a siege not long before, street-corners where the hooded men sat talking in the shade, mules ambling under stately citizens disguised as bundles of white linen, hanging lamps half-seen through horseshoe arches, negroes elbowing through the press to clear a way for riders with immense straw hats perched insecurely upon turbans, fretted doorways opening on quiet courtyards, the rich gleam of tiles above wayside fountains, and the queer procession of the passers-by, of Jews in gabardines, of tanned French soldiers, blonde Berbers from the hills, sheeted Arab women, and the little donkeys with their loads brushing against the walls on either side. He learned to know its sounds as well—the mur-

mur of the market, young voices chanting low in little
schools, the click of pacing mules on cobble-stones, a drum
throbbing in the silence, the wooden clatter of storks on the
house-tops rattling their great beaks, or a voice lifted in the
wailing music of Islam behind blind walls; and as the dark
hours went by, he heard the *muezzin*, a small figure rigid on
the minaret, quaver out the hours of prayer until the dawn
came and the thin trumpets of France sounded across
Tlemcen.

Upon this shifting background Captain Bazaine attended to
his duties at the *Bureau arabe*, wrote his reports, or watched
his visitors through narrowed eyes. His eyes were always
heavy-lidded; and in his office at Tlemcen he learned to wear
a mask. For if Arabs were inscrutable, their administrator
could not afford to wear an open countenance; and as it was
his duty to divine their purposes, he was unlikely to achieve
it if his face revealed his own. So an impassive physiognomy
marked Bazaine for life. But the mark of the *Bureau arabe*
was deeper on him. His apprenticeship in Spain had been an
unusual variation on a soldier's training; and now Algeria was
teaching him a good deal more than soldiers usually learn.
For he was graduating in the arts of management. His duties
at Tlemcen involved a grasp of politics that were not always
simple and an ability to resolve awkward situations with diplomacy that was occasionally tortuous. Native diplomacy
was far from candid, and the *Bureau arabe* could hardly risk
a higher standard. He faced his problems with a modest
establishment consisting of a French subaltern, a native judge
and some assistants, a dragoman, a clerk or so, and a few
mounted men to act as constables or escort. At one time his
assistant was a young captain of Zouaves named Chanzy. For
the *Bureau arabe* was a school of native administration
through which large numbers of young officers contrived to
pass without loss of virtue. The chivalry of Lamoricière was
unimpaired by the experience; Charras retained his republican

austerity; Bourbaki remained a model for young soldiers; and du Barail was just as dashing as before.

Not that its duties were exclusively performed indoors or behind city walls. For the head of the *Bureau arabe* dealt largely in military intelligence and participated actively in such operations as might be conducted in his area; and with Abd-el-Kader on the run the country round Tlemcen remained a busy place. The Paris boulevards were singing:

> *À cheval ou a dromadaire,*
> *Dans tout ce que l'Afrique a de l'air,*
> *Il faut poursuivre Abd-el-Kader . . .*

and the army followed suit. Bugeaud's flying columns raked the country systematically in all directions, and royal princes came out in search of laurels. Their first quarry was the Emir's *Smala*, the moving capital of Abd-el-Kader's nomadic state with his perambulating Court, arsenal, officials, flocks and herds, and a population of 30,000 men, women, and children. Early in 1843 the Duc d'Aumale was on its trail. This tall young man, whose sensitive soul recoiled from the execution of some natives guilty of signalling to the enemy (a prejudice against the death sentence which he was subsequently able to outgrow, as Bazaine found just forty years later), sought glory for the dynasty on land, whilst his brother Joinville looked for it at sea. Success rewarded him when a vast cloud of dust ahead revealed a city on the march, and startled Spahis saw the *Smala* in the very act of pitching camp. A swift charge by a few squadrons, six hundred men launched against a multitude that wheeled and scattered, ensured a splendid haul. The duke's operations had been anything but faultless, since he had risked his tiny column in perilous proximity to forces of unascertained dimensions. But success excuses all military errors; and the capture of the *Smala*, with some aid from Horace Vernet's courtly brush, assured the Duc d'Aumale his place in history as well as his square yards of canvas among the painted acres of Versailles.

With Bugeaud a Marshal and Abd-el-Kader an embarrassed phantom somewhere in Morocco the war was nearly over, though there was still work for columns from Tlemcen. Early in 1844 Bazaine was promoted *Chef de bataillon* in the 58th of the Line. His first protector, Baron Roger, was now a Deputy and had been assuring the Minister of War that he regarded the young soldier *"comme un veritable fils d'adoption."* For their relation had, it seems, been slightly informal, though it had lasted thirty years and in the interval General Conrad had stood *in loco parentis* to Bazaine, who appeared to have something in the nature of a gift for adoption. This promotion gave the *Commandant* an increase of pay and a change of uniform, substituting the red trousers of the Line for the grey of the *Chasseurs à pied*. But work went on at the *Bureau arabe*. In the next year he got a new assistant, when Captain Chanzy was succeeded by a remarkable young man named Doineau who came, like his predecessor, from the Zouaves. The war was really over now, since Bugeaud had cleared the west by routing a Moorish army 60,000 strong at Isly. But with the end of major operations there was more than ever for the *Bureau arabe* to do in administering conquered territory. The area of French control was spreading fast; and by 1845 their southward drive had reached the desert, where they looked out across a lunar landscape towards a void scribbled with the meaningless reticulations of innumerable trails, whose emptiness scared the horizon back towards vanishing point. The Sahara lay waiting in the glare, empty desolation haunted by the mirage and flanked by the unpleasant silhouette of range upon range of dun, pigmy mountains; and the newcomers turned back toward habitable country. But though the French prepared to hold Algeria between the desert and the sea, their tenure was not uneventful. At one point a false prophet named Bou Maza gave trouble; at another Abd-el-Kader still had power to bring the fighting within forty miles of Tlemcen and to confer upon a company of Bazaine's old battalion of *Chasseurs à pied* the undying glory of extermination under heroic circumstances at Sidi-Brahim.

A political officer was always on active service; and that year *Commandant* Bazaine received a step in the Legion of Honour. In 1846 his district was enlivened by a false prophet, who displayed some originality by varying the usual procedure and claiming to be Jesus; and the hunt for Abd-el-Kader, who was growing desperate, still went on. But he was flagging now. There was no shelter for him in Morocco, and the French were on the watch along the border. The next year found Bazaine still administering his district and collating his intelligence reports. For some official reason he was transferred to the 5th Infantry; but his duties remained the same. One December night in 1847 Lamoricière received a rain-sodden paper bearing Abd-el-Kader's seal and a messenger announcing his surrender; and the next day a weary man gave himself up by the fatal *marabout* of Sidi-Brahim, where the Chasseurs had died. One story was that the Emir handed his dagger to *Commandant* Bazaine. But his surrender was re-enacted with due formality in the presence of the Duc d'Aumale. For the prince had just arrived as Governor-General of Algeria, and the end of Abd-el-Kader was too good for him to miss.

But the Governor's embarrassments were only just beginning, since three winter days of 1848 ended his father's reign in the sudden landslide of the February Revolution. Marshal Bugeaud was less successful with the roaring Paris streets than he had been in Africa; Louis Philippe retired ungracefully from kingship in a four-wheeled cab and the unlikely name of 'Mr. Smith'; and whilst ecstatic Frenchmen hailed the Second Republic, Aumale was left to make his exit into the mournful land of might-have-beens inhabited by exiled princes. But these sublime events were far above the *Bureau arabe* at

Tlemcen and left its chief unmoved. His own promotion to be lieutenant-colonel came nearer home; and when this was accompanied by a charming letter from the new Governor-General, in which General Cavaignac congratulated him and expressed a more than formal hope that he would not think of leaving Tlemcen, his prospects were encouraging. The new lieutenant-colonel was attached to the 19th Light Infantry and transferred later in the year to the 5th of the Line. But something was still lacking. He had his work; he had his prospects; but what were they without a home? The colonel was still single; and when he sought a bride, he sought one in a slightly unusual quarter, redolent of a young *légionnaire*'s first sight of the *mantilla* and the comb ten years before in Spain. For his tastes were always Spanish.

One of the leading drawbacks of Tlemcen had been a lack of hotel accommodation. After some correspondence between a French general and the consul at Cartagena this defect was eventually remedied by the importation of an enterprising lady, who had kept an inn somewhere in Murcia; and the social scene was brightened by Señora Tormo and her three daughters. Bazaine became a lodger with the family; and the observant head of the *Bureau arabe* noticed the youngest of the three. She had a charming smile for everyone, danced to the castanets with grace, and though her modesty was duly safeguarded by a duenna when she tripped through the alleys of Tlemcen, she had a youthful tendency to ogle officers at the theatre. For Soledad was only seventeen. Bazaine was deeply interested. There were twenty years between them; but Achille could not deny the attraction of a small figure swaying to the click of castanets with lifted arms and stamping feet, outlined in the half-light of a *patio*, as a great honey-coloured moon rode over Africa.

But though her *cachuca* was accomplished, the remainder of her education left much to be desired; and as the colonel's intentions were strictly honourable, this must be seen to.

There were few facilities for self-improvement in Tlemcen. But Oran was only sixty miles away; and with his landlady's consent her youngest was installed there for instruction at Bazaine's expense. His duty often took him to Oran, and he was able to observe her progress in long, solitary rides. So far the course of his romance had run tolerably smooth; and there seemed no reason why he should not carry it one stage further. He was a lieutenant-colonel now; and if he wished to marry, who could gainsay him? Little Soledad was willing; so was her mother; and the only fairy that could spoil his dream was the Ministry of War. For serving officers required official leave to marry; and his application, naming Maria de la Soledad Indria Gregoria Tormo, was submitted in due form. But it must be countersigned by General Mac-Mahon. Less susceptible to Spanish charms, the general responded coldly that such a marriage would be prejudicial to Bazaine's career. Taking a highly favourable view of the colonel's prospects, he felt that the name of Tormo was a little too familiar in the army. He even went so far as to allude with some feeling to the case of an impulsive colonel married to a lady who was widely known in military circles as 'Casque en cuir.' As Bazaine's romance was quite authentic, there was an angry scene between the men, which may have left lifelong resentment on one side at least. But at the moment there were no wedding-bells for Soledad.

Quite, indeed, the contrary. For shortly afterwards she left Algeria for the Sacré Cœur at Marseilles. But there was no intention that she should take the veil, since her resourceful lover had arranged with an obliging Vicar-General for a fresh instalment of her protracted education. Vague suggestions that she was the daughter of a Spanish general, who had died fighting at Bazaine's side in his native land, might render a demure *pensionnaire* from Marseilles more acceptable in official circles than a well-known, if highly valued, feature of the night-life of Tlemcen. Meanwhile, he had his work to do. While France settled down under the Second Republic, exchanging the stern rule of Cavaignac for a Prince-President who smoked innumerable cigarettes and talked low behind a large moustache, Algeria was turning from a seat of war into a colony. In 1850 Bazaine became a colonel in the 55th Infantry; but his duties were still political, as he was now in charge of the department of *Affaires arabes* for the whole province of Oran. It was eight years since he had quitted regimental life; and an inspecting general reported that he had been too long away from soldiering, commenting harshly that Bazaine had lost some of his military feeling in the *Bureau arabe* and was even lacking in practical experience. Pélissier recommended that he should be returned to his unit; and he spent the remaining months of 1850 in France. But this unfavourable view of him was hardly shared by Mac-Mahon, who wrote offering Bazaine the command of a battalion at Tlemcen in friendly terms that showed no traces of hard feelings on the subject of Señorita Tormo. His days in *Affaires arabes* were numbered; and soon he emerged from his prolonged initiation into Arab ways and native problems. It left him with something of a politician's mind and something of a policeman's. He would quote Arab sayings to the end of his life; and his later critics attributed anything about him for which they did not care to this experience. For the *Bureau arabe* was far from popular with those outside the little corporation. But now he was a soldier once again. For early in 1851 Colonel Bazaine received a new appointment; and the young sergeant, who had come to Africa nineteen years before, succeeded to Bernelle and Conrad in command of the 1st Foreign Legion.

There was always work for the Legion in Algeria. The Prince-President was busy out-manœuvring the politicians, who cackled loudly over the Second Republic until they found to their surprise that they had hatched the Second Empire; and Bazaine attended to his duties in Algeria, while

French soldiers were shooting other Frenchmen on the streets of Paris in the *Coup d'état*. In the next year obliging staff officers at Algiers amused a visiting Archduke named Maximilian with an Arab powder-play and the blond young man, who lived to see a wilder *fantasia* in Mexico, watched wheeling horsemen in the sunshine of Africa. Bazaine taught a lesson to the Beni-Snassen on the Moorish border with the assistance of his enterprising pupil, Captain Doineau, who was now in charge of the *Bureau arabe* at Tlemcen. But his thoughts turned lightly in the direction of Marseilles, where Soledad, now an extremely pretty girl, was the darling of the Sacré Cœur and a remarkable pianist. He was forty-one; and it was really time to think of getting married. But it was 1854 before his application reached the Ministry; and by that time France had an Emperor, and the Emperor had his war. (Wars seemed appropriate to Emperors named Napoleon.) But Bazaine had got his bride. They married at Versailles that summer; and as he was not the man to let a war interrupt his honeymoon (had not his predecessor in command of the Legion taken Madame Bernelle on active service with far less provocation?), Soledad accompanied her husband to the Crimean War.

SECOND EMPIRE

Le paysan voulut couronner sa légende.
JULES FAVRE.

I

IT WAS nearly forty years since the last square of the Guard
struggled off the field of Waterloo round a dazed Emperor; and in the interval France and her neighbours had forgotten a great deal. For some years, whilst Waterloo was still
the best-remembered battle in history, the bitter flavour of
defeat lingered in French mouths. But gradually, as the past
receded, the nightmare of their failure began to fade; and
French memories played agreeably over the long roll of Napoleonic victories without undue attention to the fact that
they had been the prelude of defeat. The Empire, in fact,
became a legend; and legends are not always wholly true.

More than one circumstance assisted this distortion of the
uncomfortable facts. It was consoling in the empty years that
followed 1815 to recall that France had conquered Europe
without noticing that Europe in the end had conquered
France. Once the memory of Waterloo grew faint, a golden
age of Imperial anecdote began; and there were enough survivors of the great adventure to regale respectful listeners
with a tale of unbroken glory from Marengo to Wagram.
The dismal epilogue of Spain, of Russia, of destruction on
the Beresina and defeat at Leipzig, of France invaded twice
and Paris occupied by foreign armies was gradually overlaid

by the splendour of the Napoleonic years that had gone before. It was all foretold by Béranger in his shrewd prediction,

> On parlera de sa gloire
> Sous la chaume bien longtemps,
> L'humble toit, dans cinquante ans,
> Ne connaîtra plus d'autre histoire.

Besides, it was a comforting resource for Opposition writers to remind a Bourbon monarchy that things had been very different under a Bonaparte; and though Bonapartism as a programme did not re-enter politics for many years, there was already a great deal of Bonapartism as a sentimental retrospect. France was suffering acutely from a nostalgia of glory; and the emotion was appropriated with some skill by the adroit Louis Philippe. He emphasised the difference between himself and his old Bourbon cousins by recalling the lost laurels of those twenty years of history which their strict orthodoxy forced them to ignore and by bringing back the tricolour. True, he could not adorn it with the eagle. But though his cockerel was a poor substitute, he did his best. There was a vast outpouring of Napoleonic imagery, of prints, statuettes, odes, epic poems, melodramas, oil-paintings, book illustrations, and monuments. Now the Emperor lay beneath the great dome of the Invalides; his effigy returned to his column in the Place Vendôme; great blocks swung into place, as the Arc de Triomphe rose slowly in the long perspective of the Champs Elysées; and a new wing of the palace at Versailles was dedicated to French victories recorded in life-size upon a wilderness of painted canvas.

These heartening activities, by which the prospects of Napoleon's surviving nephew were inadvertently improved, induced a feeling that French military power was still supreme. There was not much in recent military history to confirm it, since French armies had scarcely been engaged in Europe since Waterloo. A military promenade had taken

them to Spain in order to suppress a revolution and adorn
Paris with the name of its sole event at the Trocadero; an
uneventful siege of Antwerp enabled them to disentangle a
new kingdom from the Dutch; and the siege of Rome had
just demonstrated that French troops were equal to dislodg-
ing Italians behind improvised defences. But Africa was the
main theatre of their activities. The conquest of Algeria absorbed French military energies for twenty years; and after
some initial failures a technique had been developed by Bugeaud and his assistants which gave satisfactory results and
made new reputations. The *razzia*, the flying column, the
night march, the steady square, and the dashing charge were
now the school in which a younger generation of French soldiers learnt their business. Their elders were still telling stories
about Napoleon. But they did better than their elders who,
trained in European warfare under the Empire, were often
unequal to the demands of active service in Algeria. That,
however, scarcely proved that their own training in Algeria
would qualify them for success in European war. It might be
good enough to beat Abd-el-Kader. But if a more formidable
enemy set larger forces in motion, would they know how to
handle them? Their experience, like that of British soldiers
in India, was all in the small change of war; and their military
education left much to be desired. For savage warfare is an
imperfect school. All brave, nearly all ruthless, a few were
clever, and more than one of them could read a map. Their
enemy, though enterprising and extremely mobile, was indifferently armed; and who could say how far they would be
equal to conducting major operations against a European adversary with arms as formidable as their own?

Bronzed, decorated, exquisitely tailored in the martial mil-
linery devised to gladden eyes in France, the heroes of the
jeune Afrique helped powerfully to restore a feeling that
their country was invincible. Hussars were as elegant (if not
a trifle more so), Lancers as dashing, and Dragoons as hel-

meted as anything that the Empire had known; white-aproned Pioneers still wore beards and bearskins; and big drum-majors paced majestically under tall tricolour plumes. Algeria added its own embellishments—the scarlet *chéchia* and short, blue jacket of the Zouaves, and the red burnous of the Spahis. If appearances counted for anything, France was still formidable under Louis Philippe. Foreign statesmen appeared to think so; and Wellington, who looked further than appearances, passed sleepless nights over his country's unprotected state in dangerous proximity to such a neighbour. But Wellington was nearly eighty; and perhaps the French were not quite so dangerous as they appeared. In any case, a timely outbreak of French politics reduced the danger. For in 1848 the King gave place to a republic; and there were grounds for thinking that the Second Republic was too well-meaning to present a military menace to anyone except those of its own citizens who went too far for General Cavaignac.

But the busy wheel of politics revolved once more. Well-meaning republics are apt to be short-lived in Paris no less than in Berlin; and Cavaignac had been succeeded by a Prince-President who bore a name of military significance. True, his ideas were less Napoleonic than his name. For the bronze syllables of the Emperor's record bore few traces of the vague enlightenment accumulated by his nephew in forty years of exile. But princes are often more enlightened in exile than on the throne. Napoleon at St. Helena had been positively progressive; and his nephew's day-dreams in Switzerland, in a French prison, and in the West End of London moved with the times and even ahead of them. Indeed, the miscellany of opinions that Louis Napoleon had accumulated were almost revolutionary, inclining towards socialism of a sort and those drastic rearrangements of the map of Europe which were favoured by political exiles in Leicester Square. But he was back in Paris now; there were sentries at his door instead of creditors; and it was just possible that his Bonapartism might take a turn for the Napoleonic. His opportunities were limited so long as he presided decorously over the Second Republic under the blameless tutelage of elder statesmen and continued to officiate (in his own phrase) as 'the Prince Albert of the Republic.' But this role, however agreeable to a Saxe-Coburg-Gotha, failed to suit a Bonaparte; and presently, in his unhurried way, he made arrangements better suited to his name. When the shots of the *Coup d'état* rang out in Paris, France knew that it was ruled by a First Consul once again, although he still retained the title of President; and twelve months later the anniversary of the night before Austerlitz and the *Coup d'état* ushered in the Second Empire.

France had an Emperor once more; and it would be interesting to observe how far Napoleon III was going to resemble Napoleon I. There was already a distinct resemblance in externals. The crowned N, the eagles, and the bees returned; there was a Court again with a Grand-Almoner and a Grand-Marshal of the Palace and a *Grand Veneur;* and the Emperor's becoming sense of antiquarian propriety had collected bearers of Napoleonic names to run his errands. A Ney, a Murat, and a Meneval were found, whose fathers had accompanied his uncle. His collection even comprised a few originals. For ghosts still walked, where old Excelmans who had ridden with Murat sat his horse in the old style, and Marbot told his stories, and King Jerome exhibited the Napoleonic profile that had once ruled Westphalia. But the most substantial item was the army, which became the army of the Empire once again. There were eagles on French standards now, and the Imperial anthem clanged above the drums. They were more elegant than ever, as the *Guides* trotted past in green and gold to Rossini's new trumpet march, and the tall bearskins mounted guard at the Tuileries. It was not long before the Emperor had his Guard. But their battle-honours were still the old Napoleonic victories. For until 1854 the Second Empire had no battle-honours of its own.

2

The Crimean War is one of the bad jokes of history. Nobody quite knew what it was about; and when the belligerents discovered that they were at war, nobody seemed to know what to do next or where to do it. The forces on both sides appeared to have some difficulty in making contact; and when they did, their operations were often marked by delirious incompetence. This difficulty was inherent in the fact that Great Britain, France, and Turkey found themselves at war with Russia. It was comparatively simple for the Russians to bring force to bear upon the Turks. But when the Western Allies faced the problem of devising operations against Russia, the hard facts of geography were notably unhelpful. As Germany was not at war, they could not invade the western provinces of Russia by a march overland; and the only points at which they seemed to have a hope of getting near their unapproachable opponent lay at his exposed extremities along the Black Sea or the Baltic. Since Turkey needed their support and Russia's northern approaches were uncomfortably fortified, there was a good deal to be said for concentrating in the south; and Franco-British forces moved into the neighbourhood of Constantinople with a vague idea that, when they got there, they could be usefully employed.

There was not much to encourage this belief either in their composition or in their command. For while French experience of war was mainly African, the British contribution to a land campaign was still less appropriate in 1854. It was almost forty years since Waterloo; but the military mind had scarcely noticed it. For Wellington was only two years in his grave; and what had been good enough to beat the French was always good enough for Wellington. After the crowning mercy of Waterloo time stood still at the Horse Guards; and it resulted that the British force which took the field in 1854 was very largely what it would have been in

1814. Queen Victoria might sit in the seat of George III; the
Royal Navy might not disdain the use of steam in small quantities; but the British expedition was Wellington's army without Wellington. Although the Duke could not be present,
this defect was remedied so far as practicable by securing the
assistance of as many of the Duke's contemporaries as still
survived. French tradition might be satisfied by adherence to
the military doctrine of Napoleonic veterans (someone had
found old Jomini in a Paris restaurant and elicited a plan of
campaign in his best Empire style); but British piety retained
them in the flesh. For the army was commanded by Lord
Raglan, long familiar at Peninsular headquarters as Lord
Fitzroy Somerset; and those of his colleagues who had not
lost an arm at Waterloo belonged no less to the heroic age
and embarrassed their allies from time to time by alluding to
the enemy, from sheer force of habit, as 'the French.'

If the British suffered from too much experience, the
French had too little. For Saint-Arnaud, who was in command, was by no means the best-founded of the military
reputations made in Africa with the added drawback that he
was a dying man. His whole campaign was a protracted cal-
vary of pain alternating with unnatural outbursts of energy;
and if this command was his reward for the military preparation of the *Coup d'état*, republicans might feel that it was
handsomely avenged. Arriving at the seat of war in Turkey
before his army was in any state for operations, as the men
had been thoughtfully embarked in steamships while their
horses and supplies followed more leisurely by sail, he found
them in the vicinity of a dispirited little town named Gallipoli. This position would enable them to defend Constantinople, if it was attacked from that direction. If, however, it
was not, their presence was quite pointless; and as the Russians did not oblige with an offensive, Allied strategy still
faced the problem of where they were to fight. For they
could hardly win a war without a battle; and the French, who

were not greatly interested in the Eastern Question, wanted a victory. "*Depuis Waterloo*," as a patriotic socialist wrote from his prison, "*nous sommes les vaincus de l'Europe, et, pour faire quelque chose de bon même chez nous, je crois qu'il est utile de montrer aux étrangers que nous savons manger du poudre.*" This heroic demonstration was hardly practicable at Gallipoli, as the enemy was not in sight, but they had the cholera instead.

The Foreign Legion, like much else in the Crimean War, was an afterthought. Saint-Arnaud had objected to their inclusion in his command; and when their sailing-orders came in June, 1854, a large proportion of the army had already started. But though they came late, they came in time for the cholera. Bazaine commanded his new regiment; and as his honeymoon had just begun, the bride came with him. Feminine society was not unusual in the Crimean War; and it is a romantic error to represent Miss Florence Nightingale as a solitary figure with a lamp in a wilderness of men. The appearance of Madame de Saint-Arnaud at the seat of war might be accounted for by her husband's health; but that of other ladies had no reason except pure domesticity. For General Yusuf, the cavalry commander from Algeria, had brought his wife; other officers were thought to have even sprightlier companions; and presently reviews were brightened by the riding-habits of the English ladies.

But if the presence of Madame Bazaine was not surprising, that of her piano was. Nor was she content with the metropolitan security of Constantinople, since the colonel's bride was found beside the colonel in a house at Gallipoli. Her education at the Sacré Cœur had included a strong dose of music; and she was a notable pianist. The amenities of her new home included a piano, although it is not easy to believe that this instrument formed part of the original equipment of a Turkish house in a small sea-side town; and its appearance at Gallipoli was in the nature of a triumph of transportation

from Stamboul across the Sea of Marmora, unless the French
(who left behind a lot of more essential instruments of war)
had brought it all the way from France. But shortly after the
beautiful Madame Bazaine and her pianoforte were installed,
cholera broke out; and her medolies tinkled across the
stricken streets. When a son of Marshal Ney succumbed, she
moved him from his lonely billet to her house and comforted the dying man with a sonata of Mozart or (as some
said) of Beethoven. News of this melancholy scene reached
Paris in his obituary; and her performance under trying circumstances was favourably compared with that of a gifted
lady who had recently consoled the dying Chopin with his
own compositions.

Presently the Legion sailed with the rest of the Allies for
the Crimea, where it had been decided to attack the fortress
of Sebastopol; and one September morning drums and bugles
sounded a loud reveille at the Alma. The Russians were assaulted frontally with a mechanical precision which reminded
Canrobert of a Hyde Park review; and the Legion did extremely well. A costly victory was followed by a flaming
sunset; and as Saint-Arnaud turned back to die, the Allies
moved without undue haste (and without maps to guide
them) towards Sebastopol, covering their siege operations
with a fight at Balaklava better calculated to inspire popular
recitations than to produce tangible results.

As winter shut down on the freezing trenches, the Spahis
were sent home to Africa. Not so the Foreign Legion, whose
strength was presently increased by the arrival of their second
regiment. Bazaine's command now ranked as a whole brigade;
and early in 1855 he was promoted *Général de brigade*. The
new general's command was trying, since the Legion's shortcomings were more visible in European warfare than in the
easier conditions of Algeria. Desertion was not unknown (one
deserter from the Legion revealed French mining operations
to the Russians with disastrous consequences); their addic-

tion to the bottle became more than usually glaring; and the fastidious Canrobert, who noted in their ranks thieves, murderers, ruined noblemen, and an ex-Prefect of Police from Rome, was shocked to encounter on parade a thirsty *légionnaire* who had sold his boots in order to buy brandy and blacked his feet for the sake of appearances, a sacrifice illsuited to the Crimean winter. But Bazaine struggled through the dreadful months before Sebastopol; and his sufferings were mitigated by the presence of his dauntless bride. For Soledad, who had managed to keep up her piano at Gallipoli, was still undefeated by the war, the winter, or the Russians. She crossed the Black Sea and contrived to make a home for him in the Crimea. If she could not be with her husband in the trenches, at least he had not far to go; and one night it was unkindly whispered that he went there when he should have been commanding in the line and that this untimely domesticity earned a stern report from the unbending Forey, which may have lingered in Bazaine's memory when they served together seven years afterwards in Mexico. But Canrobert, to whom his lapse was reported, left it unpunished; and when the command passed to the impetuous Pélessier, ampler opportunities of glory opened before General Bazaine.

The new commander had a noticeable taste for Soledad's society. It was a pleasant way of his to write poetry for ladies. Besides, he had known Tlemcen and Oran in the old days; and she was often entertained by the Commander-in-chief at dinner in his hut, where the pair laughed like children, and she put on his cap and let him pinch her chin, or watched his little dog jumping over rows of chairs at his command, which was a good deal easier than capturing Sebastopol; and sometimes they waltzed to a regimental band. During these agreeable exercises Bazaine was otherwise employed. His steadiness in face of danger had already earned distinction (an order of the day praised his conduct in a night attack); and Pélissier gave him every opportunity to exercise it. But whether this was due to interest in his career or in Soledad is not entirely clear. For Spanish types appealed to Pélissier, who subsequently paid her the compliment of marrying another Spanish beauty. But such favour was highly advantageous to Bazaine, since it obtained him a prominent position in the assault upon Sebastopol, which he managed to survive. When the place fell, he was appointed commandant of the ruined fortress and promoted *Général de division*; and shortly afterwards Pélissier's continued interest in his career secured him a command at some distance from Sebastopol.

The siege was over; and as the Second Empire had secured its laurels, the French inclined towards negotiations with the Czar, although their British allies (always a little slow to notice things) were just getting interested in the war. Since it seemed possible to strike another blow at Russia by attacking two more fortresses a hundred miles away on the north shore of the Black Sea, an expedition was despatched to Kinburn in October, 1855, with Bazaine in command. He sailed with two brigades, one English and one French, and an Allied fleet. Feinting at Odessa, they landed from a rough sea at Kinburn; and three rudimentary French ironclads opened a bombardment presently continued by the whole fleet, whilst infantry on shore attacked the fortress. Its guns were silenced in five hours, and the place surrendered. The Russians saved them further trouble by blowing up the adjacent coast-defences at Ochakov; and Bazaine returned in triumph after an effective operation, in which he had commanded 8,500 men with complete success and reached all his objectives in a fortnight. Pélissier, a Marshal now, was particularly complimentary. Indeed, his sympathy had prompted him to visit Madame Bazaine every afternoon during her husband's brief absence, arriving shortly after three o'clock each day in the only carriage on the peninsula, an ancient coach captured from a Russian prince and now harnessed to a gun-team. This picturesque conveyance brought the playful Marshal to pay his daily call on Soledad in sight of the whole army. But she knew what soldiers were; for Miss Nightingale's was not the only reputation made in the Crimean War.

3

The world of Frenchmen was gay in 1856. Another European war had ended; and this time France was indisputably on the winning side. They were no longer '*les vaincus de l'Europe*'; the dark memory of 1812 had been effaced; and France, an Empire once again, appeared to have the casting vote in world affairs. For Paris was the capital of Europe, when the diplomats assembled to put the world in order and compose a peace-treaty. It was a new Paris, though, with fewer corners where a few angry men behind a barricade could hold out against the police, and troops would have little difficulty in clearing the broad avenues. But when the Guard came marching home from the Crimea in a hail of flowers, and it heard the bands come down the street and saw the bearded faces under the long line of bayonets, Paris was itself again. For the imperfections of the war, the gross inadequacy of supplies, and the incompetence of most of the commanders were all forgotten in the splendid fact that it was over and that it had been won.

Now all the world had come to Paris for the Congress, which was to answer the Eastern Question once for all and to ask (if Count Cavour knew his business) the Italian Question. The Emperor, a charming host, received the delegates and displayed the beauties of his capital, already honoured by a visit from his ally, Queen Victoria. Diplomacy assured his place among the sovereigns of Europe; and showmanship was rapidly replacing the Empire in a milder version of its old supremacy. But something was still lacking. For Napoleon had no heir except his unpleasant cousin, who had not done particularly well in the Crimea and nearly always managed to be rude. But his lovely Empress with the sloping eyebrows was not receiving; delegates enquired discreetly after her health; and Paris waited for the news. All day long the crowds stood outside the Tuileries; and early one spring morning the guns thundered at the Invalides. Paris counted twenty-one (that meant a princess) and waited for the next. There was a dragging silence that kept them all on tip-toe, until the gunners launched into the full Imperial salute of guns, which told the world that the Empire had an heir. The old gunner in command, who kept Paris breathless in March, 1856, had served the battery that banged close on fifty years before for the heir of the First Empire as well as for Louis Philippe's son and grandson. None of them had reigned; and it was two centuries since any son had succeeded to his father on the throne of France. But now there was a prince in the Tuileries once more. The town was putting out its flags, as busy workmen fixed rows of gas-jets on official buildings or hung monuments with strings of fairy-lamps. It was a sunny afternoon; and the palace gardens filled with a crowd of children and their nurses in long streamers, hoping vaguely that, if they could get near enough to the great building, they would see the baby. The hawkers were still selling toy balloons, and one inspired retailer did a brisk trade by crying, "*Demandez le ballon rouge du Prince impérial!*" until the air, the green trees, and the spring sky above the Tuileries were full of red balloons.

That was a victory which called for celebration no less than the Crimean War and the peace that followed it a fortnight later and set guns booming at the Invalides once more. Paris settled down with gusto to an immense round of parties. The Emperor danced at the British embassy in the blue ribbon of his Garter; the dark loveliness of an Italian countess named Castiglione came upon the town in every sort of costume, draped and undraped, occasionally shocking her delighted followers, who stood on ballroom chairs to see. For Paris could be shocked in 1856, when open fans hid blushing ladies all round the audience, because the lines that Dumas *fils* had written were too daring and left the *salons* gossiping for weeks about the memorable '*soirée des éventails*.' One evening two generals from the Crimea dined at the Tuileries; and before they left the table, Canrobert and Bosquet were both Marshals of the Empire. On the next day they were admitted to the Prince Imperial himself, the cradle flanked by two rigid aides-de-camp in full uniform, and the infant barely visible beneath the broad red ribbon of the Legion of Honour. Sometimes he took the air in his own carriage trotting smartly behind two blue and silver *Cent-gardes*, who rode ahead with lifted pistols; and a respectful capital watched his passage through the bright air of 1856.

As the spring stood over Paris, all the world was dancing, dining out, and making bows. March had been gay; and April showed no signs of falling off. One day (it was April 24) Marshal de Castellane, the old martinet in command of the troops at Lyons, was reading a letter from his married daughter, who was having such a wearing time in Paris with a round of parties that seemed likely to go on until the Imperial infant was safely christened in the summer. She had been meeting Princess Mathilde and all the Russians, and after dinner they went on to a delightful ball at Morny's. As the old man read her letter in his room at Lyons, the gay air of Paris seemed to waft into the provinces. But the French provinces were not all quite so gay that April day in 1856. For in a home, where there were already three children and four more were to come, a child was born at a small village in the Pas de Calais, to whom his father gave the melancholy name of Henri Philippe Benoni Omer Joseph Pétain. As St. Omer was not far from Cauchy-la-Tour, there was an excuse for Omer. But Benoni was a depressing appellation:

"And it came to pass, as her soul was in departing (for she died) that she called his name Benoni."

"That is," a dismal margin adds with italic emphasis, *"the son of my sorrow."* True, its original recipient was later renamed Benjamin. But the small Pétain continued to be called Benoni all his life.

4

These splendours were a long way from General Bazaine; and while Paris danced, he still wore his uniform in the discomfort and disease of the Crimea. He would soon be going home, splashed by a few bright drops from the Allied fountain of honour. For that year he became a K.C.B. and advanced a grade in the Legion of Honour, to say nothing of the Queen's Crimean medal and a Sardinian decoration in prospect. It would not be long before he took his lively lady home to France, to Paris, to the Tuileries, where they might hope to make a bow before their sovereigns. They had both come a long way from Tlemcen; and Paris with its lights and parties seemed the very place for Soledad. Or was it? Paris did not ask too many questions under the Second Empire, since the answers might sometimes have been peculiar. But Paris talked; and though her musical achievements at the death-bed of the Duc d'Elchingen had got an admirable press, there was just a risk that it might talk about Madame Bazaine. Spanish beauties were in fashion; but had she been a shade too popular in the Crimea, to say nothing of the old days in Algeria? Besides, her husband had risen from the ranks. Whilst it was undeniable that the First Empire had recruited its nobility from troopers, there was something a little doubtful about a sergeant in the Foreign Legion. They made their *début*, though, with complete success. For she was charming and could be discreet; and the Bazaines were safely launched in Paris.

At the moment he had no command, although he was appointed to inspect troops at home and spent a few weeks in Algeria late in 1857. The long conquest was really over now.

Marshal Randon had finished it that year; and they were all discussing the extraordinary case of Captain Doineau, who had served under Bazaine in the *Bureau arabe* at Tlemcen and was convicted at Oran that summer of murdering the Agha of the Beni-Snouss. The two men had been on uncomfortable terms; and there could be no doubt that the Agha had been murdered with another passenger in the *diligence* that plied between Tlemcen and Oran. That lumbering conveyance with its yellow sides had rumbled down the silent streets behind eight horses a little after three o'clock of a summer morning; and as day began to break a quarter of an hour later, they were overtaken on the road by some mounted men who fired a few shots. As blank shots were a normal form of native courtesy or high spirits, the passengers were not unduly alarmed. But when bullets began to whistle through the coach and hooded figures seized the leaders, while someone shot at the postilion, things were plainly growing serious. The *diligence* was stopped; somebody shot and killed the Agha; a French passenger was dying; three scared survivors scrambled off for help; and as the sun came up, a yellow coach was left forlornly standing on a lonely road.

There were enquiries and arrests. But the wayside tragedy at Safsaf was not remarkable, until the native prisoners began with strange unanimity to identify their ringleader as Captain Doineau, head of the *Bureau arabe* at Tlemcen. As highway robbery with murder was not a speciality of French officers, the charge was singular. But Doineau's dislike of the Agha had been notorious; and when a search disclosed a hoard of 30,000 francs, for which the captain could only account by an unlikely story of a legacy that he had kept uninvested for at least four years, his prospects were not improved. Civil courts are rarely blind to military imperfections. Besides, the prisoner was head of the *Bureau arabe;* and that institution had its critics. The case plainly had the makings of a *cause célèbre;* and as wider issues were involved, the authorities provided

Doineau with a distinguished advocate who had once acted for the Emperor, while the chief native prisoner, Bel-Hadj, whose acquittal depended upon Doineau's guilt, was represented by Jules Favre. This eloquent republican, one of five intrepid partisans just elected to the Chamber, made the rafters ring with his denunciation of the captain; and the court-room at Oran became a sounding-board from which the world might hear the crimes of an Imperial regime based on the abuse of military power. The trial lasted for a fortnight; and the public, less interested in the relevant eye-witnesses of the murder than in the fine irrelevance of generals at issue with Jules Favre on the duties of *Bureaux arabes*, enjoyed itself immensely. French households were divided by the *cause célèbre*, and the unfortunate Doineau attained a vast celebrity. Bazaine had been unable to give evidence for his former subordinate, although it is not easy to discern any point on which he could have testified without transgressing the permitted limits of irrelevance, which are the glory of French jurisprudence. But the case could not go on for ever; and after a sublime appeal to the civilian virtues by the shaggy eloquence of Jules Favre the captain was found guilty. French opinion, which is always partial to a trial with political implications, was thrilled by the spectacle of an officer holding a high administrative post under sentence of death; and when the Cour de Cassation dismissed his appeal in Paris, the story seemed to end.

But Doineau's story was not over yet; and just a fortnight after his old chief was appointed to command the troops at Bourges, they told him that his sentence had been commuted by the Emperor to imprisonment for life. Bourges was a promising appointment for Bazaine, as his predecessor was a duke. But while the general's position was fairly assured, his lady's was less certain. For society at Bourges lived in the shadow of the cathedral. The Cardinal-Archbishop might not take to Soledad, who was an unlikely denizen of a French

Barchester in 1858. But he was charmed at once. Had she not been a *pensionnaire* of the Sacré Cœur? Her pious eye was quick to notice that Bourges lacked a spiritual agency that had been highly beneficial at Marseilles, and she pressed His Eminence to form one out of hand. This met in the Cathedral, where young ladies of the best local families assembled regularly to sing sacred music to organ accompaniment. What could be more fitting than that Madame Bazaine should play the cathedral organ? Society capitulated to this edifying spectacle; and as the diapason thundered gently down the aisles, her career had been aided once again by her more than ladylike accomplishments.

As Bazaine went off to Bourges, Doineau was shipped to Toulon *en route* for French Guiana; and their paths diverged once more, though less widely than might have been expected. For someone managed to mislay the key of Doineau's cell on the day that his ship sailed; and it left without him. The convict was returned to Africa, where somebody saw him working in a penal settlement outside Algiers wearing his Zouave tunic and the Legion of Honour. His misfortunes had engaged Bazaine's sympathy. After all, they had been together at Tlemcen. Doineau was his own successor in the post that he had held for years; and there was always a fellow-feeling between members of the *Bureau arabe*. (Even the virtuous du Barail, who belonged to the fraternity, risked a general's displeasure by contradicting him about Doineau.) The captain's brother, who was in the Guard, made some approaches to Bazaine about appealing to the Emperor again. But there was nothing to be done at present, as Bazaine was not yet a personage and Napoleon had other things to think about in 1859.

He was still brooding, in his silent way, over the map of Europe which had been so grievously misdrawn by the peace-treaties of 1815. For these instruments, by which his dynasty had been effaced, entirely failed to recognise the existence of

a country which was his ruling passion. He had fought for
Italy as a young man; but Italy was still a chess-board of unimportant kingdoms, Austrian dependencies, and Papal States.
He must do something for the Italians. Perhaps their notion
of inducing him to do it by throwing bombs at him was not
persuasive. But when Orsini was defended by Jules Favre, he
was a more rewarding client than Bel-Hadj. True, his counsel
failed to persuade the court to acquit the incompetent assassin.
But his advocacy of Orsini's deeper purpose seemed to leave
the Emperor reflecting still that he must do something for
the Italians. That could not be done without war with Austria;
and war was never far from his calculations in those years
of French rearmament, of autumn manœuvres at his new camp
of Châlons and Napoleonic readings out of Thiers' latest
volume to his new Marshals after dinner. Now he had a cause;
he had an army; and in 1859 he found a *casus belli*.

5

War, as the Emperor had written with some penetration a
few years earlier, is an affair of detail—"There are more details about an army than about anything in the world"—and
detail was not the forte of the French army in 1859. But it was
to be hoped that this would not matter very much, as they
only had to fight the Austrians. Now that Russia was defeated, Austria possessed the most considerable army on the
continent; but somehow it was always beaten. The Hapsburg
monarchy had taken part in every European war for centuries,
and it was rarely on the winning side. Napoleon's career of
victory had been practically uninterrupted so long as he confined himself to fighting Austrians. The long roll of his Italian
victories from Montenotte to Marengo, followed in brilliant
succession by Ulm, Austerlitz, and Wagram, had all been won
at Austrian expense; and why should not his nephew, who

had been handling troops with some ability at Châlons, follow in his footsteps?

It was not quite so easy as it looked, as Napoleon III had graduated in a less exacting school than General Bonaparte. True, he had served with the Swiss army and written about gunnery. But more might be required in order to command success in 1859. For one thing, European war was now a more elaborate affair than it had been when Napoleon I subdued the continent with cannon-balls and muzzle-loaders. The First Empire had been a sustained improvisation; but it was by no means certain that the Second Empire could rely with equal confidence upon impromptu methods. The world was not so simple now. Equipment was more complicated and munitions bulkier; railways supplemented road-transport; and the electric telegraph transmitted orders and intelligence with embarrassing frequency and speed. A rich confusion brooded over the French preparations, to which the Emperor contributed by introducing new weapons at the last moment. A despairing Minister of War opined that they were short of everything but courage; and it was typical of the *imbroglio* that, as Canrobert left for the front, orders reached him at the railway-station candidly confessing that no plan of combined operations with the Italians had yet been evolved and adding gravely that the Minister "notes with regret that the troops under your command are not organised for active service. You will remedy this situation."

Was this to be the nemesis of haphazard military methods, of easy victories over Abd-el-Kader? Old Marshal de Castellane, who was left behind, reflected angrily that this was what came of undue reliance upon Algerian experience, upon *"les principes d'Afrique,"* where no one ever learnt the art of war. For it was one thing to deal with Arabs and quite another to confront a European adversary on the continent. True, they had fought in the Crimea; but that had only been a siege, not a war of movement. Now they had to defeat an enemy in the field somewhere in Italy, and it was by no means certain how they were to do it. Old Jomini, who was still alive, had given them a plan in his best Napoleonic style, which totally ignored the railways (as an improper innovation) and would only work provided that the Austrians kept reasonably still, while they were being outmanœuvred. Perhaps the Austrians could be relied on, since most Frenchmen were convinced that there was little to be feared from a white-coated enemy, who wore tight blue trousers and preposterous headgear. But there were at least 100,000 of them with 400 guns in Italy; and if they were to be defeated, the French would have to get there somehow.

One day in April General Bazaine sailed from Toulon for Genoa in command of his division, which consisted of four battalions of the Line. His corps commander was an irritable veteran named Baraguay d'Hilliers with one arm and water on the knee; and the Emperor, more impulsive in war than in politics, insisted on immediate operations, although their artillery had not yet arrived from France and its place was imperfectly supplied by two batteries of museum specimens borrowed from the Italians. They moved up-country; and this time Bazaine was unaccompanied by his "*chère Marie*," who got no further than Genoa. The Austrians attacked one of Baraguay d'Hilliers' divisions at Montebello; and as it was a thoroughly confused affair, there was some uncertainty as to whether Bazaine moved up to its support (it was commanded by Forey, his old Crimean acquaintance) or was prohibited from doing so by his corps commander. A fortnight later, after the Austrians (who ran mercifully true to form) had obligingly allowed the French to march across their front, a sanguinary and decisive battle at Magenta cleared them out of Lombardy. Bazaine's corps was not engaged. But three days later, while the bells were pealing in Milan and Napoleon rode through a storm of flowers in the roaring streets that ended in the great cathedral square, Bazaine saw some fighting. An Austrian brigade was still at Melegnano (where the French of long ago had won the victory of Marignano over the Swiss pikes); and Bazaine with some infantry arrived before the rest. They had been marching since dawn in driving rain. But it was nearly six o'clock; and if they waited for support or artillery preparation, the light would fail. This was the kind of warfare that he understood. Generals in 1859 charged in the old heroic style with drawn swords and lifted *képis;* and Bazaine, who had learnt the art in Spain when Conrad took the Legion into action, was no more backward than the rest. Going in with the bayonet, they stormed the village in the face of a well-posted enemy. A Zouave battalion lost half its strength; Bazaine was wounded in the head; but the corps had avenged their enforced inactivity at Magenta.

A second grisly pounding-match at Solferino shook the Austrians at the approaches to Venetia; and this time Bazaine was in the thick of it again. Perhaps it was not clever to assault a village cemetery without endeavouring to breach its walls by gun-fire. But it was gallant; and in 1859 gallantry appeared to be the whole art of war. The deadly strong-point in Solferino was eventually carried by Bazaine's division, and he came through without a scratch. He wrote about it afterwards to a relation from his headquarters on the road to Verona:

"The battle of Solferino was long and hard, but victory soon makes you forget fatigue, and two days afterwards we were fit to start again. I was lucky enough to get through without losing any bits of myself (*sans y laisser un morceau de mon individu*); a bullet went through my left holster and lodged in my saddle quite close to my left leg, and my horse's right leg was grazed. It was lucky to come through so lightly, especially under such a fire. The *flies* (which is the soldiers' name for bullets) were buzzing and stinging like a swarm of bees. This great battle was really grand! But when the excitement of the fight is over, what a dismal sight is the battlefield covered with dead and wounded. In these days war is really an evil, and the men who drive nations to it are very guilty.

"The young Emperor of Austria lit out (that is what the soldiers call it), and the day after the battle he was back in his own capital, leaving his generals the job of making good as far as possible the damage to his military honour. It is really funny.

"From the Palace where I have my headquarters, which is just a farm-house, because any large house is called a *Palazio* in this country, I can see the gorge of the Adige, the Tyrol, and the plateau of Rivoli. It is an admirable view, and you would love to see it. Why should not Angelo take advantage of my stay in Italy and take a trip? I should love to see him, and he could come by way of Genoa, where my dear Marie is staying. Then the railway will bring him as far as Brescia, and from there to Desenzano on Lake Garda, or he could drive to my camp before Peschiera. For my Division is to besiege the place. In spite of all the fatigues of a campaign which has been so very active I am quite well, and all that I ask is to give the Austrians such a dusting (*tellement brosser les Autrichiens*) that they and their anti-Liberal principles will give no more trouble for a long time to come."

Cheerful, confident, warm-hearted, slangy, General Bazaine with his eye for landscape and his dislike of war and his progressive principles sat writing in his headquarters on a summer day in 1859. He thought the war would soon be over. But it ended rather sooner than any of them thought. For inside a week two emperors had met by a road-side, and a hurried peace was signed at Villafranca. Austria was disinclined for further shocks; and the intelligence that Germany was mobilising to stop Napoleon from going further was a warning to the French. For they had managed to defeat the Austrians, and that was quite enough.

6

Another war was safely over; and French prestige was intact. That was something to be thankful for in view of all that might have happened. Had the enemy been anyone except the Austrians, the result must have been very different; and if Napoleon had pushed on to Venice, France might have been invaded by the Germans. But though the margin had been narrow, he had won the war. Indeed, the world at large was much impressed by a campaign in which the Emperor had commanded his own armies in the Napoleonic fashion and won two victories that gave their names to Paris streets and bridges, to new members of his nobility, to the latest colours created by the aniline process for feminine delight. But though Mac-Mahon was Duc de Magenta and the Pont de Solférino spanned the Seine, France was by no means unassailable. There was one more triumphal march through Paris, and the Emperor's head was laurelled on his coins and postage-stamps. But Napoleon had seen the muddle and known black moments of uncertainty during the campaign. He had withdrawn before the German challenge for the simple reason that his forces were unequal to a European war on two fronts. Indeed, there might be grounds for fearing for them in a war on one. He saw their limitations plainly. When a cavalry commander displayed unusual incompetence, the Emperor's comment was revealing. For as he dismissed the *beau sabreur* as "very second-rate," he added bleakly, "*C'est un bon général d'Afrique.*" Soldiers of that calibre had been good enough to beat Abd-el-Kader; but was it quite enough for Europe?

Untouched by these misgivings, his subjects packed the streets to watch the conquerors march by. Bronzed Zouaves were all the fashion, and swarthy Turcos became the cynosure of Paris omnibuses. But some of them were still in Italy; and early in 1860 General Bazaine was writing sadly from Pavia, where he had been joined by his Marie:

"You will have heard from Georgina about my dear Marie's accident; our hopes are disappointed once again, and we are very sad. My dear wife's health is still uncertain. What she needs is warmth and more distraction. There is nothing of the

sort at Pavia, where the sky is always as grey and the air as
damp as Holland. You would be surprised; but we have none
of the blue sky of Italy. I believe it only exists at Naples and
Florence.

"There has been some talk lately of the return of the army
to France. We shall be moving soon, because my Division has
been at Pavia for eight months, with fever in the autumn and
snow all the winter (there is still some left in the garden and
on some of the house-tops). The question of peace seems to be
settled, and unless the Devil takes a hand in the Pope's affairs,
there is every hope that Central Italy is now free and has seen
the last of the Austrians. The whole country is full of enthusiasm; and I have great hopes of its future, if they do not drive
it ahead too fast to want to liberate Venetia and take in the
Papal States and the Kingdom of Naples; because, make no mistake about it, *that is the object of the Italian extremists*. They
may be right. But before anything else it is indispensable for
this new group of twelve million people to organise itself and
to become a national unit, both from the military and the administrative point of view; and in order to achieve that they
must have some years of internal calm and peace.

"The King of Piedmont has given me the Grand Cordon of
his Military Order of Savoy. That will be a souvenir of this
fine campaign of Italy. But these honours do not make us
richer, as one has to pay big fees to the Chancery for leave to
wear them; and nowadays we do not get the big money-grants
of the First Empire."

Perhaps the cautious warrior withheld his dues, since he was
never authorised to wear the Order of Savoy in France. But
three months later he was back in Paris with his division;
and when the command came to an end, he inspected troops
in France for the next year or two.

General Bazaine was quite a figure now, with his handsome
wife and his ability to pass shrewd judgments on political
events in foreign countries; and when another move was made
to do something for poor Doineau, who was still serving his

life sentence in a convict prison at Tours, Bazaine took some part in bringing it before the Emperor. The captain was released, entered the Spanish service in Morocco, and had the pleasure of helping Queen Isabella to defeat the same tribesmen he had dealt with in the old days on the French side of the frontier. Then he disappeared into the unmilitary duties of managing the gas-works at Monte Carlo, while Bazaine progressed sedately on the higher levels of his profession. But though their paths diverged once more, they had not crossed for the last time.

CHAPTER III

MEXICO

Toreador, en garde,
Et songe en combattant
Qu'un œil noir te regarde
Et que l'amour t'attend.
CARMEN.

I

FOREIGN investment is by no means an unmixed blessing either to lenders or to borrowers. It frequently involves investors in losses they can ill afford to bear; and it leaves borrowers with the distasteful obligation of repayment. Indeed, by the mysterious operations of finance the only profit often lies with those intermediaries by whom those burdens are transmitted to either party. These unfortunate phenomena were all present in the case of Mexico. Large numbers of investors had lost considerable sums of money, as the orderly development of its natural resources was inconsistent with a chronic state of civil war; and the promptitude with which successive governments repudiated one another's obligations rendered any hope of recovery extremely faint. It was not even clear that the financiers were making anything, when a Paris house with a Swiss proprietor named Jecker went bankrupt in 1860. But as its assets consisted largely of an astronomical number of bonds issued by President Miramon and repudiated by President Juarez, the best solution for the creditors appeared to be a change of President.

75

French policy was interested in M. Jecker's claims against the Mexicans, because his operations had been conducted on the Paris market and he had influential friends. The Duc de Morny was the Emperor's half-brother; he had helped to save society by the *Coup d'état* of 1851; and having saved it, he saw no reason why he should not continue to enjoy its benefits. He had been in business before the Second Empire; and though there was no reason for a high Imperial dignitary to remain in business, he had a *flair*. Unhappily his *flair* included Mexico; and Morny had a large financial interest in the successful prosecution of M. Jecker's claims. Who was to prosecute them? Jecker was a Swiss; and the Swiss Confederation rarely intervenes decisively in international affairs. But his creditors were largely French; he was a Paris banker; Morny's interest had been enlisted; and as M. Jecker was in process of becoming a French subject, these happy circumstances united to wrap him in the tricolour and to make his claims against the government of President Juarez a matter of official concern to French diplomacy in Mexico.

But the last word was with the Emperor. Napoleon's control of French policy was absolute; and no step was ever taken which did not form part of some design emanating from the vague reflections of that great, if somewhat cloudy, thinker. Palmerston once wrote that his "mind seems as full of schemes as a warren is full of rabbits"; and its crowded population was even livelier than usual on the subject of the Americas. He had been thinking vaguely about the Western Hemisphere for years. Whilst he was in a French prison, he had received a deputation from Ecuador in search of an imposing President; about the same time some gentlemen from Nicaragua interested him in an inter-oceanic canal, which was to bear his name and cross the Isthmus by a route far superior to that by way of Panama; and his lifelong taste for brooding over maps impelled Louis Napoleon to trace its course and write a pamphlet on the subject. But its utility was not to be confined to world communications, since he had a large conception of unfolding prospects for Central America. This region seemed to lie, like a latter-day Byzantium, half-way between east and west. Besides, it might perform an even nobler function in its own hemisphere by lying between north and south. For North America, it seemed, was largely permeated by the Anglo-Saxons. He had seen something of them, when he was in New York; and it appeared unnecessary for the remainder of the continent to become entangled in the sprawling growth of the United States.

This might be avoided, if a solid Latin unit could be created somewhere. Why not (he was still brooding over maps) in Mexico? True, a weak Mexican republic had just failed to withstand the rising tide of American expansion in the course of an injudicious war with the United States, which ended by withdrawing Mexico's frontier six hundred miles across the whole width of the continent and leaving California, New Mexico, Texas, and Santa Fé to the United States. But this distasteful process need not be repeated, if French policy succeeded in erecting something stable between the oncoming Yankees and the helpless mass of South America. They had got no further south than the Rio Grande; and if they could be halted there, a grateful hemisphere would look to France. Most of Napoleon's errors were due to his illusion that nations are capable of gratitude. A kindly man himself, he looked in vain for kindliness in international relations. *Les nations*, as somebody had said, *n'ont pas de cousins*. But in spite of this unpleasant truth Napoleon III was always trying to do something for some foreign nation in the hope of winning an ally for France. The results hitherto were disappointing. The Russians appeared to be unmoved by a generous peace settlement; the Italians rewarded him for their liberation by loud demonstrations of ingratitude; and when the time came, Mexicans were strikingly ungrateful for his touching anxiety for their cultural integrity in face of Anglo-Saxon penetration.

But his plans were rarely simple; and there was more than one thread in the web Napoleon was weaving about Mexico. If stability was desired, it was plainly unattainable under President Juarez; and the last forty years of local history appeared to indicate that it would be equally remote so long as Mexican affairs were in the hands of a republic. After all, the Emperor was a convinced monarchist. Had he not destroyed the Second Republic, and was not France a better place than it had been in 1848? Outside M. Jecker's native country there were no republics left in Europe; and in 1861 it was not easy to resist a feeling that republics were not doing very well elsewhere. The United States had just disintegrated into civil war, a state from which most of their Spanish-speaking neighbours only intermittently emerged. The notion of a monarchy in the New World has come to look a trifle odd. But there was nothing odd about it in the days when the largest state in South America, occupying nearly half of the sub-continent and rather larger than the United States, was governed by the Emperor Dom Pedro of Brazil. Why not an Emperor of Mexico? King-making was always an amusing business. Besides, his uncle had surrounded France with a constellation of Imperial satellites; and where the First Empire had shone with benign radiance upon the Kingdoms of Spain, Naples, Holland, and Westphalia, why should not the Second Empire go one better and, calling the New World into being to redress the balance of the Old, see its own brilliance reflected in an Empire of Mexico? There had been one for a few stormy years under Agustín de Iturbide; and if Napoleon could only constitute another, it would be (like his own) a Second Empire.

That was not all. If there was to be an Empire, there would have to be an Emperor; and perhaps he would be able to find somebody who would not only be grateful for his elevation, but might leave others with the same emotion towards his benefactor. Moved by his eternal craving for gratitude (and a haunting sense that his work for Italy had been left half-done in 1859), Napoleon was still endeavouring to do something more for the Italians. True, he had helped them to Milan. But his pledge to recover Italy from the Alps to the Adriatic was still unredeemed. For German solidarity had checked him before he could reach Venice, and the Austrian white-coats were still on the Grand Canal. If he could only manage to get Venice for them, surely the Italians could not help being grateful. Then his task in Italy would be complete, and France might have a faithful ally. But this could only be achieved with Austrian consent; and that depended on the Emperor Franz-Joseph. There could be no question of another war with Austria; but diplomacy might do the trick, if he could find a way to win Franz-Joseph's gratitude.

This potentate had an Archducal brother named Maxi-milian, whose popularity was sometimes a shade embarrassing to the reigning Hapsburg; and if Napoleon was only instru-mental in transferring him to the next hemisphere, it was just possible that a grateful Emperor might see reason about Venice. That strange, lovely city he had never seen haunted Napoleon, as he sat smoking endless cigarettes over his maps. One Hapsburg crowned Emperor of Mexico might mean an-other grateful Hapsburg in Vienna, who would have it in his power to yield Venice to the Italians; and if that dream came true, Italian and Austrian gratitude would mean two European allies for France, to say nothing of a Latin *bloc* in the New World under French patronage. It was all as insubstantial as the blue smoke of his cigarette. His thought was always shadowy; but there was no denying that the thinker, who sat smoking in the Tuileries, had come a long way from his start-ing-point. He had always been a schemer; and as the greatest of his schemes had ended in the Second Empire, who could say there was no chance for one more dream? A loyal minister termed it ecstatically *"la plus grande pensée du règne"*; and as it beckoned, Napoleon moved slowly forward like a sleepwalker, launching his country, his army, Maximilian, Charlotte, and Bazaine into the Mexican adventure.

2

The slope was gradual. At first there was a notion that France, Spain, and England might secure the desired result by a joint expedition to Mexico. But as the results desired by each of them were entirely different, their collaboration was short-lived. There was a tripartite treaty justifying European intervention on the customary ground of a desire not to intervene; and the expedition sailed. The British, who were not greatly interested in their fellow-subjects' claims against the Mexicans, sent a few Marines under a commodore; the French, whose claims were larger, sent Marines and some Zouaves under an admiral; and the Spaniards—with a hazy notion that there might be a chance of recovering their lost colony—sent a brigade under a general, which was not only the largest of the three contingents, but broke all historic records by arriving first. This unique phenomenon startled the French into sending out a general with reinforcements. As yellow fever was the only coast-defence at Vera Cruz, their landing was unopposed. Indeed, the Mexicans politely agreed to their advance into the less pestilential *hinterland* in order to discuss the points in dispute. But before they were effectively discussed, the alliance had disintegrated. For the French began to show their hand; and there were rumours that they had a likely claimant for the throne of Mexico. Eager emissaries had been tip-toeing about the Continent; the Archduke Maximilian had been approached; Napoleon had murmured his approval; Franz-Joseph was understood to be favourable; the sagacious Leopold, who had once been offered Mexico as well as Greece and now ruled Belgium in the intervals of writing to instruct his niece, Victoria, on the art of ruling Great Britain, was not averse from the bright prospect of his daughter, Charlotte, as an Empress in the New World; and dark, eager Charlotte looked on, while Maximilian stared at the Adriatic from the tall windows of Miramar and turned his thoughts to Mexico. All this was very damping for the Spaniards, since it left no opening for a Bourbon, and still less for General Prim in spite of the hopeful circumstance that his consort was a Mexican; and while Spanish interest in the affair evaporated, the British were frankly shocked. For it was no part of British policy to take sides in Mexican disputes; and when their allies sailed away, the French were left alone in Mexico.

Their problem was simple, although it was not altogether clear that they had assembled all the elements for solving it. If the Mexicans were only reasonable and consented to dispense with President Juarez and to pay large sums of money for the benefit of M. Jecker and his creditors, it seemed as though they would get off with nothing worse than an Austrian Archduke. But if they found this diet unpalatable, there would be no alternative to force. In that event the only question was whether the French could bring sufficient force to bear; and it soon became obvious that they could not. Their first objective was the capital, since decisions of the nature contemplated by the French could hardly be reached elsewhere. Mexico City lay more than two hundred miles from Vera Cruz; and it was demonstrated in the course of 1862 that 6,000 bayonets were insufficient to cover that distance in face of opposition. For when they had got halfway, they were checked decisively before the Mexican positions at Puebla. It was an unpleasant surprise to find that President Juarez was not nearly so unpopular at home as his fellow-countrymen abroad had given them to understand; and it was still more humiliating for a French brigade to be defeated by the Mexicans. This reverse could hardly be ignored; and there was plainly nothing for it but to send out more reinforcements and to hope devoutly for the best. For whatever misgivings Napoleon might feel about his army in a European war, even

Algerian practitioners should be able to command success in Mexico; and after midsummer General Forey was hurried off from Cherbourg, entrusted with almost vice-regal powers and two divisions. The first of these was to be commanded by General Bazaine. His name had been proposed by Marshal Randon, who had long African experience and was Minister of War; and when Napoleon III wrote, "*J'accepte Bazaine*," he changed the course of Achille's life and, perhaps, of European history.

It was a great opportunity for a rising soldier, since Mexico might suit Bazaine. Its problems were, to some extent, political; and he had developed a considerable aptitude for politics in the *Bureau arabe*, to say nothing of his old familiarity with Spanish factions in the Carlist War. Besides, he spoke the language. Other Frenchmen might be at a disadvantage with the Mexicans; but Bazaine was quite at home. If military reputations were to be made in Mexico, there were grounds for hoping that this burly man of fifty-one, who spoke good Spanish and had a way of penetrating other people's motives with his narrow stare and charming manners, was on the point of making his.

As wives were not encouraged to accompany an expedition to the tropics with a long sea voyage and a high mortality from yellow fever, he left his dear Marie behind and sailed from Toulon in a warship with four hundred infantry on board one August day in 1862. They were nearly eight weeks on the way. If Toulon had been hot, it was still hotter at Teneriffe, where a tall mountain watched them from the sky and nobody went ashore. But they all landed at Martinique, and official wisdom directed them to discard the massive shako in favour of straw hats, speedily replaced by white linen covers for their *képis*. The voyage could not last for ever, though; and halfway through October they saw the breakers on the reefs and the low foreshore and the crowded masts of all the transports in the roads of Vera Cruz. Seventy miles

away the snow looked down from Orizaba. But before they
could breathe the thin, exhilarating upland air, the tropics
welcomed the newcomers with a rich repertory of rain, hurri-
cane, and yellow fever in the empty streets, where dogs and
buzzards scuffled in the dust of Vera Cruz. This was hardly
what impulsive Zouaves, who had been writing to their
families about "the conquest of the richest country in the
world," were anticipating; and as the rain drove down on
Vera Cruz, it was not easy to appreciate the Emperor's great
idea. But it persisted; his instructions to Forey dwelt lingeringly on the benefits to be derived from the survival of an
independent Mexico under French patronage, contrasted with
the odious alternative of domination by the United States. It
was not easy at the moment to imagine that anyone could
covet Vera Cruz. But, after all, that unpleasant seaport was a
mere frontispiece; and enthusiasts continued to view the
expedition as a brilliant *coup* in spite of heat, damp, mos-
quitoes, yellow fever, a lack of practically every form of
nourishment except a few unlikely vegetables and drinking-
water whose properties were mainly medicinal, and an alarming landscape with a foreground populated by a few dazed
Indians.

General Bazaine waited in the insanitary lowlands for his
division to disembark. He was to command eight battalions of
infantry and two batteries; and he employed the interval in
clearing the neighbourhood by a few minor operations in
driving rain against stray *guerrilleros*. Then, diverging from
the road to Orizaba, he made a sweep with a small column in
order to impress the region of Jalapa. It was an operation of
the type conducted by French columns in Algeria for years;
and it held no surprises for Bazaine. He rode with the advance-
guard, which was duly ambushed; and one of his staff officers
was killed. On the next day (there was a heavy fog that turned
to icy drizzle) large quantities of mounted Mexicans were
scattered by a fraction of their number; and after that a

nonagenarian fort was captured without incident. The sole military problem had been to choose his moment for launching a squadron of Chasseurs d'Afrique against a wheeling mass of Mexicans; and he was perfectly at home. For Bazaine had spent twenty years in Africa; and the operations of a column of 4,000 men against a disappearing enemy were well within his range.

But Puebla was a harder nut to crack. Lorencez's 6,000 men had made no impression on its outer forts in 1862; and when Forey moved against the place in the next year with 26,000 men, he proceeded with immense deliberation. For General Forey was not taking risks; and in pursuance of this cautious policy he took steps calculated to identify his subordinates with such consequences as might ensue by summoning them to a council of war for the endorsement of his plans. Forey was a conscientious soldier. Had he not reported Bazaine seven years before for preferring home and beauty to the trenches one winter night before Sebastopol? But if there was to be another failure before Puebla, Forey did not propose to be a lonely scapegoat. When the day arrived, however, a well-timed call of duty prevented Bazaine from attending the conclave. For if General Forey was not taking risks, neither was General Bazaine.

If they were to conquer Mexico, there was really no alternative to an attack on Puebla, which lay astride the route from the coast to the capital. Its belfries gleamed in the spring sunshine behind a ring of formidable forts, watched by the square bulk of Malinche on the sky; and the French slowly drew their net round the fortress. Bazaine, a master of the *petite guerre*, systematically cut and held the outlets to the west and then presided imperturbably over a successful assault on the first fortified position. But their success was limited by the apparent resolution of the Mexicans to ignore military science by defending every building in the city; and as these were solidly constructed and Mexicans were always formidable behind walls, there was every prospect that Puebla would attain distinction as a New-World Saragossa. Progress was extremely slow; and as the gunfire rolled round the city, the French knew some anxious moments with diminishing supplies of ammunition in the interior of a strange continent four thousand miles from home. A relieving army lay somewhere to the north of them; and there was a risk that it might be able to run the gauntlet into Puebla and to introduce supplies, which would enable the fortress to prolong its defence indefinitely. Bazaine was detached to dissipate this menace. His command consisted of two mountain guns, a battery, three squadrons, and four battalions. Its strength was almost exactly that of one of Marshal Bugeaud's typical flying columns in Algeria, which had normally contained two mountain-guns, two squadrons, and three or four battalions. If his force's composition was African, its proceedings were equally familiar. Marching an hour after midnight as though they had been moving out of Tlemcen to catch Abd-el-Kader before dawn, they surprised the Mexicans at sunrise and assaulted a position held by twice their own numbers. Bazaine had ridden with his advance-guard on the night-march (night-marches were no novelty for him); and he launched his 3,500 men confidently at the height of San Lorenzo, which was held by at least 6,000 Mexicans. The bold attack succeeded. Eight guns, large quantities of stores, some flags, and 1,000 prisoners formed a gratifying haul; and Forey's order of the day paid tribute to Bazaine's precision and success, with special mention of the favourable influence exercised on the troops under his command by his inspiring qualities—"*son coup d'œil, son sang froid et sa bravoure entraînante.*" The troops, indeed, were vastly impressed. For they saw little of Forey. But Bazaine had ridden with them; they had seen him under fire; and he was always strolling round among them with his friendly air and a stick in his hand, as Conrad used to stroll among the *légionnaires* in Spain. That was where he had learnt to handle men, as he had learnt the art of war in Africa. Bazaine was a good learner; and while the Foreign Legion had taught him how officers make themselves popular, his Algerian experience pointed the way to victory with a flying column and a night-march.

The siege went on, as spring deepened into summer. The ring tightened round Puebla, and the Mexicans surrendered. There was a French *Te Deum* at the great cathedral in the square; and Bazaine rode behind General Forey between two lines of French bayonets. Then they moved on towards the capital. Bazaine went with the advance-guard; and after an icy night in the dank, cutthroat defile of Rio Frio (which was mercifully undefended) a carriage-load of foreign consuls bore down upon them flying the white flag and bringing news that President Juarez and his government had left Mexico City for the north. When they ventured on superfluous political advice, Bazaine replied with something less than his customary urbanity that their official duties were confined to the care of their own nationals, that the French proposed to enter Mexico, and that their subsequent proceedings would be quite independent of consular advice. A week later his division marched into the city. There was no ceremony, as Bazaine was careful to leave all formalities for the Commander-in-chief, who was to follow in a few days. But the Chasseurs d'Afrique were brushed and polished to distraction; their officers were exquisitely gloved; and the white linen of their cap-covers gleamed (as their proud commander wrote) "like new-born butterflies." There was some cheering in the narrow streets. But three days later, when Forey rode in with bands playing, all the bells were reeling in the city's belfries and the balconies were packed with exquisite brunettes in ball-dresses, who pelted the marching columns with bright flowers, until the streets of Mexico were carpeted with colour and the limbers rolled in muffled silence, as the guns went by. In the great square between the palace and the cathedral that

King Philip built on the site of Montezuma's sanctuary they could see robed clergy waiting in the porch to honour their rescuers. For the Church had no love for President Juarez. There was one more *Te Deum;* and that night General Forey slept in the palace.

But Mexican affairs were never simple; and perhaps the gruff Forey was not quite the man to handle them. It seemed easy to appoint a Regency of three Mexicans—two generals and an archbishop—who assembled two hundred notables. These worthies promptly voted for a monarchy with Maximilian as Emperor of Mexico. But things were not so easy with President Juarez adrift somewhere in the north and a lively outbreak of guerrilla warfare at any point in the vast territory where French sentries were not posted. There was something to be said for a fresh start and a new method before Maximilian could safely enter on his Empire; and in the autumn Forey was informed by the French mail that he was now a Marshal and that he was ordered home on the polite excuse that its conqueror was not the man to organise the country. The command in Mexico was transferred to his enterprising junior, General Bazaine. There was an uneasy interlude, while Forey struggled vainly to retain his post. But he went at last; and one Sunday in October, 1863, the French staff rode with him out of the city and down the road to Vera Cruz. Then they turned and rode back to Mexico with General Bazaine.

On the day that he took over the command a deputation of hopeful Mexicans arrived in Trieste. Two days later they were privately received at noon under a gleaming chandelier in the blue *salon* of Miramar; and that highly castellated edifice had never witnessed a more romantic scene. For ten dark strangers were inviting their blond, bearded host to come to Mexico as Emperor. Their invitation was supported by written evidence of the assent of no less than two hundred of their fellow-countrymen, in which five towns and thirty-seven villages between the sea-coast and the capital concurred. But they were slightly damped when Maximilian appeared to stipulate for a free vote of the whole country, adding that his notions of a monarchy were strictly constitutional, not to say progressive. This was not what his callers meant at all. For the *fine fleur* of Mexican reaction, if only they could manage to get rid of President Juarez, had other notions of a Mexican holiday; and the deputation left hoping privately that Maximilian would feel differently, when he knew Mexico a little better.

3

The new commander would need all his cleverness. For Mexico in 1863 was not, and was unlikely to become, a bed of roses. While Maximilian wrestled with his doubts, Napoleon had come to a clear vision of realities. He could see now that he had been ill-informed about the state of Mexican opinion, although he still retained a hope that it would rally round a monarchy. This happy consummation would enable him to withdraw his army, leaving a small nucleus behind for the formation of a local force under the new Imperial flag of Mexico. "*Je me suis couché dans un mauvais lit,*" he ruefully observed, "*je le comprends, mais l'affaire doit être liquidée.*" That process, however, could not begin before an Emperor was on the scene in Mexico; and Maximilian was lucidly informed that if he hesitated, someone else could play the part. For there was more than one prince with a taste for travel; and Napoleon (who was broad-minded about Bourbons now) had been thinking of the Prince de Joinville. This pressure was designed to put the hesitating Hapsburg, as a French minister remarked, "*au pied du mur,*" though nobody in 1863 foresaw that the wall would be at Querétaro, and that there would be a firing-party too.

The situation in Mexico was uninviting; and if its attractions were not yet clear to Maximilian, its complications were

quite sufficient to occupy Bazaine. That resourceful man was
diagnosed this year by a brother-officer as *"un homme d'une
grande intelligence; très fin, très habile, sachant tourner les
obstacles lorsqu'il ne peut les renverser, mais arrivant à son
but."* His prestige was high with the Mexicans as well as with
his own command; and when his first official banquet heard
the new Commander-in-chief make a speech in Spanish,
everybody was impressed. The problem at the moment was
to reconcile the country to the coming Empire; and this was
not facilitated by the Regency's insistence upon confiscating
its rivals' assets and disseminating doubts as to the title under
which large numbers of the population owned Church property duly purchased from the previous regime. His own
politics were distinctly liberal; and eager clerics in pursuit of
their endowments made them still more so. Bazaine even ran
far ahead of contemporary views in his belief that the future
of Mexico lay with the patient Indians and that the prospects
of the new Empire would be assured, "if it emancipates this
good Indian race." It was more than half a century before the
discovery that Mexico belongs to the Mexicans dawned on
the world at large. But a torn letter of Bazaine's records his
opinion that "Mexico . . . to-day is no longer the Mexico of
the Span . . ." This was almost visionary in 1863. But he had
little time for visions with his daily effort to mitigate the
Archbishop's asperity and to keep Maximilian's supporters
together. Nor was life rendered any simpler by increasing
evidence of North American sympathy for the republicans or
by indications that Jules Favre's unsparing criticism of the
expedition might have a financial origin.

But the main problem was military. For though President
Juarez had left his capital, he had taken the republic with him
in his waggons; and it survived at the headquarters of his army
in the north. The French controlled a strip of territory between the capital and Vera Cruz. But the rest of the vast
country was still governed, if at all, in the name of the repub-

lic; and until this menace was disposed of, the new Emperor could hardly hope to reign. Three-quarters of a million square miles was a large area to control with 40,000 men. Half as big again as Algeria, its dusty spaces were not unlike the scene on which Bazaine had learnt the art of war; and if its nomadic President was as elusive as Abd-el-Kader, there were some grounds for hoping that the trouble might yield to the same treatment. Bazaine's grand strategy was wise. For he declined to dissipate his strength in pursuing stray *guerrilleros* or holding a front from the Gulf of Mexico to the Pacific. His design was simply stated:

> "It would be a military blunder to extend our line, which is already lengthened by the necessity of covering our base. We cannot have our right at Vera Cruz and our left on the Pacific.
> "We are confronted in the north by troop concentrations, and they must be dealt with first . . . First we must preserve our major interests and attend to details afterwards. . . . I repeat, when I have finished with the regular forces in the north, I will consider operations against the bands which you report."

Late in the year, when the rains ended, Bazaine opened his campaign. Setting 14,000 French and 7,000 Mexicans in motion, he formed his forces in two columns. Each of these consisted of five infantry battalions and two or three squadrons of cavalry, almost precisely the same numbers as he had handled with success at San Lorenzo, and only one battalion more than Marshal Bugeaud's standard column for operations in Algeria. For Bazaine was true to type; and he proposed to clear the country by the method which had served so well in Africa. A few nights before he left the capital he gave a dinner to the Regency; and his officers watched him exchanging Spanish courtesies with the three *caciques*, as Bazaine's burly figure and dark imperial moved between the plump Archbishop and the Indian mask of a Mexican general. The French columns were already thrusting north; and the General combined their operations deftly, shepherding the repub-

licans further and further from the centre of the country.
They moved fast without much fighting, capturing large
quantities of arms; and as the French advanced, Juarez fell
back helplessly towards the deserts of the north, his capital
receding two hundred and fifty miles from San Luis Potosí
to Monterrey. It was a new version of the old hunt for Abd-
el-Kader; and just as the Emir had been driven into the
Sahara or off the board into Morocco, the President was
swiftly edged towards the inhospitable desert spaces lying
between Mexico and the United States. Behind him the
French columns pounded through the chaparral, watched by
the gaunt mountains; and as the area of French control extended, its populations were invited to indicate their acceptance of the new Imperial regime. A few signatures did duty
for entire communities; and as the tide ran northward, an
impressive list of cities seemed to show that Maximilian could
count upon support in Morelia, Guanajuato, Leon, San Luis
Potosí, Aguascalientes, and even Querétaro.

Bazaine's task in 1863 was brilliantly performed. It took
Marshal Forey nearly six months to cover the short road between the coast and Puebla; but General Bazaine had cleared
the centre of the country in six weeks. He was soon reporting
to Napoleon that there was every ground for hoping that the
military problem would be definitely solved in the first weeks
of 1864 and that Mexico, if not pacified, was at least conquered, since the enemy had been driven from his bases into
the desert or the hills, where he would ultimately vanish after
a guerrilla phase. Indeed, Bazaine's diplomacy seemed to afford some prospect of an arrangement with the republicans,
with whom he was in contact. Instructing his supporters to
abstain from steps calculated to identify them with reaction,
he caused a leading colleague of President Juarez to be informed that the French "inclined to generosity and that the
Commander-in-chief hoped to surround himself with good
citizens of moderate liberal opinions." This was a shrewd

démarche according with Bazaine's political convictions; and it was consistent with the views already indicated by the new Emperor. Besides, the General had full authority from his own sovereign, who had already assured him with unusual freedom of his "complete confidence; act as you think best; I shall always approve." A free hand from Napoleon III was a rare privilege; and what more could he require for the discharge of his viceregal duties?

The war was nearly over; and he would soon be seeing his Marie again. She had always been with him in Turkey and the Crimea and at his headquarters in Italy; and soon her dark beauty would reign beside the latest viceroy of Mexico. It was a long way from the widow Tormo's at Tlemcen, where he had first set eyes on her, to the pink stone façade of Cortés' palace in Mexico. She was older now; and they had been together nearly fifteen years. She was still delicate; but he hoped she would be coming out that winter with the new French minister. It was not long since Bazaine had asked a young gentleman of the Chasseurs d'Afrique, who was invalided home, to take her a parcel of gay Mexican materials and strange Indian jewellery. With any luck the wounded hero should reach France just before she sailed; and when he got to Paris, he heard that Madame Bazaine was staying with one of her husband's relatives in the suburban peace of Chatou. He set out with the parcel. But it was undelivered. For when he arrived, they told him that Madame Bazaine would never sail for Mexico, as she had just died very suddenly.

An unkind world preferred to detect a tragedy. She had always smiled at gentlemen since the distant days when she ogled officers in the theatre at Tlemcen; and it was whispered that this time she had smiled at one with an irritable wife at the Comédie Française, who had achieved success as the heroine of *The Barber of Seville*. But it was one thing to declaim Beaumarchais' sentiments about romance, and quite another to discover a romantic correspondence on her own premises in Madame Bazaine's handwriting. Rumour added that the incensed artiste promptly posted it to General Bazaine, informing his impulsive wife of this thoughtful action, and a haggard woman rushed to Compiègne, saw the Emperor, and begged him to stop the mail before the fatal news could reach her husband. Napoleon, who had occasionally strayed himself, was sympathetic. Besides, it was important that Bazaine should not be unduly worried. But his orders came too late; and in this tragic version when Marie heard that her unhappy letters were on the way to Mexico, a frightened woman went home to die.

Her fears were quite unfounded, since no correspondence ever reached Bazaine. He was away on active service; and if any package came it was opened by his faithful staff. For Bazaine had his intimates. Indeed, his military circle bore the impress of his strong family instincts. An ugly little major named Boyer, son of a general of the First Republic, worked with two of Bazaine's nephews and a lean, long-bearded captain named Willette (whom everybody called 'the Padre') in the General's private office. Bazaine had learnt to be secretive in the *Bureau arabe;* and his confidences were confined to his own subordinates in Mexico, where secrecy was still more imperative. When the mail arrived and Bazaine was in the north they opened it. A wise precaution, it was whispered, spared him further pain by burning Marie's letters. A week afterwards word came that she was dead; and another nephew on his staff broke the sad news at a dusty bivouac in Guanajuato. Bazaine was prostrate. For so much of him lay dead with his Marie—all their plans for Mexico, the house in Italy, cathedral days at Bourges, the hut before Sebastopol, the Turkish house where her piano used to tinkle at the Dardanelles, long rides together near Oran, and the sharp note of castanets in a moon-lit courtyard at Tlemcen. All that was over now; and his royal master wrote gracious condolences from Eugénie and himself to a heart-broken subject. Mac-

Mahon had once objected to his marrying her. But Mac-Mahon was always stupid; and when he lost her, sovereigns condoled with him. The widower responded dutifully that he felt his loss so deeply that he could only thank Their Majesties, assuring them that the remainder of his life belonged to them. The cloud was on him for some time. But afterwards (he may have heard the dreadful tale) the burden seemed to lift; and Bazaine walked with a lighter step.

His private tragedy apart, he had every reason to feel satisfied in the early weeks of 1864. He was in supreme command; Napoleon appeared to have unbounded confidence in him ("I have only to give you *carte blanche* and to tell you to act for the best in the light of your own judgment"); and his trust had been brilliantly discharged in a campaign of six weeks. Swift, effective, and involving strikingly few casualties, Bazaine's operations wholly justified his method. The well-planned advance of his converging and diverging columns swept the vast country like a drag-net; the republicans were herded away from market-towns and driven out into the wilderness or up into the hills, where they could be hunted down at leisure; and behind his swift-moving lines the central provinces of Mexico were cleared and ready to receive the new regime. Whether that was capable of holding all the French had won and keeping what passed in Mexico for order was another question, which Bazaine was not called upon to answer by himself. But the unbroken success of his campaign, coming after the mixed fortunes of his two predecessors before Puebla, showed him to be a brilliant practitioner of the class of warfare that was required in Mexico. Unlike them, he seemed to see that the vast, empty *terrain* called for a repetition of Algerian methods, though he did not disdain local innovations, indulging in the picturesque expedient of Colonel Dupin's big-hatted *Contreguerrilla* and Turcos on horse-back and other military monstrosities. Success is the sole test of military wisdom; and Bazaine's campaign of

1863–4 was a complete success in planning and in execution. Few commanders in recent times had reached their objectives in shorter time or at lighter cost; and it was tragic that his personal bereavement shadowed this brilliant performance.

The tangled skein of politics brought him back to the capital, where the Regency was always tiresome. (Bazaine's outcries about the Regency of Mexico bear a strong resemblance to Wellington's about the Regency of Portugal.) Monsignor Labastida, with the fatal inability of archbishops to recognise their own limitations, encroached in all directions. But Bazaine was lucidly resolved to confine this enterprising cleric to "the spiritual direction of his flock." The crucial question of Church property was always present; and politics in Mexico, which were never simple, threatened to become still more complicated, when General Santa Anna, a one-legged veteran of Mexican disorder, returned from exile with profuse announcements of his loyalty to the new regime. But old habits were too strong for him; and when he could not resist publishing a manifesto, Bazaine promptly had him arrested and returned to outer darkness in a French warship. For the General was not easy-going, and his tolerance did not extend to civil war.

His immediate duty was to make Mexico a land fit for Maximilian to reign in. For the adventurous Archduke had overcome his hesitations now. A treaty regulated the new Emperor's relations with the French, providing that their forces would remain in Mexico until the situation could be stabilised in the early future by the recruitment of an army under Maximilian's own flag. The rate of French withdrawal was prescribed in a secret article and would leave him with at least 20,000 French soldiers at the end of 1867; and the treaty undertook that, "whatever events may occur in Europe, the assistance of France will never fail the new Empire." Napoleon's diplomacy was not Bazaine's affair. He was four thousand miles away in Mexico when the Convention of

Miramar was signed in Paris; and if there was to be any breach of faith, it would not be Bazaine's. While Maximilian and Charlotte toured Europe collecting benedictions from their royal relatives, he was hard at work preparing Mexico for the blessings of monarchy. His sole contribution to the removal of their doubts was the transmission of evidence, assembled on the simple principle of multiplying any area that his troops controlled by the number of its population, that 6,500,000 Mexicans desired their presence. But he gave an explicit warning that this impressive total was by no means the result of universal suffrage, although it indicated, in his view, the opinions of a majority; but when there was a tendency to remedy this defect by a poll, Bazaine urged that it would be unwise to disturb a decision which had been obtained in consonance with local practice.

The war was practically over now excepting for a ring of distant provinces beyond the reach of French columns, where Porfirio Diaz fought on in the south-east and Juarez still maintained the republic in the north with his back to the United States. True, the State Department at Washington coldly refused to recognise Maximilian as Emperor. But he might be able to dispense with Mr. Lincoln's recognition, as it was not long since General Lee had threatened Washington itself, and the Confederates were likely to be more amenable. Bazaine's immediate problem was to govern Mexico until the Emperor arrived. He was an able viceroy, and French subordinates were shrewdly taught their duty:

"Your duty at Guadalajara is just the same as mine at Mexico towards the Regency. You have to supervise the administrative authorities with a view to preventing them from making errors that might unsettle opinion and disturb the country. This supervision must be exercised with tact and without hurting the feelings of highly-placed officials. You know enough of Spanish pride and local moods for me to indicate this difficulty without going into further detail.

BAZAINE IN MEXICO.
(From an old print in the author's possession)

"It is your right and duty to offer sound advice and to give warnings as to any measure inconsistent with the broad principles of Intervention policy.

"You have no right to dismiss officials; but when serious facts come to your notice, you should put the case to the Prefect with a request for action against the officials concerned and for a change of staff.

"As to any action taken by the Prefect himself which you may consider contrary to Intervention policy, harmful to the public good, and likely to produce dangerous consequences, you are entitled to notify the Prefect that action must be suspended whilst you refer to me. I will then take up with the Regency any points involving a difference of opinion; and everything will be settled without dispute, all parties bearing their due share of responsibility."

There have been worse manuals of inter-Allied conduct; and Bazaine's subordinates appeared to have a chief who knew his mind and had a firm grasp of procedure, tempered by the arts of management and a fair understanding of Mexican peculiarities.

His reign as viceroy of Mexico lasted for eight months; and it was a remarkable achievement for an ex-sergeant of the Foreign Legion. If bereavement still left him with ambitions, these were fairly satisfied by the exercise of power over a large population and an immense territory. He had few illusions about Mexico, deploring the inertia to which each applicant for public office happily succumbed after obtaining it, no less than the unworthy appetites of certain leaders. But, given wise leadership, he did not despair of the country's future. Its visible defects were firmly dealt with, as he encountered them; and Bazaine struggled manfully with unruly subordinates, imperfect sanitation, and a strong local tendency to transfer the criminal classes bodily into the armed forces. For this was Mexico, where it seemed advisable that year to prohibit the celebration of Easter Saturday by the customary immolation of unpopular public characters in effigy to the accompaniment of large quantities of fireworks (an edict wisely mitigated, at Bazaine's instance, by the subsequent payment of compensation to disappointed holders of large stocks of squibs); and he was not guilty of a facile belief that the country could be Europeanised by a form of words. That, perhaps, was to be Maximilian's illusion; but Bazaine was too clear-sighted to share it. He did his best with the available material, though his enthusiasm was reserved for the troops under his command. "These expeditions," he wrote buoyantly to Napoleon, "suit us; and if Your Majesty despatched us to the world's end, with soldiers like this we should go with the confidence of certain victory. We are so happy that the Emperor is satisfied with the conduct of his legions, and so proud to see our victorious eagles soaring over the two hemispheres." This was almost Napoleonic; and Bazaine had his Napoleonic moments. For he projected the creation of a commission for the encouragement of art, science, and literature in Mexico. French commanders and officials were incited to collaborate in the collection of interesting material for publication, exhibition, or transport to France. After all, Egyptology had been a by-product of General Bonaparte's descent on Egypt. Might not New-World learning owe an equal debt one day to General Bazaine? He attended the first meeting, flanked by the impassive mask of General Almonte. Nor were his interests confined to the past, since the sciences were amply represented, and a progressive outlook rare in 1864 included photography among the arts.

But time was passing, and Maximilian was on the way to his new Empire. Before May was out, an eager couple landed at Vera Cruz; and one afternoon in the second week of June, after an exciting and uncomfortable journey, they were receiving a heavy-eyed man in a French uniform at the chapter-house beneath the great dome of the Guadalupe a mile or so outside their capital. Two hundred carriage-loads of loyal

Mexican ladies and five hundred black-coated gentlemen on horseback had come to greet them; and the road was lined with cheerful Indians waving green branches. There were cries of "*Viva Maximiliano primero*" and "*Viva Napoleon tercero*"; and everybody shouted "*Viva*" and lifted their enormous hats. On the next day they drove into the city, Bazaine riding with drawn sword at the right-hand door of their carriage. It was his wedding-day; but his Marie was not there to see him ride beside an Emperor into his cheering capital.

4

Maximilian (it cannot be denied) was not clever. Had he been, perhaps he would not have come to Mexico. But life offered him few opportunities after his brother's heir was born. Now he would not reign in the Hofburg after Franz-Joseph. That glory was reserved for Rudolph; and Maximilian was left to his own resources, which were not inexhaustible. A sailor prince, he had written casually on his travels and published three pamphlets upon naval questions. But Austria is an unsatisfying *terrain* for a naval expert; and he found employment as a provincial Governor in Italy, where he was inclined to treat Italians reasonably rather than to rule by force of arms. This career was discontinued when the provinces he governed began to disappear in the disintegration of the Hapsburg Empire. For the world was growing less inclined to be ruled without apparent reason by Hapsburgs. Previously all they had to do was to inherit. But he was unlikely to succeed his brother now; and it was anything but clear what Maximilian could do next. That was how his services had come to be available for Mexico. Strictly Nordic in appearance, he possessed a magnificent blond beard, more suitable to large oil-paintings than for wear in the tropics; and as their folklore led the Mexicans to look forward hopefully to the arrival of a fair-haired stranger from the east, he seemed to fill the bill. Cortés had been a disappointment; but they might do better with Maximilian.

Besides, there was his handsome wife. For the new Emperor had brought his Empress, whose restlessness had a good deal to do with their acceptance of the new situation. Dark, active-minded, and intelligent, Charlotte had found residence at Miramar unsatisfying. She was her father's daughter; and King Leopold of Belgium accepted his royal destiny without complaint. If only his first wife had lived to become Queen of England, he would have been Prince Consort; and though Brussels was a second-best, he seemed to be related to practically every throne in Europe. For Coburgs married wisely; and while their Orleans connections seemed a little out of date since the disappearance of King Louis Philippe, one of his nephews was Prince Consort in England and another in Portugal. His Charlotte was a Saxe-Coburg-Gotha too; and when she married Maximilian, he was Franz-Joseph's heir. But that bright vista faded, when a son was born to her sister-in-law, Elizabeth, and her Max became just another Hapsburg. He could not reform the navy all the time, and they could not always be travelling. What were they to do all day at Miramar? Her botany and his collections somehow failed to satisfy; and even when he took to sculpture, there was still a void. For Charlotte was a Coburg, and what she really needed was a throne. When Mexico appeared to promise one, it gave them a great deal to think about. There had been hesitations. But all that was over now; and the young couple (he was thirty-two and she twenty-four) walked graciously between bowing Mexicans and saluting Frenchmen into their Empire.

Mexico might be a shade unusual. But if they had their way, its Court was going to conform to the best European models. The Empress (she was called Carlotta now) had her Grand Chamberlain, her Wardrobe, and her ladies. Some of them might look a little fierce and swarthy in their fashionable crinolines; but they were decorated with her Imperial cypher, and they bore the best names of Mexico. For if Señoras de la Peña de Hidalgo, Tagle de Adalid, and Gutierrez Estrada de Gonzalez Gutierrez sounded like a Court, there was no reason why they should not look like one. If they failed, indeed, it would not be for lack of effort upon everybody's part. An Austrian count, provided with a liberal supply of gold braid and aiguillettes and surmounted by an operatic helmet, commanded the palace guard and looked for all the world like *Lohengrin;* and old General Almonte in a large pair of epaulettes sustained the dignities of Grand Marshal of the Court and Minister of the Imperial Household. A year after their arrival a copperplate communication from the Emperor transmitted an impressive handbook, bound in green and stamped with a gold Imperial crown, containing full instructions upon what to do at Court and by whom it should be done, briefly conveyed in three hundred quarto pages of text and twenty diagrams. This solemn masterpiece adapted the grave decorum of the Hofburg for use in the New World; and if it was only followed, Charles V would be perfectly at home at Chapultepec. There was a splendid inventory of Court dignitaries, with Imperial Highnesses, Cardinals, and Collars of the Mexican Eagle all ranged in their due precedence and members of the ex-Imperial family of Iturbide ranking as Highnesses (a depressing reminder of what sometimes happened to Emperors in Mexico). All kinds of functions were provided for—balls, birthdays, concerts, public holidays, gala performances, and dinner parties. Everything was duly classified, official etiquette acknowledging three classes of guests at Court banquets, of whom two received the nicely balanced honour of a written invitation, while the third got no more than a printed card. There were three grades of dinner, too, with diminishing illuminations and progressively less interesting wine-lists; and everyone was told precisely how to dress for each occasion from vespers at

the Guadalupe to a third-class dinner in the yellow fever belt
at Vera Cruz. Everything was foreseen by the all-seeing eye
of etiquette; and a careful student of the *Reglamento de la
Corte* would know exactly who had to hold the Emperor's
sword and hat, should he venture on a dance, and just where
the happy functionary would be standing. For a series of
exciting diagrams charted the Court, plotting the course of an
arriving diplomat or Cardinal, to say nothing of a debutante's
excited footsteps. It was all prescribed, and there were no
surprises left for Maximilian. Six final regulations even dealt
conclusively with the subject of public mourning after he was
dead.

Few documents are more revealing. For this manual was
not the pastime of their voyage out. That might have been
excusable, as there was mild entertainment to be found in
elaborating rules of deportment for an unknown land; and if
such had been its origin, the *Reglamento* would throw little
light on the mentality behind it. But when this strange com-
pendium was issued, its authors had already been ten months
in Mexico. They had seen the queer, dusty country over
which they had been called to reign, the crumbling churches
and the cactus and the Indians with sandalled feet. They
could see quite well, if they could see at all, that this was not
Vienna, that the splendid edifice of Hapsburg etiquette was
somehow out of place in the clear light of the New World
with the mournful *ahuehuetes* of Chapultepec standing at
their palace gates. Yet they deliberately reproduced it in a
handbook that bore no relation to reality. It might have been
composed for Offenbach's delicious *Grande-Duchesse de
Gérolstein*. For there was not the slightest hint of Mexico
anywhere in its crowded pages; and though careful charts
told everybody where to stand on all occasions with meticu-
lous distinctions between their respective magnitude that
strained the typographical resources of a local printer to

breaking-point, there was no provision anywhere in this majestic fairyland for a French general.

But it was highly doubtful how long Maximilian would last without Bazaine. At the moment the General was highly confident, reporting the inauguration of the new regime hopefully to Napoleon and even indicating that it might soon be possible to repatriate some of the French troops. A Mexican republican observed ruefully that order had been so far restored under Bazaine's vice-royalty that the telegraph was functioning, road traffic comparatively safe from brigandage, and railway construction in progress. His subordinate commanders were advised that their guardianship of Mexico was ending and that there was no need to continue their administrative supervision. They had found Mexican officials a sore affliction; but the new Empire must learn to rely on its own personnel.

Now Juarez was no more than an embarrassed phantom flitting in the distant north, and Maximilian could begin his reign with confidence. His notions were enlightened. The Emperor once termed himself a Liberal, adding archly that his consort was a Red. Maximilian's attempt to reconcile Italians to Hapsburg rule had been interrupted by a war. But there seemed no reason why the progressive methods he had favoured at Milan should not be applied in Mexico. True, Mexicans (as he would learn one day) were nothing like Italians; but Maximilian and Charlotte had not yet found that out.

Meanwhile, the presence of the French was reassuring; and when their friend Bazaine was made a Marshal (the good news reached Mexico in October, 1864), Maximilian's congratulations were shadowed by a fear that this promotion might be the prelude to his departure from a country where his services were "so necessary." The Marshal had been charming. Had he not given Charlotte a delightful lunch under canvas, of which the impressionable Empress (she was only twenty-four) was positively moved to print a full description from the royal hand? Besides, he made an admirable speech at an official banquet. Anyone could see that he was quite devoted to them; and his young mistress, conscious of her station, added privately that he had every reason for it, since they actually treated him as a friend. But royal tact is often less compelling than its owners think; and Bazaine was not gratified when Maximilian informed him that the new army would be organised by a stocky little Austrian named von Thun, because there was no Mexican or French officer to undertake the work.

Besides, the Marshal's optimism had begun to fade a little. Maximilian was touring his dominions giving conscientious demonstrations of affability, which convinced his wife that he was winning every heart. That was how Coburgs usually managed to persuade their European subjects that they were respectively English, Belgian, Portuguese, or of whatever nationality had called them to its throne; and how her Max was "truly Mexican." But Mexico was somehow rather different. Perhaps royal graciousness, expressed in acts of charity and appearances in public with a large sombrero, was not enough for Mexico. For there were burning questions to be settled, and Bazaine noted a disturbing tendency to let them slide:

"There has been no indication on the part of the Government that the Emperor has taken any step with regard to the grave questions by which the country is disturbed. No order, no decree has yet been issued to announce the Sovereign's intentions and to reassure opinion as to the future.

"So I observe a sort of uneasiness and general discontent, indicated by an attitude of increasing reserve and a tendency of the Liberals to draw closer to the reactionaries for opposing, but equally thwarted, purposes.

"The Liberals will make use of their rivals to overturn the

edifice that has been so laboriously constructed, and it is undeniable that energy and intelligence are on their side . . .

"Everywhere there is a sort of indifference that I can only
attribute to the cause which I have mentioned; the absence of
any decision on the great questions which divide the country.

"Confidence is only established under the influence of French
bayonets, by which safety is ensured, and under the authority
of French commanders, by whom public and private interests
are protected. But it is impossible to leave garrisons everywhere; and I do my best to convince everybody that, when a
country desires to save itself, it must help itself and make its
own contribution to the work of regeneration."

This was a mournful diagnosis; and when it was made, the
new regime was already nearly four months old. But there
was no improvement, and Bazaine's next report was in the
same depressing strain:

"The same spirit of uneasiness is universal with no visible
symptom beyond a sort of apathy, which appears to have overcome even the Government's personnel. For nothing is done,
and there is no indication that anything serious is going to be
done . . .

"I am continually telling high officials that a country that
wishes to be saved must prove that it is making an effort to
save itself instead of relying exclusively on Providence."

But this was Mexico, where Spain's unhurried rule had lasted
for three centuries among uncomplaining Indians; and the
one consolation for the French was that they were able to
send home three battalions of infantry and some guns before
the end of 1864.

Now Maximilian was growing almost embarrassingly
Mexican, and his French protectors were sometimes made to
feel that they were unwelcome guests. His relations with
Bazaine were less idyllic, though Charlotte was anything but
reassured by the prospect of being left alone in Mexico with
no protection from her husband's subjects beyond that

afforded by local troops and two rather miscellaneous units from Belgium and Hungary. For her Belgian soul had thrilled at the sight of a French regiment marching behind its tattered colours; and she was not too patriotic to confess that Austrians and Belgians were all very well in quiet times, but—"*vienne la tempête, il n'y a que les pantalons rouges.*"

The subjugation of the south, where Porfirio Diaz still maintained himself in Oaxaca, promised a last crop of laurels, which a spiteful colleague suspected Bazaine of reserving for himself in order to adorn his Marshal's *bâton*. He took command in the first days of 1865, directed a force of 5,500 men against the fortress, which was skilfully surrounded and disposed of inside a week. Swift, competent, and inexpensive, this operation, which netted 8,000 prisoners and 60 guns at a price of 50 casualties, was an exercise in Bazaine's familiar manner. It might not loom very large beside the costly and precarious victories of French armies on European battlefields. But it showed conclusively that the latest Marshal was, within his limits, an efficient practitioner of war upon the scale required by overseas expeditions.

His conquering return to Mexico was followed by a gentler sequel. For Bazaine was courting once again. His eye for beauty had always favoured young brunettes; and Pepita Peña was both. Just seventeen, she had no money, large eyes, and an uncle who had once been President. The Marshal, who was fifty-four, began to pay her marked attention. For the widower had started dancing once again and never missed an Habanera with Pepita. After the fancy-dress ball, where they danced no less than two quadrilles, an Habanera, and the lancers (to say nothing of the supper-dance), Mexico could not be blamed for talking. Charlotte knew all about it, though when she asked the Marshal if they could congratulate him, he refused to give himself away. But when he found that she was on his side, he told her the great secret, asking her to intercede with the Empress Eugénie, whilst he wrote officially to

Paris for leave to marry Señorita Maria Josefa de la Peña y
Barragan y Azcárate. This time the course of true love ran
smoother for an eager Marshal than it had run nearly twenty
years before for an amorous colonel. No superior authorities
refused him leave to marry; no less than four Imperial Majesties blessed his union; and at midsummer they were married
by the Archbishop in the private chapel of the great palace
in the square. At the wedding breakfast Charlotte kissed the
bride and Maximilian toasted the happy couple. For when
Achille married Pepita, it was an altogether more brilliant
affair than when he claimed his Marie. A kindly royal thought
presented them with an imposing town residence at the
Buenavista palace, once occupied by General Santa Anna
and decorated to his taste. But as they might not live out all
their lives in the New World, the thoughtful giver undertook
that if they had to leave their home in Mexico, a grateful
government would pay the happy owner 100,000 piastres. It
was a noble wedding-gift.

5

Skies were bright above Bazaine in 1865. For he had
reached the very top of his profession. It had taken the recruit
thirty-three years to become a Marshal of France, years of
active service in the glare of Africa, the biting wind of Spain,
the Russian snow, the blue skies of Italy, and the raw sunlight
of Mexico. The Foreign Legion had formed him. It was a long
time since a young sergeant of the Legion had landed at
Algiers; and here he was, not far past fifty, reading old Marshal Randon's letter enclosing the Imperial decree that named
him Marshal. He was the first Marshal who had started as
a *légionnaire*. For he had risen from the ranks, like the great
Marshals of the First Empire. Bazaine had not travelled the
easy road that led direct to a commission from the *écoles
spéciales*. For he had failed to pass into the Polytechnique

when Louis Philippe was king. But Napoleon III made him a Marshal; and he was younger than the others. Old Pélissier, Duc de Malakoff, had just died at Algiers; Randon was Minister of War; Bosquet was dead; Niel was a sapper; Canrobert had failed before Sebastopol; Mac-Mahon, Duc de Magenta, was safely relegated to Algiers; and when French armies in the field next needed a commander, Bazaine was well in line. He might have been a duke as well, since Maximilian offered to make him Duke of Mexico. But he did not relish the idea of a foreign title; and there have been dukedoms that looked more promising.

Just fifty-four, he was married to a girl whom he adored. The prospect was inviting; and the retrospect was highly satisfactory too. For he had discharged his duties with success. Efficiency, suave manners, and a grasp of local politics had placed him where he was; and it was pleasant to doze after lunch with a cigar behind a newspaper and then to surprise his staff, when news suddenly arrived that the rebels were in Matamoros and the whole province of Tamaulipas was up, by dictating swift orders for troop movements in the north without calling for returns or looking at a map. It was all in his head; and he could be Napoleonic, when he chose. It was flattering to feel that a whole country looked to him. This was better than the deference of a few Kaids in the *Bureau arabe* at Tlemcen. Now ministers watched his expression; he confronted prelates instead of dusty *marabouts;* and the burly Marshal saw himself as the guardian of an Empire. Young Albert Bazaine said proudly that his uncle had a party of his own in Mexico; Boyer, who wrote his letters, boasted to someone after dinner that his own pen and the Marshal's sword controlled the country; and envious subordinates began to whisper that his pretty wife might lead him on, that having had one President in the family she would be glad to have another, that other Marshals had not disdained a foreign throne, and that what Bernadotte had done in Sweden could be done again in Mexico. The story even reached the Tuileries from General Douay, and Prosper Mérimée retailed it as an exciting piece of gossip. But French generals were always spiteful about one another; and Bazaine's success had been far too conspicuous to escape malicious comment by less fortunate contemporaries. He was always conscious of their resentment, writing long afterwards to his sister about the professional jealousy to which he was exposed:

> "I cannot deny my humble origin; and no doubt it is because I have risen from the common people and the ranks that the envious pursue me, especially since my promotion to be Marshal; the officers who come from the special schools" (Polytechnique and St. Cyr) "cannot forgive me."

Other men with more advantages had not got so far; and it was easy to drop unpleasant hints, as the Marshal went about his business in Mexico. Anyone could see that his career, when he returned to France, was likely to be less spectacular; and it might appeal to a doting husband to set his dark young bride in front of all her fellow-countrymen, if that was what she really wanted. But was it? No doubt it was highly gratifying to parade her massive conquest, as he danced a creditable Habanera, and to condescend to her own contemporaries. For Pepita would have been less than human, if she had not derived immense enjoyment from the status of *Madame la Maréchale*. She was young; she had been poor, but well-connected; and now she was the first lady in Mexico after the Empress.

But was Mexico the only place where she could shine? For the world had a brighter centre; and it might be sublime to swim into the ken of Paris on a Marshal's arm. Meanwhile there was Mexico, where her position was unchallenged and her friendly aptitude for match-making found congenial employment. What could be more entertaining than to find impressive husbands in the French service for her contemporaries? Besides, there was some evidence (if the peevish Douay could be believed) that her relations favoured a prolongation of their stay in Mexico. This was not surprising, since a family committed to the Intervention's side by a conspicuous French marriage would be unlikely to prefer a return of the avenging Juarez. Local politics were apt to be ungentle; and *Madame la Maréchale's* relations could scarcely view with equanimity the departure of the French. It was whispered that soft hands retained Bazaine in Mexico, to say nothing of his own ambitions. For while brother-officers accused him of prolonging Maximilian's Empire by exercising undue pressure to prevent him from abdicating in despair, less restrained critics have suggested just the opposite by imputing to the Marshal a diabolical design to make Maximilian fail in order to succeed him on the throne. Both stories cannot be true at the same time; and the second (and far graver) charge is answered by the fact that Bazaine knew far too much of Mexico to be romantic on the subject. Indeed, the utmost indicated by the evidence is that he favoured at one stage the substitution of a French protectorate. The preference was natural in a French soldier; and if this solution was adopted, no doubt a French proconsul acceptable to the Mexicans would be required. The choice was obvious. But when Mac-Mahon was Governor-General of Algeria, it could hardly be an unworthy ambition for Bazaine to be Governor-General of Mexico, the new Bugeaud of a new Abd-el-Kader. The latter role seemed to fit President Juarez to perfection; and need his conqueror disdain to fit the cap?

But would Bazaine conquer the phantom President? He had done so once already, to all intents and purposes, in the victorious campaign of 1863-4, which cleared the central steppes of Mexico and backed Juarez up against the Texas frontier at El Paso del Norte. At that stage there was a fair prospect that Maximilian would be able to govern Mexico with the Confederate States as a good neighbour on his northern border. Those had been the happy days when all was smiles at the palace of Chapultepec and Mexican society observed with awe the heavy draperies and handsome statuary, the rich carpets and sumptuous alabaster vases, to say nothing of the Gobelins chairs (a gift from Napoleon himself) tapestried with stories from La Fontaine's Fables. A suave Marshal took his place beside two young sovereigns; and the victor of Oaxaca had a charming letter from the Empress that confessed her inability to send a laurel wreath, because he had gathered his own laurels, and enclosed instead her father's Order of Leopold.

But as 1865 went by, the outlook was less promising. His shrewd political advice was mostly unregarded; and a new shadow began to fall across the Empire. For Richmond fell that spring; General Lee surrendered at Appomattox; the Confederate States ceased to exist; and when the Civil War was over, Maximilian lost the hope of a good neighbour in the north. The United States had never recognised the Empire, since Washington had always frowned on European intervention, disapproving equally of the presence of French armies in the New World and of a Hapsburg monarchy that seemed to mar the republican simplicity of Mexico. Secretary Seward's disapproval was not important so long as Texas formed no part of the United States and the Stars and Bars floated on the north bank of the Rio Grande. But when the Civil War was over and they were replaced by the Stars and Stripes, it became certain that Juarez would receive powerful support, to say nothing of an unpleasant possibility that the United States might take a hand themselves. This prospect had been foreseen in Paris; and Napoleon was already warning Bazaine to concentrate his forces in view of possible invasion from the north. It had been one thing to clear the interior of Mexico with flying columns. But it would be quite another to confront the armies of the United States, hardened by four years of active service in the Civil War; and Bazaine began to watch his northern frontier anxiously and to view without enthusiasm the possibility of a last stand by the Confederates in Texas just across the Rio Grande and even the imminent arrival of the Confederate ex-President as a refugee.

On this darkening scene, while Maximilian refused to face his problems or mishandled them, the Marshal continued to manipulate the army with interludes afforded by General Brincourt's frequent resignations and the Court's selection of a colour indistinguishable from the Legion of Honour for the ribbon of their new decoration. (This *imbroglio* entailed protracted correspondence between Mexico and Paris, bringing into play the full intelligence of European royalty on the sort of question that it could really grasp.) But things could not go on for ever, with the Minister of War writing him from Paris that French forces must eventually be withdrawn from Mexico; and that event was brought appreciably nearer by the vigorous diplomacy of the United States. The Marshal's problem was not simplified by Napoleon's inconsequence in writing just the opposite, with a vague indication that he might be sending out more reinforcements. For the moment, though, Bazaine's main preoccupations were less military than political; and the politics in which he dealt were largely of the unpleasant variety engendered by financial stringency. For the Empire of Mexico had very little money; and, of what it had, it seemed to owe a large proportion to the French. Since the relation of debtor and creditor rarely makes for mutual esteem, Franco-Mexican relations deteriorated rapidly; and no improvement was effected by a succession of French experts, who usually tended to grow acrimonious shortly after their arrival in Mexico. The altitude at which the city stands is often fatal to good temper, a circumstance unnoticed by historians and highly influential on the course of politics in Mexico.

Bazaine's relations with the Court grew more unhappy, though when Pepita's son was born, Maximilian and Charlotte

gave the baby an Imperial christening. His instructions to evacuate the army became more definite; he was even authorised
to leave himself; and by the early months of 1866 Maximilian
could see that his protectors were under orders to desert him.
This was serious. For a few Belgian volunteers would scarcely
fill the gap. The cost of a French army might be inordinately
high, and there was something to be said against the Marshal's
"*système arabe*" and "*fantasias militaires*," as Maximilian termed
them angrily with a sound diagnosis of the Algerian sources
of Bazaine's military inspiration. But if his army were withdrawn, what would happen to Maximilian and Charlotte left
to the tender mercies of their subjects? The United States, unwilling to admit their sovereignty, did not greatly care. For
Secretary Seward was not unduly troubled by the fate of
European princes adrift in Mexico. But as Napoleon had placed
them where they were, he must really be induced to leave
them with the military means of staying there. True, he had
written to explain that he must soon recall his troops. The
expedition was increasingly unpopular in France; and Europe
was not quite the place in 1866 that it had been when the
great idea was first conceived five years before. It was growing evident, as the new star of Prussia climbed the sky, that
France might have to face a challenge nearer home and that
French troops were likely to be more needed on the Rhine
than on the Rio Grande. Napoleon's reflections were un-
enviable; but the moral claims of Mexico (to say nothing of
his treaty obligations) were obvious; and if Maximilian could
contrive to reach his conscience, the Empire might yet be
saved.

One last expedient remained. For if Charlotte found little
savour in being Maximilian's wife, she was his Empress still;
and it was just possible that Napoleon might listen to a royal
voice. That was now their only hope, since Bazaine merely
obeyed orders. Dark, determined, and a shade distracted,
Charlotte drove down the dusty road to Vera Cruz and sailed

alone for Europe in order to persuade Napoleon to change his mind and save her husband's throne. It was a desperate errand that failed tragically because, when she arrived in Paris, she found a desperate man. His world had crumbled in those summer weeks of 1866 that saw the first swift Prussian victory over the Austrians at Sadowa. Napoleon had lost his magic. The indefatigable conjurer still waved his wand; but nobody paid much attention. His health began to fail as well; and a pale man at St. Cloud sat watching his excited visitor, as she pleaded for the help he could not give and then trailed wildly off into delusions about lurking poisoners from Mexico. The same incoherent horror was repeated at the Vatican before a sad-eyed Pope; and Charlotte's fate, harder than Ophelia's, wandered in the shadows for a dim half-century.

Four thousand miles away Bazaine was peering north across the desert for the rising tide of rebels. Juarez and his big-hatted avengers would soon be coming that way, as the French withdrew; and there was an ugly possibility that they might be followed by the blue columns of the Union armies. The Marshal's first idea had been to leave with the first contingent of French troops. But he decided to preside over the evacuation, which was likely to be an operation of some delicacy. For it would not be simple to withdraw 28,000 men from a large area in face of an advancing enemy. Bazaine was fully authorised to return home, leaving the joys of the retreat to General Douay; but he preferred to be the last to go, though he had no illusions about the future of the Empire. That was, he said eloquently, *"une agonie dans l'impossible"*; and even Maximilian appeared to see it, when news came that Napoleon was obdurate about the French evacuation. There was graver news as well that autumn. For when a cipher telegram arrived from Europe, a scared secretary muttered vaguely that it was about one of the Emperor's ladies, that she was unwell, that . . . Maximilian said sharply that he could face the worst and, when they told him, sent for his doctor. Who, he asked was

Doctor Riedel, of Vienna? The answer came that he was head
of the madhouse; and Maximilian knew the truth about Charlotte.

His first instinct was to abdicate. The valuables were packed
and carted down to Vera Cruz for embarkation; and the Emperor went as far as Orizaba after writing a heart-broken letter
to Bazaine. But the game was not so simple now, as there was
another player. For Napoleon was losing faith in Bazaine's
promptitude and, with his inveterate belief in secret missions,
had sent General Castelnau to liquidate the wretched business
with over-riding powers to effect a prompt evacuation. The
Marshal's feelings were not considered in this appointment
of a junior to be his taskmaster, though Bazaine blandly
offered to accommodate him in his own quarters, an attention
which the wary Castelnau declined. Indeed, the brigadier's
precautions went so far as to send his communications to
Napoleon by hand to New Orleans for direct delivery to the
French packet, as he had little confidence in the official mail
from Mexico. It was his fixed belief that Bazaine was less impressed than he should have been with the urgency of Maximilian's early abdication and an immediate withdrawal of the
troops; and in this orgy of cross-purposes it was not surprising that the Marshal, who always had a taste for proverbial
wisdom, reported ruefully:

> "The Arabs have a saying, 'When two are on the road, mis-
> trust your fellow-traveller; when there are three, choose a
> leader.' Here there are four of us—the Commander-in-chief,
> H.M.'s aide de camp, the French minister, and the head of the
> financial mission, each with his own instructions and his own
> point of view ! ! !"

His own attitude was not unaffected by his long experience
of Mexico and by his local affiliations. For it cannot have been
easy to destroy the whole work of the last three years; and he
knew too much of Mexican affairs to doubt that a premature

collapse of the Empire was likely to be followed by an interlude of anarchy. It might be wise to play for time. Besides, he
had to extricate the army from its scattered garrisons and to
embark it safely at Vera Cruz. Swift solutions might precipitate disaster for the troops under his command and for his
friends in Mexico; and Bazaine was never rash.

A fresh complication appeared, when Maximilian changed
his mind. An enterprising German priest was busy with his
conscience, and an exciting letter from his mother told him
that the Viennese had cheered his name that summer after the
Austrian defeats. If this was so, if there was something greater
left at home for him to live for, he must not deface his name
with an abdication. He might yet save the Church in Mexico
from its oppressors by a heroic fight; and he resolved to make
it. There could be no abdication now. For he resolved to fight
Juarez to a finish; and if he lost, a meeting with the President
might end the Empire honourably and leave him free to follow
a higher destiny in Europe. An interview with Juarez became
his ruling passion; and an ignorance of Mexican politics prevented him from appreciating the extreme rarity of honourable ends.

That was Maximilian's dream, whilst angry Frenchmen
waited for him to abdicate and Castelnau suspected Bazaine
of inspiring the delay and of an undue interest (which was
not surprising) in the contents of his own private correspondence with Napoleon. Bazaine, who had graduated in the
Bureau arabe, became aware without undue effort of the
uncomplimentary terms in which his junior reported on him.
But his legitimate complaints were answered with a round assertion by Marshal Niel, the new Minister of War in Paris,
that his royal master's confidence in him was unimpaired. It
might be wise to avert a general breakdown in Mexico until
the French could get away and even to come to some arrangement with the next regime. There were indications that
Bazaine was active in both directions. But it was beyond them

now to exercise the slighest pressure upon Maximilian, intent on his heroic rearguard action. As the French drew nearer to the coast in the first weeks of 1867, the deluded Emperor went back into the interior. His last interview with Bazaine was not unfriendly, and the two men were seen arm-in-arm. But at ten o'clock one winter morning French drums went rolling through the streets of Mexico for the last time, and Maximilian lifted the corner of a palace curtain to see them cross the square. A fortnight later he was at Querétaro, and Bazaine was halfway to the coast.

The Marshal managed to withdraw his army without loss from a collapsing country; and 28,000 men were shipped from Vera Cruz in eight weeks. It was a notable performance, which deserved more gratitude than it received. Bazaine left in the last convoy; and when his warship reached Toulon after a voyage of six weeks, the Marshal walked ashore without military honours. The same reception had greeted old Pélissier after the Crimean War. But it was an unpleasant homecoming, and Bazaine could hardly be expected to understand that both his country and his Emperor hoped to forget Mexico and Maximilian.

Mexico was not forgotten, when Querétaro fell a month later and his gleeful subjects put Maximilian on trial for his life. With some humour they made play with a stern decree issued by the Emperor himself at Bazaine's instance and imposing the death penalty for armed resistance to the authorities. There could be no doubt that Maximilian had been taken in arms; and the case (like all politics in Mexico) appeared to turn on who were the authorities. As the penalty was death, the death sentence was duly passed after a protracted display of military justice, civil eloquence, and Latin jurisprudence on the stage of a provincial theatre. The story ended with a ragged volley on a sunny hillside; but the prescriptions of the *Reglamento de la Corte* for Court mourning were not observed, because there was no Court.

Now Mexico was herself again; and the experiment was over. It was more than forty years since Mexicans had shot an Emperor. The sad news (they kept it from Pepita, to whom another little boy was safely born) quite spoilt the prize-giving after the Paris Exhibition, graced by Napoleon and the Sultan of Turkey. For the world heard that day that an Empire had fallen; and, what was worse, it was a Second Empire.

CHAPTER IV

METZ

Dies iræ, dies illa
Solvet sæclum in favilla.
MISSALE ROMANUM.

I

THREE times within seventy years the Germans have launched Europe into war; and in each case there is a strong resemblance between the antecedent symptoms. Each outbreak is preceded by a period of apprehension, in which a nervous world sees German appetites increase alarmingly and it becomes obvious that war cannot be avoided. The outbreak of 1914 followed three years of alarming incidents from Agadir to Sarajevo; that of 1939 was the culmination of a series of unpleasant shocks beginning three years earlier with the occupation of the Rhineland and proceeding by way of Vienna, Prague, and Munich to the final challenge; and the preliminaries of 1870 were not dissimilar. For there is no essential difference between the German way as practised by Bismarck or by Hitler.

The first intimation that the German tribes were on the move came in a gratuitous aggression against a small nation, when Denmark was attacked and summarily robbed of Schleswig-Holstein in 1864. This unprovoked assault was militarily unimpressive, as the Prussian army had not yet been re-made by von Moltke and von Roon; and it is possible that strong European action at the moment when the Danish frontier was violated might have checked the unwholesome growth of German appetites. But Europe in 1864 was incapable of collective action. For while Britain strongly disapproved of the aggression, Napoleon III was vaguely favourable to Prussian aims, which seemed to rest upon his own sacred principle of nationality and to challenge the dead hand of the peace-treaties of Vienna. (A similar divergence, with the parts reversed, prevented Anglo-French action when the Germans marched into the Rhineland in 1936.) This milestone safely passed, Bismarck proceeded on his way. A quarrel deftly picked with Austria in 1866 gave him a second opportunity. This time the prize was larger. For if he could win, Berlin would replace Vienna in the leadership of Central Europe. Once more Europe had its opportunity to call a halt before a Prussian victory could destroy the counterpoise of Austria. It was the climacteric of the whole process; but it was allowed to pass without effective intervention. For while Napoleon fumbled with the cards (it was the tragic summer of his illness and Charlotte's desperate appeal), Benedek was beaten at Sadowa and the scales of Europe tilted sharply towards Berlin.

Sadowa was to Bismarck's series of aggressions what Munich was to his successor's. For a swift, unqualified success indicated plainly that something had grown up in Germany which its European neighbours were unable to control, and that there was worse to come. The victory was paralysing proof that the Prussian army, which nobody had thought about since Waterloo, was capable of defeating the second army of the continent in a campaign of seven weeks. The term *Blitzkrieg* was unknown in 1866; and it might have been unduly flattering to apply it to the slow convergence of the Prussian armies by way of Gitschin and Nachod upon Benedek's last stand at Sadowa. But there was no doubt of the result or of the terrifying brevity of the most decisive campaign of the last half-century. Hitherto regarded as a slightly comic force with a tendency to wear spectacles in combination with unsightly helmets and ill-fitting uniforms, the Prussian army had shown as little of its true quality against the Danes in 1864 as Russian armies showed against the Finns in 1939. But the substitution of von Moltke for von Wrangel worked wonders; and the needle-gun, with which their infantry was armed, gave rise to an uneasy feeling that they might be better armed as well as better led.

The gravest consequences of Sadowa were political. Like Munich, it transformed the balance of Europe. For in 1866, if Austria had been defeated in the field, France was still more disastrously defeated in the diplomacy that followed. While Prussia rode off with the prizes of victory—Schleswig-Holstein, Hanover, and the headship of a new North German Confederation—all French attempts to secure a return engagement of Napoleon III as the arbiter of Europe were contemptuously repelled before a watching world. It might have saved a fragment of his dignity, if he had only been permitted to award Venice to the Italians, his eternal protégés, who had attached themselves to the winning side. (That instinct that never failed them until 1940.) In one way or another Napoleon had been through so much in order that they might get Venice. It inspired his choice of Maximilian for Mexico; it underlay his unselfish blessing of the recent transfer of Italian affections from France to Prussia; and it was the unkindest cut of all when they marched into their latest acquisition without waiting for their unwearied benefactor's leave. His efforts to obtain the French some compensation for Prussia's new prosperity were equally unsuccessful, as he made vague passes in the direction of outlying fragments of German territory or controlling rights in Belgium. Never an altruist, Bismarck was not inclined to dispense 'Trinkgeld' (as he elegantly termed it) in order to obtain possession of something he already held; and Napoleon rose from the table empty-handed. If he wanted anything for France, he would have to fight for it.

Not that he had the least wish to. For Napoleon's ambitions, as the light of evening fell on the bright fabric of the Second Empire, were far less enterprising. To keep up appearances, to satisfy his subjects that they had not been publicly humiliated by the swift rise of Prussia, to prepare the country for a smooth transition to the next reign, and then to fade into the background as his Empress took her place as Regent beside the pallid boy who was to be Napoleon IV, these were his modest aspirations in the troubled years after Sadowa. The uncertainties of a European war were the last thing he wanted. But his subjects, more susceptible and less well-informed, saw things rather differently; and a conviction grew on most Frenchmen that they would have to fight the Prussians before very long. (A small Pétain, who would soon be ten, was relatively unaffected.) The prospect did not cause them serious concern, as it was natural for Frenchmen to assume their own military superiority. Was not their army the direct heir of Napoleon, the inheritor of all the victories engraved upon the Arc de Triomphe? Had it not won battle-honours of its own in Italy and the Crimea, to say nothing of outlying exploits in Algeria and Mexico?

But the Emperor, an incurable romantic in many things, was a realist on military matters. Acutely conscious that his army of 288,000 men was now confronted by an enterprising neighbour with 1,200,000, he pressed feverishly for an increase of numbers. But the Empire, just in process of converting his autocracy into a parliamentary government, was in a state unpropitious to rearmament. Few transitions are more awkward than the passage of dictatorships towards democracy; and the *couronnement de l'édifice* was an operation of unusual delicacy, involving a new degree of consideration for his subjects' feelings. Their representatives, quick to point out where the nation's prestige had suffered from the shortcomings of Imperial diplomacy, were less eager to impose an added burden of military service on their own constituents; and

French rearmament in the uneasy years after Sadowa was effectively retarded by the representatives of France. Universal military service was a distasteful novelty to citizens accustomed to rely for their defence on others, on the unaided efforts of a small army of professionals; and the most that could be obtained by Marshal Niel from the politicians was the addition of a half-trained *Garde mobile*. It was their last chance to confront the Germans on equal terms, since French population had not yet fallen below the German level. But the opportunity was missed by the reluctance of French legislators to impose an equal burden on French shoulders; and their hesitations preserved a glaring inequality of numbers between the armies of the two nations.

Numerically weaker, the French were not so well equipped, since change had been distasteful to a military caste of high prestige and limited intelligence. Besides, rearmament cost money; and it was doubtful if their new masters in the Chamber would acquiesce in any large expenditure. The Empire in its latest phase was in pursuit of popularity, and high taxation has never been the road to popular affection. But as the Prussian victories were generally attributed to the needle-gun, the Emperor was able to impose on his advisers the admirable Chassepot rifle. He was an indomitable amateur of military novelties; and when it was submitted by its inventor during the Crimean War, he had it tested. The official experts promptly rejected it. But Napoleon persisted in his quiet way, armed a squadron of Guard cavalry with the new weapon in the war of 1859, induced the experts to reverse their view of it a few years later, and caused his army to adopt the Chassepot eight weeks after Sadowa. (He had taken just eleven years to get his way; but he got it in the end.) It was a better weapon than the Prussian needle-gun; and there might still be time to make enough of them, although there were none for the *Garde mobile*. Artillery was a still graver problem, as it was even more expensive. But it was clear that the Krupp gun was formidable; and the Emperor was reduced to financing the development of a new weapon, named the *mitrailleuse* and credited with almost miraculous powers of destruction, out of his private funds. This stealth combined the advantages of avoiding undue publicity and outflanking parliamentary economies, by which all projects of fortifying the frontier were systematically obstructed. When war came, the only fixed defences on the eastern frontier constructed within recent memory were five unfinished forts at Metz. For the French scorned the thought of a defensive war. It would be more glorious, as well as a good deal cheaper, to conduct the war in Germany. So why fortify the frontier? The high command appeared to share this view, since the maps issued to French officers on mobilisation were all of Germany.

But was the army equal to conducting a successful European war? That was the riddle which confronted anxious military men in the years after Sadowa; and it was answered four years later by a German officer in an ambulance at Wörth, who startled his French neighbour by observing, "You will get the worst of it; your army is not a European army." That unpleasant fact was not apparent to gallant cavalry commanders, as they put their men, exquisitely tailored and burnished to distraction, through all the mazes prescribed by the Field Service Regulations of 1829 (which owed a great deal to the principles of equitation prevailing under Louis XV), although a British visitor had once made everybody laugh by persistently enquiring of his hosts what it was all about. "*Mais l'hypothèse?*" asked General Hope Grant that summer, as he watched two thousand mounted men wheeling with faultless precision in the dust and sunshine of Châlons.

"*Comment, l'hypothèse?*" replied a startled French commander.

"*Mais oui,*" the Scot persisted doggedly, "*l'hypothèse! Dans quel cas, à la guerre, executériez-vous ce mouvement?*"

"*Mais il n'y a pas d'hypothèse*," the general replied; and all was made plain. The cavalry of the Guard were just manœuvring for art's sake without a sordid thought of actual warfare to mar the purity of their manœuvres; and when the persevering visitor continued to enquire, "*Mais l'hypothèse?*" his host returned with equal regularity, "*Il n'y a pas d'hypothèse*," until their dialogue was overheard in the ranks and grinning troopers, affecting English accents, echoed, "*Mais l'hypothèse?*"

What military purpose underlay the whole army of the Second Empire with its obsolete equipment and its elderly commanders? The day would come when Bourbaki, the dashing Bourbaki, who was only fifty-four, outlived the elegance that had once made them sing,

> "*Ce chic exquis*
> *Par les Turcos acquis,*
> *Ils le doivent à qui?*
> *À Bourbaki!*"

On the night of Rezonville his eyes were full of tears, as he muttered bitterly, "We are too old for a war like this." They were all too old—too old and too inexperienced. For their experience of European war was limited to the static heroism of Sebastopol and two scrambling victories over the Austrians. Their military education seemed to be confined to a few readings after dinner from Thiers' *Consulate and Empire*. Their staff-work was deplorable, because it did not take much staff-work to send out a flying column after Abd-el-Kader or Porfirio Diaz. Some of them were shy of map-reading; and they called Jarras, who was fond of paper-work, 'the Archivist.' Haphazard methods had been quite good enough in Algeria or Mexico; they knew no others; and they had made an army in their own image.

Like its generals, the army of the Second Empire was brave, uneducated, and adapted to the special purposes of colonial warfare. But it was almost wholly out of place in Europe. The older men (and there were far too many of them) had shown bravery in the Crimea and Italy; and they were full of Algerian experience and Mexican adventure. Its uniforms, perhaps, were a reminder of Napoleonic glories; but as a military instrument it was little more than a picture of its own past, when French armies rode across a conquered continent under another Emperor. But what a picture, when the Second Empire showed off its military paces to the Czar of Russia and the King of Prussia one June day at a Longchamps review. It was in the Exhibition year of 1867, and all Paris came to see. Marshal Canrobert was in command; and as he took his place, there was a roar of cheers, sharp orders, bands playing in all directions, and the slow booming of the guns from Mont Valérien. Three sovereigns were on the ground. For the Emperor was well enough to ride again, although he drooped a little and his hair was dyed an unconvincing shade of chestnut and his colour was occasionally a trifle better than the grey reality. But he sat his horse between his tightly buttoned royal guests, as thirty thousand men went by at the salute. They saw the marching bearskins of the Guard behind a flaunting drum-major and the beards and axes of white-aproned Pioneers, the flaring red and blue of the Zouaves, trim shakoes of the Line, and green Chasseurs under the long bayonets, and little *vivandières* in their gay regimental petticoats; and then the mounted men came charging straight for the saluting-base in an immense line that ran clear across the race-course—big, burnished Cuirassiers, helmeted Dragoons, light cavalry of every shade in bright accoutrements and all kinds of headgear, furred, frogged, and braided, with sling-jackets and without, all thundering towards them, until the racing horses checked at a shouted order, and all the sabres lifted above a roar of *"Vive l'Empereur!"* in the June sunshine on a field ablaze with every colour—the painted army of a painted Emperor.

2

A few weeks earlier, in the spring days of 1867, Bazaine returned to this distracted scene. The Marshal's home-coming
was not particularly pleasant, as he had been officially informed on reaching France that there would be no military
honours at his landing. For the Empire had cut its losses in
the New World; and Bazaine's feelings were a small item in
the debit balance. The main thing, since few governments
dwell on their failures, was to forget Mexico; and if this involved a slight on a successful soldier, it could not be helped.
But that was a memory which Opposition leaders would not
willingly let die; and as ministerial advocates were tending to
transfer the Emperor's responsibility to Bazaine, republicans
and royalists began to argue vehemently that the Marshal was
a first-rate soldier and that the Empire alone had been to
blame. Bazaine had useful contacts with the Opposition, since
his elder brother, a distinguished engineer, was a friend of
Jules Favre (and the wary soldier had preserved documentary
proof of that austere republican's financial interest in Maximilian's defeat). Besides, he had risen from the ranks; he was
not a Court general like Frossard and Castelnau; and his name,
unlike Canrobert's, was unsullied by direct association with
the *Coup d'état*. A republican named de Kératry, who had
served on his staff in Mexico, published abroad (out of reach
of the French censorship) a damaging account of the whole
episode, which vindicated Bazaine and opened with a glowing
tribute from the most brilliant pen among the Liberals to "a
tried servant whose strong hand and calm resolution may
shortly render France great service." Nor were the royalists
behind in their appreciation, since Berryer praised him in
glowing terms, which left it to be understood that the Marshal
had known better all the time.

But the most flattering approach came from the Orleanist
leader, M. Thiers. The frosty little man, whose pen had

glorified the First Empire, was an unwearied critic of the
Second. A specialist in foreign policy and military matters, he
intoned an endless Jeremiad which has much in common with
Mr. Churchill's unheeded warnings to a later generation.
Deeply patriotic and apparently excluded from all further
chance of holding office, he denounced the growing series of
Imperial failures with mournful gusto; and a forthcoming pro-
nouncement on the theme, "There are no more blunders left
to make," would plainly have to touch on Mexico. Knowing
one of Bazaine's staff officers, Thiers sent him to the Marshal
with an intimation that he proposed to speak in his defence,
if Bazaine would only call on him or let him have some documents. But though the Marshal resented his own treatment
deeply, he retained his loyalty; and his sense of military discipline was too strong for him to lend himself to such proceedings. Thiers' emissary was informed that, though his kindness
had profoundly touched the Marshal, he could not meet the
statesman or supply confidential papers without committing
an act of indiscipline towards the Ministry of War, by which
the Marshal's actions had uniformly been approved. (Obedience to orders had always been his *forte* from the distant days
when a young captain of the Foreign Legion urged that it was
as well to be covered by a written order; and it was undeniable
that he had done no more in Mexico than his orders had required.) This rebuff impressed the statesman deeply. For
when he was informed of Bazaine's attitude, Thiers' respectful
comment was, "*Voilà un vrai militaire.*" His high opinion of
the Marshal, which dated from this incident, never wavered
afterwards; and he alluded habitually to "*notre glorieux Bazaine.*"

But though the Empire grudged him any laurels after
Mexico, Napoleon received him kindly at St. Cloud; and he
was even furnished with a copy of Frossard's plan of campaign
in the event of war with Prussia. For the French military mind
concluded that it would be as well to have a plan; and one

had been prepared by a gifted sapper, who was the Prince Imperial's tutor. The communication of this highly secret document was a sign of official favour, though Bazaine was still unemployed. He was seen with Pepita (now safely installed in France with her little boy and an inseparable Indian maid, named Dolores) at official functions in that resplendent season of the Exhibition. There was even a notion of silencing his critics by a full enquiry into events in Mexico, which was to be held on his demand. Marshal Vaillant spoke to him about it with the Emperor's approval, and Bazaine undertook to make a formal application; but nothing came of the idea.

That winter he was posted to command the 3rd Army corps at Nancy (succeeding Forey, as he had already done in Mexico) with responsibility for the first line of defence on the eastern frontier or for the first thrust into German territory. He collected information about Coblentz and Rastadt and other points in Germany and promptly inspected every fortress and garrison between Thionville and Strasbourg, riding over all the ground in order to familiarise himself with the terrain and recommending various improvements to the Minister of War. He noted the defects of Metz and Strasbourg; and he complained vigorously of the lack of any maps of eastern France at his headquarters. For the Ministry was busy at the moment on its masterpiece, an admirable map of Germany, which satisfied the conscientious Jarras and might be extremely useful, if the war was only fought on the right side of the frontier.

As 1868 went by and the Minister of War struggled with the reluctance of French legislators to make rational (if costly and uncomfortable) preparations for a war that seemed increasingly inevitable, a broad-shouldered Marshal was riding round the roads of Lorraine, studying the country. He had always been a strong believer in personal reconnaissance; and this was the ground over which he would have to operate, if war broke out. At one point near Longuyon (it was re-

membered against him afterwards, when all his acts had to
be twisted into an indication of incompetence, or worse, to
soothe the vanity of a defeated nation) he startled a young
captain with his head full of grand strategy by pointing to a
little wood and observing that he would put a company of
skirmishers just there. In the next year he found himself commanding the manœuvres at Châlons, where he handled
25,000 men, the largest force that he had yet commanded in
the field, and did his best to emphasise the importance to generals of an eye for country, as well as the desirability of their
acquiring the habit of commanding all arms in combination
(there were too many specialists) and the utility of shelter-
trenches. The latter was a lesson of the American Civil War,
which had not yet penetrated the professional intelligence of
most European soldiers. Indeed, it took them nearly forty
years to learn the virtues of entrenching-tools; and even when
the lesson had been enforced by the Russo-Japanese War, it
came as a complete surprise to large numbers of them in 1914.
But it was clearly stated in Bazaine's instructions of 1869. For
he had been closer to the Civil War than most Continental
soldiers; and he was evidently capable of learning its chief
military lesson, although his taste for trenches in no way indicated a defensive bias in his mind, as the Marshal dwelt upon
their value "for the defence of a position or for the preparation
of an offensive."

He saw something of the Emperor that year, when Napoleon took his cure at Plombières. Bazaine had been invited to
one of the Imperial house-parties at Compiègne in 1868. But
this was more intimate than that stately alternation of sport,
dinners, and dramatic entertainments; and for some days the
two men talked quietly about the army. The Marshal made
a number of suggestions. But the Emperor seemed helpless in
face of departmental inertia, and nothing came of them. There
was some talk of his succeeding Marshal Niel as Minister of
War that summer. Bazaine himself made no move in this

direction; but it was felt that, as he seemed to be the Opposition's favourite soldier ('*notre glorieux Bazaine*' had become a commonplace in those quarters), it might be a good appointment. The lot, however, fell upon Le Bœuf; and that moustachioed and downright warrior succeeded to the grim inheritance, while Bazaine applied for the command of the Imperial Guard. The Emperor consented graciously, and the Marshal left Nancy for the capital.

If war broke out, Le Bœuf informed him that he was to command the Army of Lorraine. Meanwhile there were worse fates than commanding the Guard in Paris, although they had their private sorrows. For they lost their elder boy that year; but when a little girl was born his gracious sovereigns stood god-parents to a small Eugénie Bazaine. He had been a member of the Senate for some years; and he was seen at Court with Pepita. She was only twenty-two; and now she entered great assemblies on her Marshal's arm. But Paris was not all enjoyment. For politics were most absorbing in the first weeks of 1870, as M. Émile Ollivier took office with a new ministry that was to bring the Empire up to date; and they grew still livelier, when a disreputable cousin of the Emperor incautiously shot a young republican named Victor Noir, whose political associates decided joyfully that the funeral would afford unrivalled opportunities for rioting. Political funerals were classic fixtures in Parisian disorder. But the new ministers were disinclined to be indulgent; and the military authorities made comprehensive arrangements to disappoint an eager public. Le Bœuf, Canrobert, and Bazaine were consulted; and the Marshal, who displayed no partiality for his Opposition friends, enquired indignantly of the Emperor why there had to be these half-measures. The rioters, he felt, should be cut down wherever they appeared, and then the revolution would be left without a head. He spoke from some experience of revolution in Mexico; but the Emperor, who had come a long way since the *Coup d'état*, responded meekly that he could

only act upon his ministers' advice. The day, however, passed
off admirably; and the revolution melted off the streets, as
Bazaine's troopers showed themselves at the right moment.

As 1870 wore on, the Second Empire resumed its even
course; a plebiscite confirmed it by an immense majority;
Pepita was seen at the first Court in Lent wearing a confection
of gauze, taffeta, and satin in three shades of green with a lace
mantilla on her shoulders and green velvet foliage in her hair;
her Achille continued to command the Guard; and one Thursday at the end of June M. Ollivier announced that European
peace had never seemed more certain.

3

The blow fell swiftly. Bismarck was a quick worker; and
his successes hitherto had been obtained by admirable timing.
The defeat of Austria in 1866 had caught France at a disadvantage, and since that time he had gone from strength to
strength. (The years between 1866 and 1870 irresistibly recall
the troubled interval between Munich and the outbreak of war
in 1939.) A British diplomat reported gloomily that Germany
"looms out like some huge ironclad from which no sounds
are heard but the tramp of men at drill, or the swinging upon
their pivots of monster guns"; and its pilot drove ahead without the least regard to other craft at sea. There was a war-
scare over Luxembourg and another over Belgium. But the
French had lost their touch, and Bismarck won every trick.
British statesmen began to talk about disarmament; and though
Bismarck was unresponsive, France gave a sign of good faith
by reducing the conscription of 1870 by 10,000 men. It might
still be possible to save the peace of Europe, if the French
consented to be eclipsed and out-manœuvred. But would that
be safe for France? They were rearming at the modest pace
permitted by French politics; and the Emperor was groping
vaguely for allies in Austria and Italy. Time, perhaps, was on

their side; but how much time would Bismarck let them have?

That unrivalled chess-player, no less aware of how the game might go if the French succeeded in recovering their breath, moved in a new direction. His current threat to France was on the Rhine. But if he could succeed in planting on the throne of Spain a German prince who held a commission in the Prussian army, France would be seriously out-manœuvred. For the presence of a Prussian colonel in Madrid would mean another frontier for the French army to defend in the event of war with Germany, since they could hardly leave the Pyrenees unguarded. War on two fronts (resulting in what later jargon has resolved to term a 'pincer movement') was a military nightmare; and their resources were already badly strained by providing for the possibility of war on one. It was a tempting move. If France consented, she would have been out-manœuvred once again; and if she did not consent, there might have to be a war. Bismarck was by no means averse from another war, as there was a good deal to be said for fighting France while she was still relatively unprepared and before the Franco-Austrian alliance, which was in process of formation, had time to harden. Besides, a war of all the German states against a common enemy would efface unpleasant memories of fratricidal slaughter in 1866 and might elevate the King of Prussia to his proper place in a united Germany. The Prussian army was not afraid of war with France; and Bismarck dealt the cards with confidence.

Just three days after M. Ollivier's hopeful prediction it was learnt that Prince Leopold of Hohenzollern-Sigmaringen had been chosen to be King of Spain. An instant protest at Berlin was repeated in the French Chamber; and in face of this apparent firmness the candidature was withdrawn. But French tempers had been roused; and in an evil hour it was decided to satisfy his angry subjects that their Emperor, for once, had won a trick by obtaining from the King of Prussia an admission that he participated in Prince Leopold's renunciation and a formal guarantee that the Hohenzollern candidature to the throne of Spain would not be renewed. France had been humiliated so many times since 1866; and it would be pleasant to humiliate the Prussians for a change. This mission was entrusted to the French ambassador, a draftsman of the highest virtuosity named Benedetti, who had already been ordered to make contact with the King. That venerable figure was devoting his royal energies to a quiet cure at Ems; and when M. Benedetti, who had buttonholed him on the promenade one morning near the bandstand, showed a tendency to reopen the unpleasant subject of events in Spain, King William seemed disinclined for further conversation on the point. He was not prepared to discuss the proposed guarantee; and later in the day he refused politely on no less than three occasions to receive the pertinacious French diplomat. Two days later, for no apparent reason, their countries were at war.

The reason was not to be found in anything that happened at Ems, since nothing very grave had happened there. But events are sometimes of less importance than the form in which they are presented to the world; and in this case the mild sensation of the day's events at Ems was skilfully transformed into a *casus belli*. Bismarck was dining in Berlin that evening with von Moltke and von Roon; and the party was a trifle gloomy, as the episode appeared to have concluded with Prince Leopold's withdrawal and there seemed to be no chance of war. When a telegram reporting the rebuff to Benedetti arrived from Ems, Bismarck improved it with a few skilful touches making it appear that the French ambassador had been finally dismissed by an indignant monarch; and this version of the news was promptly issued to the press and to all Prussian diplomats. The story, he explained, would be in Paris before midnight, and in that form it would act like a red rag on the French bull. After this happy interlude their dinner was resumed on a distinctly brighter note, the Minister of War reiterating an expression of his renewed faith in the

Almighty, and von Moltke (whose thoughts appeared to turn in the opposite direction) offering to let the Devil carry off his old bones, if he was only spared to lead the German armies in the coming war.

Bismarck's ingenuity was more than justified, as France, maddened by the apparent insult to a French ambassador, flung into a declaration of war. The streets of Paris were full of angry people shouting "*à Berlin!*" as Émile Ollivier announced that he accepted the responsibility of war "with a light heart" and Marshal Le Bœuf stoutly expressed his confidence that the French army was prepared "to the last gaiter button." A simple falsification had enabled German statesmanship, which had already initiated the wars of 1864 and 1866, to enrich its country's history with the war of 1870.

4

Bazaine was not commanding the Army of Lorraine, as he had been warned the year before, because there was no Army of Lorraine. A last-minute change of plan eliminated the three large formations, which were to have been commanded by Bazaine, Mac-Mahon, and Canrobert, substituting a single army (optimistically termed the Army of the Rhine) under the Emperor's direct command and divided into eight Army corps and the Imperial Guard. Napoleon III had led his armies against Austria eleven years before; and the sick Emperor commanded them again, a dull-eyed imitation of his own inimitable uncle, with Le Bœuf, Lebrun, and Jarras composing a synthetic Berthier. Bazaine, the youngest of the corps commanders (exclusive of the dashing Bourbaki), was to command the 3rd Army corps with headquarters at Metz. His disappointment was expressed to the Emperor, when he took leave of him before departing for the front; and Napoleon, who deplored the necessity of war and said something about the great importance of Saarbrück as their first objective in

Germany, replied that his services were necessary and that a more important command was waiting for him later on. Some indication of this ampler prospect appeared on the next day, when he was given temporary command of all the forces in Lorraine until the Emperor's arrival at the front. That day (it was July 16) he left for Metz; and as Bazaine stepped into a train at the Gare de l'Est, he turned to someone on the platform. "*Nous marchons*," said the Marshal, "*à un désastre.*"

This was not a cheerful frame of mind in which to go to war. Bazaine was not a coward. But he was no longer young; and he had seen too much of war in three continents to view it with exhilaration. That enviable mood might animate Parisians engaged in the congenial exercise of bawling "*à Berlin!*" punctuated by the sound of breaking glass from shop-windows with names of German owners and by eager view-halloos, as they flushed a German spy. But the Marshal knew what it was like. Ten years earlier he had recalled the horrors of a battlefield after an action, and he had seen more since then. Those actions had all been victorious; and how could he be certain that the battles of the next campaign were going to be victories? After all, he knew as much of the deficiencies of the French army as any of his contemporaries. Had he not commanded the frontier Army corps for two years? He had seen its incomplete defences and its defective organisation; and he knew that it was still much as he had left it in 1869. What grounds were there in July, 1870, for feeling that they had any chance of winning? The public might believe it and shout itself hoarse in the belief. But an intelligent professional could be forgiven an overwhelming sense of inferiority, as he confronted the victors of Sadowa with the conquerors of Mexico.

European warfare had become a business of immense complexity, which Prussian methods and equipment seemed to have transformed within the last four years. Besides, the French were out-numbered to begin with; and given the

grave disparity in numbers, it might be advisable for them
to stand on the defensive rather than to run the greater risks
involved in operating on German territory against stronger
forces. A strategical defensive on the French frontier might
be accompanied by defensive tactics as well. For French military thought, observing the apparent triumphs of the Prussian
needle-gun in 1866 and the devastation wrought by the
Chassepot among the Garibaldians in the next year, was
deeply impressed by the fire-power of modern weapons; and
the official handbook for infantry bluntly laid it down that
"the advantage lies with the defence." That mood has never
been propitious to French victory, since the offensive spirit,
the *furia francese*, is half the strength of France; and when
it is overlaid either by the march of science or by a defensive
mentality disaster follows swiftly. But Bazaine was not inclined to challenge the official doctrine. He might have his
own opinions on the excessive use of trenches (another con-
cession to the devastating fire of modern rifles and artillery);
but he was quite prepared to follow where the official experts
appeared to lead in the direction of a war of strong positions.
These, it might be hoped, would hold until the Germans
withered under Chassepot fire or until the situation was transformed by the arrival of allies from Austria or Italy to redress
the unfavourable balance of man-power. True, nobody
thought of confiding any indication of the plan of campaign
to a Marshal, who was merely in command of four Army
corps upon a threatened frontier. That could wait until the
Emperor himself took over. Besides, it was a trifle fluid at
the moment in view of their uncertainty about the Austrians.
If Austria was coming in on their side, French strategy must
obviously accommodate itself to their ally's requirements,
which appeared to indicate an invasion of South Germany
and a happy meeting somewhere in the neighbourhood of
Munich. But if Franz-Joseph had learnt caution from his unbroken series of defeats, the French might have to win the

first few battles for themselves, whilst he made up his mind. In any case, the situation in the third week of July seemed to call for an attitude of caution along the French frontier.

Would they be able to defend it? Bazaine's sombre prediction at the Gare de l'Est showed that he had his doubts; and they were not diminished by what he found on his arrival. Starting off from Metz without waiting for his staff (Bazaine had always liked to see things for himself), he took a look at Thionville, a frontier fortress of primary importance. This was held at the moment by six hundred untrained men and ninety Customs officers; and work on its defences had actually been begun, although the guns had not arrived. But that was not surprising, as Metz itself was only held at the outbreak of war by a battalion of the Line, some sappers, and a few odds and ends apart from untrained *moblots* and a more respectable contingent of two hundred *douaniers*, upon whom the defence of the French frontier seemed largely to devolve. A division had just arrived; and as Bazaine surveyed the situation from his new headquarters, Metz began to reproduce in highly concentrated form the wild confusion that prevailed all over France. For France was mobilising on a system fathered in delirium, under which reservists from Alsace proceeded to Algeria in order to join a battalion of Zouaves at Strasbourg and drafts wandered about France for months on end. Regiments arrived at Metz without their transport; whole divisions had no ambulances; someone was telegraphing for a million rations; units appeared from nowhere without tents; corps commanders were unable to buy anything because they had no ready money; sugar began to run short; there would be no coffee soon, if some did not arrive from Paris; *mitrailleuses* appeared without the specialists, who knew how they should be fired, and faced them with the supreme humiliation of a secret weapon that insisted on remaining secret even from its friends; and somewhere in the railway station there were three million rounds of ammunition, which nobody discovered until two decisive battles had been lost.

In this administrative bedlam there was little prospect of active operations. Paris was informed of their deficiencies in telegrams of varying emphasis; and after five days of it Bazaine learnt with some relief that the Imperial headquarters would be arriving shortly. Upon this intimation he transferred himself from Metz to Boulay halfway to the German frontier in order to be with his own Army corps and to leave his rooms in the Hôtel de l'Europe free for Le Bœuf; and when this dignitary arrived in Metz, the Marshal was not there to greet him. Second Empire paladins were not a band of brothers; and there had been some misunderstanding about the time-table. Besides, a corps commander might have better things to do than to hang about the railway station in order to salute a man who would be shortly taking over his responsibilities. (Le Bœuf, cast to play Berthier to his sovereign's Napoleon, was chief of staff to the whole Army of the Rhine.) But no offense was taken; and Bazaine was left in temporary charge of the four Army corps in front of Metz until the Emperor arrived.

The military situation was still unchanged, because there was no means of changing it, when a tired man drove from the station to the Préfecture and Napoleon summoned his Marshals. The eager Le Bœuf sprang at him with a question about Austria, because it all turned on what the Austrians proposed to do; and when the Emperor murmured that they were still negotiating, he snapped impatiently. Bazaine was there; and as he said very little, the observant Jarras concluded that his relegation to the status of a corps commander was still rankling with the Marshal. But he had never been a talker; and the impassive manner, behind which he had learnt to keep his counsel in the *Bureau arabe* at Tlemcen and in Mexico, was new to Jarras. There was an inconclusive talk; and on the next day they had another conference in the little railway station at St. Avold. Frossard was full of his idea of a dash at Saarbrück to disorganize the German railways; and orders were prepared for a whole Army corps to operate against this small junction, which was lightly held by Prussian infantry, with Bazaine in general control of the attacking forces and of two supporting Army corps. He had no enthusiasm for the scheme, objecting that the army was in no condition to follow up any success that might be gained, although he advocated with imperfect logic a more ambitious thrust into German territory further to the north. His objections prevailed. But though all notion of a serious advance was dropped, the French steam-hammer was laboriously brought into position with the limited objective of cracking the single nut of a small railway station.

Time was passing; it would be August very soon; and the French armies were still strung out along the frontier, waiting to be set in motion. It was doubtful whether they were yet prepared to move; and if they could, it was not clear in which direction. For the Austrians might call for an immediate thrust across South Germany; and in that case it would never do to commit themselves to an advance elsewhere. French strategy was fatally subordinated to political considerations; and as von Moltke wheeled his armies into line, the French hung in the wind.

Inaction is the worst enemy of French *morale;* and when it was supplemented by a rich profusion of unnecessary marches in the height of summer, the troops began to lose their quality. For the electric telegraph was an embarrassing addition to the armoury of war, which enabled the high command to act on impulse and then to change its mind with greater frequency than had been possible without the aid of science. Modern invention, which had aided them to concentrate by rail more troops than they could handle now enabled them to give more orders than they should. Their uncertainties were all reflected in an endless series of conflicting orders; and when each of these had been translated into weary action by the movement of large numbers of perspiring men on foot to points from which they were recalled by the next telegram, discipline began to suffer. French armies were always argumentative. Unanimous in their support of the First Empire (whose victories were largely due to this unanimity), they had learnt from recent politics that the Second Empire was open to some question. True, barely 46,000 out of 331,000 serving soldiers had the temerity to vote against the Empire at the plebiscite that spring. But it took some courage for an enlisted man to cast a vote against the eagles under which he was serving; and the figures were a formidable indication of disloyalty to the regime. The tide of politics was rising; Frechmen were incurably political; and when doubts about the Empire were reinforced by doubts about the high command, a fatal brew began to simmer, whose temperature was maintained by the prescription ruefully detailed by Frossard—"*ordres, contre-ordres, marches, contre-marches.*"

But how could a command in doubt as to its own intentions act with an air of certainty? The hope of Austrian co-operation seemed to fade. Franz-Joseph felt that it would be just as well to wait and see what happened; and that disposed of the design for an advance by the French right into the Black Forest in order to meet their allies in the heart of Bavaria. But if they were to stand on the defensive in Alsace, there seemed to be no plan of active operations in Lorraine beyond an inconclusive stab at Saarbrück. The staff was working feverishly in the hot rooms of the Hôtel de l'Europe, considerately open to all comers and accessible to any foreign journalist who cared to stroll round with a view to printing full particulars of anything he could discover. But their labours were still unfruitful, so far as operations were concerned; and this lull was agreeably occupied by reassuring visits from *Mesdames les Maréchales* to their anxious mates. Madame Le Bœuf and Madame de Mac-Mahon proceeded by special train to Metz and Strasbourg; and Madame Bazaine, who had retreated to Versailles, was expected at the headquarters of the 3rd Army corps.

Other ranks at Metz were less exhilarated by two visits from the Emperor, who was not well enough to ride. But he drove round the camp in a small carriage, which he generally used to drive about the park at St. Cloud; and at the sight of that haggard mask under a gold-braided *képi* they almost forgot to cheer. The picture of an Emperor was less convincing now, as a sick man stared vaguely at them with his ragged hair and large moustache or sat painfully through inconclusive conferences with his Marshals; and his painted army had begun to lose its brightest colours. For as the August sun blazed down on Metz, the Line sweltered under heavy shakoes. Such elegance might do for Longchamps. But they were on active service now; and elegance was soon replaced by the unlovely silhouette of a low *képi*. The bearskins of the Guard were even more unseasonable. Whispering from their Napoleonic outline the last enchantments of the First Empire, they impressed perspiring wearers with nothing more than the simple fact that they were quite unwearable that summer in Lorraine. True, their forefathers had worn them in the wintry sunshine of Austerlitz and the midsummer blaze of Wagram and the full September glare of the Russian plains at Borodino. But what could be endured for Napoleon was too much for his sad-faced nephew; and a reluctant Emperor (after the order, in accordance with current practice, had been given, countermanded, and then renewed in swift succession) consented to the disappearance of their bearskins. An emblem of Imperial glory had gone back to store; and when the Guard appeared with little pointed forage-caps above their heavy facings, the Empire had lost a cubit of its stature, and a legend had begun to fade.

The operation against Saarbrück passed off without misadventure on August 2, although there was a slight uncer-

tainty about Bazaine's supervision. Not that there was much
to supervise that day, as they went briskly into action with
regimental bands playing the *Marseillaise;* and he left it all to
Frossard, occupying himself with a diversion some miles
away. They had omitted to inform him that the Emperor was
coming with the Prince Imperial. For it was to be the boy's
"baptism of fire"; and the sick man fought down his pain to
sit a horse, although he could not bear to let it move out of a
walk. It was quite a gala day for Lulu to see his first battle
and to watch his tutor winning it and to come under fire (his
mother had sent them a four-leaved clover from St. Cloud)
and keep a German shot that fell near them. This was glorious
for an excited boy of fourteen, although such experiences
were not for his humbler contemporaries. (Young Pétain
would soon be going to school at St. Omer.) But Bazaine, in
spite of a hard gallop, missed all this courtly comedy and its
bitter sequel, when Napoleon swayed in the saddle, gasping,
"Hold me, Lebrun." Then he dismounted, as the pain was
more than he could bear. They let him walk a little to ease it
before turning back to Metz. For if the affair at Saarbrück
had been won and Paris newspapers were rejoicing dutifully
in the Prince Imperial's first victory (the next battlefield he
saw was nine years away in Zululand), his father had lost a
harder battle. For he could not tell how long he would be able
to hold out against the racking pain.

This sufferer was still commanding all his armies with Le
Bœuf as chief of staff. Operations were controlled from headquarters; and French commanders enjoyed little more than
the privilege of doing as someone else commanded in their
sovereign's name. But these uncertain evolutions could not go
on for ever. Wars are not unilateral; and control passes ir-
revocably to the side that has a purpose, provided that its
means are equal to the end in view. French movements
hitherto had been almost entirely purposeless. But the German
armies were feeling for them now; and, unlike his adversaries,

von Moltke had a plan. Two days after Saarbrück an outlying French division in Alsace was roughly handled at Wissembourg; and though a reverse sustained by 7,000 French infantry at the hands of 30,000 Germans was not discouraging, the event left an unpleasant flavour. For the French commander, Abel Douay, who had been the recipient of his brother's unfriendly letters on the subject of Bazaine from Mexico, was killed; and the first real engagement of the war had been a French reverse. On the next day the Emperor reshuffled the command of the French armies, reverting belatedly to the pre-war scheme of three formations. Retaining the supreme command himself with direct control of the Guard and Canrobert's corps (which was still in rear of them at Châlons), he placed Bazaine in command of three Army corps in Lorraine, while Mac-Mahon commanded three Army corps in Alsace. But the new commanders were limited to the control of actual operations and restricted by the Emperor's supreme command. That might (and did) intervene at any time; and between engagements each Army corps reverted to its own commander. But, within these limits, Bazaine could now direct the movements of Frossard's and Ladmirault's corps in addition to his own, although no staff with which to do it was provided, and smooth working was not facilitated by Imperial headquarters' habit of continuing to issue direct orders of their own to his corps commanders. The busy scribes of the Hôtel de l'Europe, where General Jarras sat knee-deep in paper all day long, confirmed the telegram, by which his new appointment was conferred, in writing four days later and just three days after his command had been attacked.

The Marshal was now reponsible, though in a somewhat ill-defined way, for the operations of 103,000 men in front of Metz; and it was slightly disconcerting on the first morning of his new command to learn that one of his three Army corps was just about to be attacked at Spicheren. Other parts

of his extended front were no less sensitive; but Frossard's
telegrams rose in a mounting scale of apprehension towards
sheer hysteria, as he called for reinforcements through a long
summer day, and the enlightened Engineer, to whose sagacity
the military education of the Prince Imperial had been con-
fided, discovered painfully how very different practice can be
from theory. The plan of campaign, so far as they could be
said to have one, was largely Frossard's. He had given close
attention to the defensive positions in proximity to the French
frontier; and less instructed colleagues, who had endured
much from his authoritative wisdom on the subject, reflected
with wicked glee that this was one of them. For the French
command was not, as has been said, a band of brothers. Besides, it is the frequent fate of educators to be misunderstood
by those whom they have been unable to instruct; and Frossard was not popular. There was a feeling that if the able
doctrinaire had long favoured an engagement at that point,
here was his opportunity of seeing just what it was like; and
as the day went on, one disrespectful general was moved to
the disloyal comment that the professor was in a mess and
that it would be quite as well for him to stay there.

His outcries reached Bazaine in his headquarters at St.
Avold; and Frossard decided afterwards that it was all the
Marshal's fault. The later weakness of French military
thought for attributing all French reverses to Bazaine accen-
tuates this view. But it was not so easy for the new commander to go half an hour by train from his headquarters,
where the telegraph kept him in constant touch with all parts
of the front, to say nothing of the Emperor at Metz, in order
to take charge himself. Besides, he had to think of Frossard's
feelings. For it was by no means certain that a visit by the
Marshal would be welcome to a harassed corps commander.
In his new capacity Bazaine seemed to be denied the innocent
enjoyment of cross-country gallops and personal reconnaissance. All that he could do now was to sit over his maps in

St. Avold ordering reinforcements up to Frossard. If some of them were late and others slow, Bazaine was not responsible either for their march discipline or for the distances they had to travel, since Imperial headquarters had placed them before he took over the command; and the Marshal cannot justly be blamed for events at Spicheren.

But the unpleasant fact remained that Frossard had been driven off the ground with 4,000 casualties; and that did not exhaust the bad news which came into Metz that day. For while Frossard was performing in Lorraine, there was heavy fighting in Alsace, where Mac-Mahon was attacked among the trees at Wörth. As he was outnumbered by nearly two to one and his field-guns were out-ranged, a less determined character might have avoided contact with the enemy or broken off the combat at an early stage. For there are occasions when the Roman virtues are out of place. But mere facts were insufficient to discourage Mac-Mahon; and his obstinacy lost Alsace in one long summer day of lunging bayonets and drumming hoofs and pointed swords and wasted gallantry, that left him with 10,000 casualties out of 53,000 men engaged and opened a broad road into France before his undefeated enemy. This was shattering intelligence for the bewildered headquarters at Metz. There could hardly be a French offensive now; and an uncomfortable feeling spread that they might have to fall back to some point between Paris and the advancing enemy. That might mean a retreat on Châlons, leaving Metz to defend itself as best it could. But they were not yet reduced to this admission of defeat. For the army was still east of Metz, between the fortress and the oncoming Germans, and the ailing Emperor played with the notion of resisting there. But his nerves were unequal to the effort; and headquarters began to issue orders, without the least regard to Bazaine's authority, for a general withdrawal on Metz. When the Marshal heard the news of Mac-Mahon's defeat at Wörth, Le Bœuf saw his eyes fill with tears. The two men had quarrelled violently twenty years before over Bazaine's application for official leave to marry a dark Spanish girl at Tlemcen; and his enemies preferred to think that Bazaine always viewed his colleagues' ill-success with satisfaction. But there was no trace of it that morning at St. Avold.

A scared command continued to direct the French retreat on Metz; and as the sick Emperor fought down his pain and listened to conflicting plans, his weary soldiers tramped disconsolately through the rain. Now they were falling back before an enemy whom most of them had never seen; and their morale began to suffer, as the rain drove down on the retreating columns. Retreats were not their forte; and what could be more disintegrating than a retreat in pouring rain? Nothing had gone right since the war started; and after the defeats of August 6 it began to look as though nothing ever would. Overloaded and rain-sodden, they began to throw away large quantities of portable equipment; and it was not clear how far they were expected to retreat. Sometimes it was to Châlons, and sometimes to Metz. Bazaine's alternative proposal for a stand in front of Nancy, which he had studied on the ground in 1868, found no support; and he continued to do just as he was told, with elaborate precautions against surprise that rendered progress maddeningly slow and were less appropriate to large-scale European warfare than to the wary movement of small columns in Algeria.

As the days went by, the prospect darkened. It was clear that the sick man at Metz could never take the field, although his panic-stricken entourage was strongly reinforced that week by the arrival of a dapper little man in impeccable civilian clothes, whom they recognised by his wig as General Changarnier. This spirited recruit, who brought an echo of old Algerian battlefields, was promptly equipped with borrowed fragments of a uniform. (That was the season when unlikely friends rallied to the Empire in distress, and Captain Doineau, late of the Zouaves and Monte Carlo gas-works, did his best to serve in the French army once again.) But there was a growing sense among Napoleon's intimates that, if there were to be more reverses, someone else had better be responsible. They had the dynasty to think of; and no Bonaparte was likely to reign long after a defeat. Besides, the Emperor had now confessed that he was quite disabled from commanding in the field; and it was time to choose a Commander-in-chief, while there was still an army to command. A survey of the Marshals pointed to Bazaine, who was younger than the rest and had not yet been defeated. The army trusted him, and the critics of the Empire always seemed to make an exception in favour of 'notre glorieux Bazaine.' The faithful Pietri launched the notion two days after Mac-Mahon's defeat at Wörth; the Empress, who was already advising consultation with Bazaine on future operations, favoured it; and on August 9 Napoleon went so far as to appoint him to command the forces in Lorraine, emphasising the reality of this appointment by actually giving him a staff and relieving him of a corps-commander's duties by transferring his old corps to Decaen.

But the failing Emperor could not bring himself to take the last step, to abdicate his own supreme command. He had a notion that he might be able to retain it by appointing Bazaine or Mac-Mahon chief of staff, if he was forced to drop Le Bœuf. But events moved too fast for him. For politics were out of hand in Paris, where men stared incredulously at the frontier; and the Government faced an excited Chamber, in which Jules Favre pointed the moral of the French defeats with a demand for the Emperor's eclipse and his replacement in the high command "by a general, the glorious Bazaine." Émile Ollivier bowed to the storm and resigned office, leaving it to General Cousin de Montauban, whom his achievements in the Chinese expedition of 1860 had adorned with the exotic title of Comte de Palikao. In Lorraine the army was still concentrating east of Metz, drawing closer to the unfinished fortress under low, grey skies. Bazaine was their commander now, and they trusted Bazaine. One general (who lived to change his view) wrote to his wife that week about the Marshal's "luck and skill." But the Emperor was still above Bazaine, an insistent spectre haunting his headquarters every day to hasten the retreat, to drive the columns of exhausted men that plodded angrily down muddy roads in driving rain with their backs to the enemy. Old Changarnier was often with him, a wrinkled mask beside Napoleon's empty eyes and ragged hair; and the retreat to Metz went on, watched by two ghosts. But Paris was still pressing; angry republicans called on the new Prime Minister (one of them had heard from Madame Bazaine that even the intrepid Marshal was beginning to lose heart) and pressed hard for the Emperor's retirement; and Palikao assured them that he would support Bazaine. The whole country turned towards him. There was a sense that if anybody could save France, it was Bazaine. True, they had lost two battles on the frontier; but the war was not yet lost. When someone told Pepita that they were raising funds to give Mac-Mahon a sword of honour, the proud wife replied, "If that is how they reward defeat, what will they do for the victor?" All France knew who that was to be. Even Canrobert, who was his senior, refused an independent command and asked the Emperor to place him under Bazaine's orders.

It was already done. For that afternoon (it was August 12) a letter from headquarters told Bazaine that, by the Emperor's decree, he was Commander-in-chief of the Army of the Rhine. He left the front after making a few changes in the French positions, because a German attack seemed to be imminent, and came straight into Metz. He found the Emperor sunk in an arm-chair and looking deadly pale. Canrobert was still with him, when Bazaine arrived; and old Changarnier was there as well. The Marshal thanked Napoleon for his graciousness, spoke of the heavy burden of responsibility, and urged that Canrobert and Mac-Mahon were both his seniors. Canrobert replied that public opinion and army opinion both called for Bazaine, and then left the room. Changarnier opined that they would have to hurry, if they were going to get back to Verdun. Then the sick man in the chair gave judgment. Public opinion, he said, united with the army's feelings in guiding him to choose Bazaine. Mac-Mahon had done badly in Alsace, and Canrobert's reputation had suffered from indiscipline at Châlons. That left only Bazaine's undamaged. He added almost sharply that it was an order.

Now there could be no turning back. That August afternoon in 1870 had brought the ex-private of the Line, a Marshal now, to supreme command of an immense army round a threatened fortress behind a broken frontier. He had come a long way since he enlisted nearly forty years before; he had seen active service in three continents; and now his Emperor commanded him to face the crisis of a European war. This was the summit. But how many watchers envied Bazaine his eminence in August, 1870?

5

What would he make of it? What could anyone have made of it, with a discouraged army falling back before an enterprising enemy and a vague design of interposing it between Paris and the Germans at some point along the broad road into France which Mac-Mahon's defeat had opened? That was the situation which Bazaine inherited on his appointment to the French command. His nominal responsibility extended to the full strength of 250,000 men that France had put in the field; and Mac-Mahon, as he stumbled back from Wörth, was duly advised of his junior's new authority. But Bazaine's control was limited in practice to 170,000 men round Metz. This was about twenty times as many as he had ever handled under his direct control in the course of military operations and eight times as many as he had once manipulated for a few days on manœuvres at Châlons or set in motion against Juarez in Mexico. For the formidable power of rail-transport had concentrated forces far in excess of any previous experience enjoyed by Bazaine or most of his contemporaries; and matters were not simplified by the uncertainty as to how far his sovereign's authority would leave the new Commander-in-chief in control of operations.

For the Emperor was still at Metz. Exiled from his capital by a cruel certainty that the Parisians would never welcome him without a victory, the sick man lingered with the army which he had commanded for a month. That experiment had been disastrous, although there was no evidence that the un-tutored impulses of *généraux d'Afrique* were going to be more successful. Whilst operations were directed in the Emperor's name by Lebrun and Jarras with a few hints from Frossard, they had, at least, been in the hands of men who thought in terms of European warfare; and this consideration justified Napoleon's retention of nominal command long after the growing torture of his symptoms told him that he could never hope to exercise it in the field. Besides, the eternal pressure of French politics had insisted that Napoleonic armies must be commanded by Napoleon rather than by a mere Marshal of the Empire. That was the Napoleonic way. But it was over now. For the wind of politics had changed. Now the Emperor was superseded by his own decree; and, for military purposes, Bazaine reigned in his stead.

The best that could be done was to ensure his conformity to the broad strategical design formed by Napoleon and to provide him with a staff that gave him some chance of carry-ing it out. Bazaine was not consulted, when Jarras was appointed as his chief of staff, and he showed no enthusiasm for the appointment. He would have preferred Cissey or Manèque, who had served him in this capacity with the 3rd

Army corps and in Mexico, or Letellier-Valazé, with whom he had gone through the Crimea and the Italian campaign. But Jarras was imposed on him; and as a self-taught Marshal had nothing in common with that learned specialist, Bazaine elected to ignore him blandly. Leaving his new chief of staff in Metz, the Marshal kept his own headquarters two miles away at Borny; and on the second day of his command he found an instant to tell Jarras that there were no orders for him. The busy writing-tables of the staff were unfamiliar to Bazaine. A fighting soldier, he viewed their occupants without esteem and seemed to find the beneficiaries of that professional education, which he had been denied, a shade embarrassing. As in Mexico, he worked with his own intimates; and Boyer, whom jealous colleagues irritably termed his '*éminence grise*,' still presided in his private circle, where the devoted Willette stood on guard with Magnan and Mornay-Soult and two young Bazaines ran their uncle's errands.

His broad objective, in accordance with the Emperor's design, was to get the army back to Châlons by the road through Verdun. If they could get there intact, they might be able to confront the German thrust towards Paris with some prospect of success. French strategy was dominated by the threat to Paris, though Bazaine would have preferred to risk an action outside Metz with the prospect of a halt nearer to the frontier between Toul and Nancy. But his sovereign was still insistent on retreat; and a lifelong habit of obedience inclined Bazaine, even in supreme command, to do as he was told. Indeed, it was not easy for a Marshal to diverge from royal counsel based upon expert advice at Imperial headquarters on matters which might well decide the fate of France, to say nothing of the dynasty. True, he was in supreme command. But while the Emperor remained at Metz, Bazaine's supremacy still had something nominal about it; and though he might resent Imperial control—"Yesterday," he said bitterly, "it was an order; to-day it is a wish; and they are two names for the same thing"—he had the consolation that his actions were completely covered by the Emperor's express desire. Bazaine was never rash. A lifetime of military discipline had taught him that it was nearly always safe to subordinate his judgment to superior authority. Safe, perhaps, for his professional career. But was it altogether safe for the result of the campaign? That must depend upon the wisdom of superior authority; and when it was no longer there to take the blame, the entire responsibility for any failure would fall upon Bazaine.

Proceeding dutifully with the execution of the general design of a retreat through Metz to Châlons, he had his doubts. Coffinières, who was to be left in charge of Metz, had impressed him that there was a great deal to be done before the fortress could be safely left to its own resources; and Bazaine was in no hurry to fall back. He would do as he was told, of course, but without undue haste. He would have to go eventually; and his directions for the march were detailed and practical. (When Bazaine is found attending to small matters, his critics have elected to discern a limited intelligence rather than a Napoleonic sense of detail.) Indeed, the Marshal's orders, with their vigorous attempt to reduce the army's transport within reasonable limits, bore considerably more relation to reality than the tropical profusion of impedimenta with which they had insisted on campaigning in Lorraine, as though European warfare in a friendly country had been something in the nature of an expedition to some distant part of Africa.

It was Saturday, August 13, when he took command; and they began to move on Sunday, although the staff-work of their passage across the river and through the narrow streets of Metz towards the uplands on the way to Verdun was worse than primitive. Traffic problems had been airily ignored; and on the farther side of Metz 90,000 men, with 20,-

ooo horses and 5,000 vehicles, were crowded into an area measuring no more than four miles long by a few hundred yards wide. This congestion on the road may indicate that the Marshal was in no great hurry to depart, though it is equally accounted for by sheer inability to handle the immense numbers of his new command or by his reluctance to make full use of the headquarters staff. The Emperor had left that day, watched by a silent crowd, after hearing Mass in the cathedral; and an attentive Muse observed him, where Meissonier's enormous boots and streaming beard were on the lookout for a victory worth painting for the Salon of 1871. Early in the afternoon guns began to sound in the French rear at Borny. Bazaine rode up, insisting angrily that they were wasting ammunition, that someone was amusing himself by skirmishing with a few Uhlans, that he would not have a battle, and that the retreat must go on. (The Marshal's irritation, attested by at least two unfriendly witnesses, is the best evidence that he had no intention of delaying their retreat and ignored an excellent excuse for doing so.) But as the firing grew in volume, he was soon moving stray battalions and giving them the ranges under fire. A shell-fragment bruised his shoulder; and a pointless little rearguard-action ended in a few thousand wholly wasted casualties, as the retreat through Metz went on.

That night Bazaine telegraphed to Pepita that he and both nephews were well after a victory; and he made his report to the Emperor, who had got as far as Longeville just outside the town. The streets of Metz were packed with slowly moving troops under a waning moon as the Marshal picked his way across the congested town, riding on slippery pavements and up echoing side-streets. When he reached Longeville, the sick man was in bed; and Bazaine reported on the day's events. He said that he was anxious in case the Germans, who were evidently feeling for them, got across their line of march; and as his wound was painful when he rode, he asked to be relieved of his command. But Napoleon patted his shoulder with its shattered epaulette, telling him it was nothing, and that it would be better in a day or two, and that he had "broken the spell." "*Vous venez*," said the Emperor in his most winning way, "*de briser le charme*." Then he went on to warn the Marshal against unnecessary risks, against doing anything that might deter their possible allies. For he still had hopes of Austria and Italy and warned Bazaine against undue precipitation. "Above all," said the Emperor, "no more reverses; I rely on you."

Naturally cautious, this warning from his sovereign left Bazaine less inclined than ever to take risks with his command. High policy, it seemed, dictated that the military situation should be handled gingerly, that the army must on no account be unduly risked. They were all concentrated west of Metz; and he was in no hurry to risk his slowly moving caravan in an encounter with the enemy. Retiring for the night in his billet at Moulins, he did not emerge before mid-day, though he gave Jarras some orders before getting up. These indicated that the retreat would still proceed, though at a reduced pace due to the extreme deliberation of his corps commanders and Bazaine's anxiety to keep his forces closely concentrated in order to escape the fate by which Mac-Mahon had been overtaken in Alsace; and he stated categorically that they must all be at Verdun inside four days. There were disturbing indications that the Germans were moving round them to the south; and as they might have to fight their way through, he gave orders for large numbers of vehicles to be left behind. A letter to Pepita showed that his wound was giving trouble; and before starting out that day he saw a doctor, who reassured him that it was no more than a bruise. Then he rode up to see the Emperor, who was now at Gravelotte. When he arrived, the Marshal stopped to indicate their exact destinations to some straying units. Napoleon was sitting on a chair outside the little inn at the cross-roads; and an endless stream of marching men went by in a depressing silence. As it was August 15, the *fête* day of the Empire, Bazaine had brought a few flowers from his garden; and his little offering was graciously received. Then Napoleon enquired if he had better leave at once; and Bazaine replied that as he did not know what was going on in front of them, it would be as well to wait. They went indoors; and while the sullen columns still streamed past the windows, Napoleon discussed the route by which he should leave and the escort that would accompany him, should he decide to go. He saw the Emperor again that evening and learnt that he proposed to leave at dawn. Writing to his wife that day, Bazaine expressed regret for his sovereign's departure, "because the responsibility would be too heavy, the more so as all that has been done up to now has gone on quite apart from me—I have only been consulted as a matter of form." That night he repeated that he expected to be at Verdun in a few days, unless he got his forces together and drove the Germans southwards.

At dawn on Tuesday morning the Emperor sent for Bazaine, who galloped to Gravelotte. The village street was full of Lancers of the Guard and big Dragoons; and as the Marshal rode up to an open carriage, he saw a dejected man in uniform sitting beside a sleepy boy. Napoleon's face was drawn. He looked as if he had been crying and said very little to the Marshal, who sat his horse beside the carriage door. "*Je me décide,*" he murmured, "*à partir pour Verdun et Châlons; mettez-vous en route pour Verdun dès que vous le pourrez.*" He said something about the Prussians being in Briey and a last word of hope about the Austrians; and someone thought they heard him add, with a faint touch of drama, "*Je vous confie la dernière armée de la France; songez au Prince impérial.*" Then he took Bazaine's hand and gave the word to start. The drivers touched their horses; and in the early light a woe-begone procession went down the long white road, a line of *fourgons* (somebody in Metz had called one of them '*la voiture des homards frais*') with servants in the green Imperial livery, *Cent-gardes* in sky-blue, and Lancers jogging behind a landau that took the Emperor without an army out of sight.

6

Bazaine was his own master now. It was the morning of August 16; the war had lasted just a month; and his responsibility for the events of those four crowded weeks was hardly greater than that of any other corps commander and considerably less than Mac-Mahon's, whose gallant stupidity had lost them Alsace in a single day at Wörth. They were all ready to sit in judgment on him afterwards, when Mac-Mahon was a venerated President of the Republic, to blame Bazaine for every failure except Mac-Mahon's (that had really been too far away), to find sinister interpretations for his inability to save Frossard at Spicheren and to make full use of Jarras' capacity for paper-work, to deride him for undue attention to small details, when he wrote at length to Decaen about the field of fire of one battery and the destruction of a single copse or gave his infantry the ranges under fire at Borny, and to diagnose a fatal lethargy, when he did not. Bazaine at fifty-nine was no longer young; and perhaps five years of happy marriage to a bride of seventeen had helped to age him. He was stouter now; the narrow eyes were less visible than ever above his heavy cheeks. His hair was thinner. Always burly and bull-necked, he sank his head between the heavy shoulders; and who could tell what lay behind those inexpressive features? His face had never been revealing; for Bazaine had learnt to be inscrutable in the *Bureau arabe*. He had his feelings, though, cloaked in his impenetrable reserve or concealed behind that slightly mocking geniality. Feeling his origins acutely, he was unlikely to make confidants of the fine gentlemen who had enjoyed a better education than his own and thought they knew so much more about the art of war than an ex-sergeant of the Foreign Legion. How could they fail to be jealous of the Marshal whom his sovereign delighted to honour with supreme command of the last army of the Empire? He could not avoid a sense of loneliness outside the little circle of his intimates, of Boyer and Willette and his young nephews. Bazaine had been alone with his responsibilities in Mexico; and he was alone with them at Metz. He could not share the burden of command with colleagues of his own age and rank; and it lay heavy on him. Besides, he had been shaken by his wound two days before, although it seemed to leave his powers unimpaired. For on the morning after it he was telling stray battalions at Gravelotte exactly where to go. A strong and detailed military memory had always been his forte. Had he not dictated orders after lunch in Mexico for troop movements half a continent away without looking at a map, because it all stood clear in his head, as he puffed quietly at his cigar? That gift was still unimpaired; and when it had been displayed two generations earlier by a smooth-faced Corsican, the world agreed to term it Napoleonic. But something more was needed on August 16, 1870, if the French armies were to be extricated from defeat. For it may be doubted if Napoleon himself could have played the cards dealt by Napoleon III to Bazaine.

The sun blazed down on the bare uplands outside Metz. The drenching rain of the past week was over, and summer had returned. The Germans were on two, and would soon be on three, sides of them, as the French prepared deliberately to resume their westward march on Verdun. It was not easy for Bazaine to hurry, when more than one of his corps commanders insisted upon thinking for themselves and displayed unusual consideration for their weary men. The army had grown a shade dispirited. Its fighting spirit was not unaffected by continual retreats in wet weather under a command in which they were losing confidence and by the disheartening experience of leaving French fields and villages to the invader. Discipline was growing ragged; the ranks, with little reason left for faith in Napoleonic invincibility, had already begun to mutter that they were betrayed; and there had been a few disturbing instances of causeless stampedes.

About nine o'clock that morning the head of this slow-moving mass of 150,000 men, which was to get into motion once again early in the afternoon and was proceeding without undue investigation of what might be in front of them, was shelled without the slightest warning in the neighbourhood of Vionville. This unexpected welcome ten miles on the safe side (as they supposed) of Metz was disconcerting; and the sudden shock stampeded some of the cavalry and a large number of civilian waggoners. The French masses hurriedly faced to their left along the road that ran from Gravelotte to Vionville by way of Rezonville; and the Marshal, who was just sitting down to a breakfast of scrambled eggs, ordered the Guard to stand to without putting down his fork, called for the horses to be saddled, and rode down the road to see what was happening. He met a stream of fugitives and stolidly surveyed the ground. Then he posted two regiments of heavy cavalry with orders to charge anything that showed itself in front of them coming from the south. There were Germans to the east; but these were safely on the other side of Metz, which lay behind them now, as they faced west for Verdun. There was nothing to suggest that they had got round him to the north. But Bazaine was haunted by the unpleasant possibility that they might have crossed the river south of Metz in order to attack his host in rear.

That notion haunted him all day; and his first instinct was to strengthen the portion of his line which lay nearest to Metz. His later critics diagnose a fatal fascination exercised by the unfinished fortress upon a timorous commander. But though Bazaine was cautious (and he could hardly overlook the Emperor's injunction that the army was not to be unduly risked), it would have been criminally reckless to leave his rear exposed and to drive blindly forward in the direction of Verdun. Indeed, one of the sternest of his critics has argued in the full light of later knowledge that even if he had reached Verdun, he must have been trapped a few days later between the Meuse and the Argonne; and General Bonnal's calculations in 1904 are more impressive than the invective of Bazaine's contemporaries in the first bitterness of the defeat. For in the intervening thirty years many of the political motives for the denigration of Bazaine had lost their force; and Bonnal was not so much a politician or a contemporary soldier on the defensive (at Bazaine's expense) as a highly qualified military critic of the next generation. If his conclusion in *La Manœuvre de Saint-Privat* is correct, "Marshal Bazaine's solution was the only wise one, given the inadequacy of the high command and the waste of time between August 7 and 12," before, that is to say, Bazaine's responsibility began. His excessive faith in the fire-power of modern weapons impressed him with the virtues of the defensive; and he preferred to fight defensive actions near the frontier rather than in the heart of France. When the retreat to Châlons was projected, he had pleaded for a stand near Nancy; and when it was imposed, he was in no hurry to leave Metz. For it seemed sounder to fight in Lorraine (after all, Bazaine was a Lorrainer, whose ancestral village lay just outside Metz) than to demoralise the army still further by a long retreat, to abandon more French territory to the Germans, and to bring the war into Champagne within ninety miles of Paris.

That morning (the fourth of his command) he had no choice, as the Germans were attacking; and his first duty was to win the battle. His notion as to how this could be done was simple. If the Germans were attacking, they must plainly be repelled. The enemy, who seemed to have a plan of some kind, had saved him the trouble of thinking what to do next by trying to do something for themselves; and his purpose was to prevent them from doing it. That, he felt, could be achieved by making sure that all his men were in the right positions in the firing-line and by heartening them for the ordeal. All great commanders had displayed their gallantry in action; and as the day had opened with something in the nature of a panic (of which he met unpleasant evidence streaming towards him down the road to safety), Bazaine proceeded to a demonstration of his legendary courage. The Marshal galloped up the firing-line, rolling a little in the saddle and spurring with his right. When some infantry began to waver, he was there talking to the men and ordering the drums to beat; he trotted for two hundred yards in front of two field-guns, which he sited to his satisfaction; then he was off leading a battalion of infantry into action with a cheerful *"Allons, mes enfants, suivez votre maréchal."* He seemed to find a sardonic satisfaction in taking his staff under fire at a walk, though once he ordered Jarras and his cavalcade to keep clear of him. It was a brave performance in the best spirit of those ample paintings of heroic deeds at supreme moments of French history, with which the walls of Versailles were extensively adorned. A child of Versailles, he was not unworthy of his birthplace; and if Horace Vernet could have seen him in the smoke and dust, there was no reason why Bazaine at Rezon-ville should not hang beside Mac-Mahon at Magenta, or Murat charging, furred and frogged, with his riding-switch, or Napoleon himself laying a gun with his own Imperial hand at Montereau.

That was how battles had been won against the Austrians in 1859, when generals fought their way down village streets with drawn swords; and Bazaine was a fine exponent of the method. He had learnt the simple, if exacting, art of leadership when he watched Conrad, 'el bravo del caballo blanco,' steadying the Legion in the Carlist War. Almost all the battles he had ever seen in his long career of active service had been soldiers' battles. If they could only be kept steady in the ranks,

a victory was apt to follow, a new Magenta or Solferino for
their grateful countrymen to honour; or if they failed, there
was a defeat like his first disastrous experience at the panic on
the Macta nearly forty years before. That must be avoided at
all costs. He would see to that. No doubt this was not the whole
art of war. For there were larger problems to be solved; and
more learned soldiers were a trifle pained by his concentration
upon details. But war is an affair of detail; and as the day had
opened with a local panic, Bazaine might be excused for devoting himself largely to the stability of the French line.

Apart from this, his leading contribution to the course of
operations hitherto was to launch a charge of cavalry with a
muttered, "Yes, we must sacrifice a regiment; we have got to
stop them." As the Lancers wheeled into line, he was heard to
say, "The Cuirassiers will support them"; and the armoured
glory of the Empire crashed forward with a roar in one of
those despairing missions which were understood to be the
purpose for which mounted men existed. (Later critics have
found fault with the casual tone of these orders; but Bazaine
was rarely formal, and Wellington had launched his cavalry
at Waterloo with a casual, "Now, gentlemen, for the honour
of the Household Troops.") Riding forward to see what the
ebbing tide of cavalry had done, he was caught in a swirl of
Prussian hussars. The Marshal stood his ground and drew his
sword in a storm of pounding hoofs and pistol-shots; and
presently he found himself riding alongside an excited French
subaltern. "*Allons, jeune homme,*" the older man remarked,
"*du calme. Voyons, vous n'êtes plus un enfant. Ce n'est rien.*"
Then he walked his horse away and found himself near Frossard. Pointing to a cloud of dust, he said that it was Steinmetz
trying to cut them off from Metz. For he was still obsessed
by the menace to their rear. A little later he was with Le
Bœuf, suggesting that he should clear the Prussians from his
front. Bazaine even rode at the head of an infantry battalion,
ordering its drums and trumpets to sound the charge and then

having the regimental march played by its band. He was a heartening presence with his broad shoulders and unchanging look. But when old Changarnier enquired why he did not press home his attack, he galloped off shouting that he could not be everywhere at once.

He did his best to be, though. For his white linen cap-cover (it was almost as hot as Mexico that day) fluttered indomitably up and down the front. He was in the best of spirits; and when he ran across an old acquaintance from the siege of Puebla, he told him gaily how nearly he had been captured and left his companion with a cheerful sense that the old days had come again. His nerve was never steadier; and he was happily commanding some guns, when a member of his staff (which had completely lost track of him since he vanished in the sudden storm of German cavalry) discovered him at last. "*Ah ça,*" said the cheerful Marshal, who was no respecter of his staff, "*ces bougres-là vont me laisser seul en l'air,*" and promptly sent him off to tell Le Bœuf there was no need for him to hurry, because they would have to wait for Ladmirault's turning movement. More staff officers arrived with instructive historical analogies from Austerlitz and a tiresome insistence that he should press forward with his right in the direction of Verdun. But whilst his left was threatened nearer Metz, he had no taste for this manœuvre. "*M's amis,*" he answered shrewdly, "*vous ne savez donc qu'ils nous attendent avec leurs forces réunies sur le plateau de Fresnes-en-Woëvre et que ce serait se jeter dans leur gueule.*" There was not much evidence beyond his instinct; but he feared a German trap this side of Verdun, and vastly preferred to stay where he was and fight it out.

His temporary disappearance, which had lasted just an hour and was most unorthodox, shocked Jarras profoundly and sent Bazaine's young nephew, after an anguished search, to General Bourbaki as his successor. But now the Marshal had returned and was once more exposing himself recklessly.

When somebody protested, he excused his conduct, explaining that it was necessary, as the troops were wavering and needed encouragement. (That there was reason in the Marshal's view is evident from the occasional unsteadiness of the French troops that day and from the bitter fact that, though the Germans were at all times heavily outnumbered, the French line maintained itself with difficulty.) His head was never clearer; for when an anxious subaltern asked him for orders, the Marshal calmly enumerated a long string of units in their order on his left. But as the shadows lengthened, he grew steadily more anxious for his left along the road to Metz. Was it an error? A headlong march towards Verdun remained a possibility; but what lay at the end of it? The Germans would still be waiting on two sides of him; and they might catch him on the march with insufficient ammunition and impaired discipline. The light was failing now, and the long day's fight was over. What was he to do next? As he walked his horse back to Gravelotte, the road was almost blocked by a multitude of stragglers who had preferred the open country to the firing-line. He spoke to them quietly; but they left a disagreeable impression. This was not encouraging; and he told Soult's grandson, who rode with him, that he must not say they had won.

The staff, with its usual sagacity, was jubilant; and someone was saying that Bazaine would soon be Duc de Rezonville. But he was not unduly cheerful. "*Notre situation*," he said that evening, "*n'est pas brillante.*" Somebody found him upstairs attending to his nephew's injuries; and when Jarras came round for orders a little before midnight, he was dictating slowly by the light of two candles. Maps were spread across the table at which he had dined; and he kept turning to them, as he dictated in a sleepy voice. He was not far off sixty; he had been in the saddle since four o'clock that morning; and as Jarras looked at the Marshal, he muttered to a staff-captain that the man was asleep. He had already reported to the Em-

peror that they had done a hard day's fighting in which they
had held their ground, adding that he was forced to fall back
in the direction of Metz in order to replenish his supplies and
that the German concentration in front of him made it prob-
able that he would have to take the most northerly of the
roads to Verdun. But as the messenger, by whom he sent this
report, was entrusted with a letter asking the Minister of War
for a set of maps of the country round Metz, his interest in
Verdun was visibly diminishing. This was still clearer from
his orders to Jarras, which brought the whole army back from
the ground that they had held all day towards the fortress in
their rear. When he had finished, Bazaine paused for an instant,
lifted his tired eyes from the map, and said, "If anyone thinks
there is something better to be done, let him say so." Jarras
kept silence; and the Marshal added, "After all, we must save
the army, and for that we must go back to Metz." The tired
man had made up his mind, and there was nothing more to do
that night. Tuesday was over; it was Wednesday now; and
Pepita would soon be telegraphing anxiously from Versailles:

"Êtes-vous victorieux?"

Was he? At any rate, 50,000 French had held their ground
all the morning against 30,000 Germans. In the afternoon, as
more troops were thrown in, 80,000 French successfully resisted 50,000 Germans; and before the day was done, 135,000
French with 364 guns and 66 wonder-working *mitrailleuses*
held off 65,000 Germans and 246 guns. Those were the hard
facts of Rezonville, which had cost France nearly 17,000
casualties. True, the German losses were proportionately
heavier, a quarter of their total force engaged, amounting to
almost 16,000 killed and wounded. That was the result of
Rezonville; and it was enough for one blazing August day.

7

What was Bazaine to do next? Given his excessive faith in the fire-power of modern weapons and his predilection in favour of strong defensive positions, his course was tolerably plain. For though Rezonville had shown that defence was costly too, he remained convinced that the enemy would dash himself to pieces against a suitable defensive line. (That delusion was to cost France the loss of a second war in 1940.) It remained his firm belief that "when an army has not gained moral superiority over its enemy by an initial success or by greater numerical strength enabling it to execute large out-flanking movements, it is better to conduct operations systematically, as in the Seventeenth Century." Haphazard methods and bold moves in all directions might be good enough for desert warfare in Algeria and Mexico against an enemy with little more than superior mobility. But this was European war. The board was smaller; caution was dictated by the enemy's equality, if not superiority, of armament; and, slightly over-awed, the Marshal elected to make war *"méthodiquement comme au XVIIe siècle."* That meant the stately minuet which Turenne and Montecucculi had walked between Rhenish fortresses in an age that made war without the unseemly violence of battles and fought battles without the indelicacy of pursuits, or Villars' evolutions against Marlborough along the *Ne Plus Ultra* Lines. If there was a strong position outside Metz, he was quite prepared to wait for the Germans there and earn the Lines of Amanvillers a similar celebrity. Rezonville, after all, had scarcely been a true defensive battle, since it was fought on ground dictated by the enemy's attack. An encounter-battle of this character was no test of the validity of his beliefs; and the experience left Bazaine's opinions unimpaired. For he retained a feeling that "one or perhaps two defensive battles fought in positions which I regarded as impregnable would wear out the enemy by inflicting such heavy and repeated losses as would weaken him sufficiently to leave him disabled from any serious opposition to my further movements." The result two days later at St. Privat fell short of his anticipation. But that hardly proved that Bazaine's doctrine was fundamentally erroneous, since an intelligent design might be frustrated by the imperfection of his instrument or by faults in his (or his subordinates') execution.

There was no inherent vice in his decision to withdraw to a position outside Metz. His later critics diagnosed a base inertia, if not something worse associated with reluctance to expose his reputation to the risk of active operations or to share the campaign with Mac-Mahon or to remain in communication with the Emperor's headquarters any longer than he could help. But it seems superfluous to find sinister excuses for a decision that could equally well be based on rational grounds. His preference for the defensive in the circumstances in which French armies found themselves in August, 1870, was wholly reasonable. Wellington's defensive had prevailed at Waterloo; and all Lee's brilliance in attack had failed to win the Civil War for the Confederacy. If the Lines of Amanvillers held, the balance of man-power might be redressed by German casualties; and if they did not, that would be grim evidence that an army incapable of holding them was scarcely equal to the more exacting operations of an offensive.

There were intelligible grounds for Bazaine's withdrawal after Rezonville, although it would be galling for his troops to abandon ground for which they had fought so hard. The aged warrior who was in command of the artillery had sent an officer to tell the Marshal that General Soleille anticipated a grave shortage of ammunition, if they fought again on the same scale next day. True, his powers had been grievously impaired by family bereavement; his memory was failing; he completely overlooked three million rounds of Chassepot ammunition, of which he had made a secret hoard in Metz; and as he was perpetually haunted by the nightmare of an ammunition shortage in the field, he had taken to his bed after a brief excursion, in the course of which he warned the Marshal and implored his battery commanders to observe a strict economy. Besides, his outlook was deeply coloured by an unhappy mysticism, which left him with a mournful certainty that, as the Emperor had failed the Pope by withdrawing a French garrison from Rome, his God would surely fail the Emperor. A stern conviction that all subsequent calamities were the just punishment of Heaven prepared him for the worst, a mood of resignation to which the French military mind seems occasionally prone. But though Soleille was a pessimist, his intimation that ammunition was beginning to run low could scarcely be ignored by a responsible commander.

They had fought all through Tuesday; and Wednesday was occupied with the withdrawal to their new positions. A fresh retreat was almost more than they could bear; and the troops, disappointed by this apparent waste of all their efforts, expressed their dissatisfaction in loud complaints and a general decline of discipline, which took the form of looting and widespread desertion. French soldiers always had a way of thinking for themselves; and though their indiscipline was inexcusable, they might now be pardoned for a certain loss of faith in the command. Their movements were effected in the usual chaos and with incredible deliberation, while Bazaine spent the day in his new headquarters at Plappeville. He was occupied with a mass of minor business relative to decorations and promotions; and he reported to the Emperor once more that he had fallen back to strong positions in order to renew supplies and would be able to resume his march in a more northerly direction by Friday. But Soleille was assuring him with gloomy iteration that Metz contained little more than three-quarters of a million rounds of Chassepot ammunition, which would be consumed in one day's fighting. He pressed his corps commanders to protect their new positions with field fortifications. For if the Lines of Amanvillers were to serve their purpose, no advantage of a strong defence must be over-looked. The spade had been a leading lesson of the American Civil War; and though its use was less familiar to French soldiers, at least two of Bazaine's corps commanders employed it adequately for the preparation of their sections of the front. Frossard's instincts as an Engineer and Le Bœuf's as a gunner ensured that their portion of the line was sufficiency prepared to meet attack. But the fiery Canrobert disdained more than a single length of trench and a few loop-holes in some walls. True, he was short of tools; but he made no effort to repair his needs either from local farm-houses or from army stores.

The night was quiet; and when Bazaine heard the first news of a German attack on Thursday morning, he did not seem to take it very seriously. He repeated that they were in a strong position and that no attack could possibly succeed. They could hear the guns at Plappeville; but when Jarras tried to get him to go out, he insisted that it was not serious and that the staff had better go on working out promotions. This time he would not scandalise them by undue activity in the firing-line, as there was no surprise and his own presence at the front was not demanded by any threat of panic. They should see that he knew how a Commander-in-chief should behave. He was at his head-quarters now; and he kept scrupu-lously in touch with the telegraph, which told him what was going on all round, as watchers on the cathedral tower in Metz telegraphed their reports to Plappeville. All the morning he continued to observe developments. He warned Canrobert to establish his positions *"le plus solidement possible"*; and the definiteness of his order left nothing to be desired, although Bazaine's instructions to men who were his seniors and, per-haps, embarrassed him by social superiority occasionally erred on the side of mildness. For he was always suave; an ex-*légion-naire* could not be peremptory with well-connected officers; and it was easy afterwards to argue that his light touch in command was attributable to a base desire to leave responsi-

bility with the men to whom he too frequently addressed
polite suggestions and requests instead of ineluctable commands.

In the afternoon he rode up the hill behind his headquarters,
commanding an extensive view of the country from which his
left might be threatened. For the army would not last long in
the field, if it was separated from the stores of Metz. Food
and ammunition were necessities for which there was no
substitute; and his immediate concern was to retain his communications with their nearest source. Meanwhile the German
thrust at the Lines of Amanvillers had not been conspicuously
successful. Up to five o'clock, indeed, it failed completely at
enormous cost; and Bazaine was convinced that the enemy,
having satisfied themselves of the strength of his position, had
finished for the day. True, Canrobert was calling loudly for
support. But Bazaine, always level-headed, was a little apt to
think that his subordinates cried out before they were hurt.
Besides, Canrobert was on the right; and Bazaine's gravest fears
were always for his left.

The pressure on Canrobert at St. Privat grew, as the long
summer day came slowly to an end. Bazaine could see men
streaming off that portion of the field, as he rode back to headquarters. "What can you do with troops like that?" he said.
He had not been disposed to risk his last reserve, the Imperial
Guard, in support of Canrobert, since he judged St. Privat
to be a point of secondary value in comparison with the road
to Metz. For if that were cut, they would all be disarmed and
starving; but if St. Privat went, they could still fall back and
kill more Germans in another defensive position nearer Metz.
Bourbaki had been equally reluctant to throw in the Guard,
having witnessed a disturbing exchange of compliments in
which the routed Line reviled the Zouaves of the Guard as
'dirty Prætorians,' and they responded to this tasteless excursion into classical history with loud intimations that they
had been betrayed. Left to its own resources, the French right

collapsed under relentless German pressure, as Canrobert and Ladmirault were forced back. But Bazaine refused to view it as a disaster, insisting sturdily to someone that there was no need to be down-hearted, as they would have had to fall back in any case and the Prussians had small cause for satisfaction in a French retreat on Thursday night, which would otherwise have taken place on Friday morning. Would it? The Marshal was quite right to put a face on their defeat. But if the Lines of Amanvillers could have been securely held, he would, no doubt, have held them. Since he could not without taking risks which he regarded as excessive, there was nothing for it but a fresh withdrawal towards Metz.

In one sense, the result was less disturbing than that of Rezonville, as they had been outnumbered this time. For the French had only 127,500 men engaged against 185,000 Germans. But the army had failed to demonstrate its ability to hold the Lines of Amanvillers, although they had inflicted 20,000 casualties at a cost of 12,000 to themselves. The Germans had attacked them on ground chosen by Bazaine; and the result had been a German victory.

8

Bazaine had played for safety. Sound policy, the Emperor's commands, and his own instinct all pointed the same way. France had no margin for running risks in 1870; and Bazaine was not the man to run them. It was no time to risk a gamble with the army under his command, as it was highly doubtful where France would find another. Besides, the military situation was obscure; and he preferred to gamble upon certainties. "*Je ne voulais agir*," as he said afterwards, "*que presque à coup sûr.*" Certainties are rare in war; and as he was reluctant to act decisively until he saw one, he might be excused for not risking more than he could help in the haphazard encounters of Rezonville or staking his last reserves in a final encounter at St. Privat. For the essential, as he saw it, was to preserve the army in order that it might live to fight again another day. Those had been the Emperor's instructions; and in retrospect it is not easy to find fault with them, although contemporaries could hardly be expected to applaud the strategy by which their main army was immobilised in an encircled fortress after two indecisive battles. But what else was there to do? Mac-Mahon's defeat at Wörth had let the Germans into France. And how else could the war be kept away from the defenceless centre of the country, whilst an army was concentrating in Champagne for the defence of Paris?

He had played for safety; and now the wisest course appeared to be to play for time. "I thought," as he said later, "that if I gained time for the Army of Châlons to form, it might be strong enough to come to our relief." That was his objective now; and though the Army of Châlons foundered inside a fortnight at Sedan, Bazaine's defensive served a larger purpose. For it detained an army of 200,000 Germans in Lorraine until the winter; and that respite, in General Bonnal's considered view, "alone enabled the Government of National Defence to organise resistance and to prolong it until February, 1871." The war was lost when Germany defeated the armies of the Empire in August and September, 1870. But that defeat was not followed by an ignoble surrender, since the war went on. For when the Second Empire was struck down, the Third Republic stepped into the breach and angry Frenchmen, symbolised by a stern-featured young woman in a Phrygian cap, fought in the ruins. Their effort, which was without effect upon the military situation, saved the soul of France; and that could not have happened unless Bazaine had kept the Army of the Rhine in being.

His problem was now agonisingly simple. If he was to keep his force together and to draw the German pack away from Mac-Mahon in Champagne, he must fall back from the positions which had been gravely compromised on August 18.

The Lines of Amanvillers had proved to be untenable; and he sought safety nearer Metz. Meanwhile he reported to the Emperor that he was still in hopes of fetching a wide circuit to the north by way of Montmédy in order to pass the Argonne and to rejoin him in Champagne. Mac-Mahon was warned that he was still on the defensive; and Bazaine added, in a tone of growing caution, that he would inform him of his line of march, if it could be safely undertaken *"sans compromettre l'armée."* That was the main thing. For there would be little sense in leading them to shipwreck in the open country outside Metz and, incidentally, sacrificing that valuable fortress to the enemy. Work proceeded hurriedly on its defences; and a few days later he was able to report that these were almost complete and that he hoped to leave by the northern route.

The Germans were all round him now; and his communications with the rest of France were precarious. Mysterious civilians, whose local knowledge enabled them to slip through the German lines with tiny messages concealed about them or rolled in cigarettes, came and went at headquarters. His hopeful tone encouraged Mac-Mahon under the goad, unsparingly applied from Paris, of the *plan Palikao* in a wavering advance towards the northeast with the fixed design of breaking a way through to Metz. For Palikao, the new Prime Minister, who had a long life (he was just seventy-four) and a successful expedition against the Chinese to his credit, imposed a wild strategical design by which Mac-Mahon was to swing a hammer of 120,000 men at the Germans and break them on the anvil of Bazaine at Metz. Perhaps the hammer was not quite as solid as it looked; and Mac-Mahon hesitated. Then, as the direct road to Metz seemed to be blocked, he felt his way uncertainly towards the Meuse at Montmédy hoping to disengage Bazaine or, if that failed, to slip back and cover Paris; and though there is some controversy as to the exact state of Bazaine's knowledge, he knew that Mac-Mahon was on the move towards him.

He was seeing a good deal of the pessimistic Soleille and of his imposing colleague, General Coffinières de Nordeck. That warrior, to whom a long moustache in the old Gallic mode lent added dignity, was now Commandant of Metz; and his legitimate anxiety for the great fortress entrusted to his care inclined him to oppose all measures calculated to reduce the forces in its immediate vicinity. Such counsellors were hardly likely to encourage an unduly enterprising mood in the Marshal; and when an old Algerian acquaintance found him in their company, Bazaine was indisposed to adopt Lapasset's heroic remedy of a mass sortie without baggage, sweetened by a few summary executions of those soldiers who had left the firing-line at St. Privat to loot. The Marshal answered genially that his interlocutor had never held a large command and did not know how to handle it, because 150,000 men (as he had discovered to his cost) did not manœuvre like a *goum* of African irregulars. But he sent one of his staff-officers to survey with Canrobert the possibility of a break-through to Thionville and held an inconclusive meeting, at which Le Bœuf enquired if Mac-Mahon was on his way to Metz with a large army. If so, their duty in his view would be to move towards him. This scandalised the cautious Coffinières, and a vociferous debate ensued. The meeting dealt with relatively unimportant matters, enlivened by a vigorous complaint from Canrobert that he had been left unsupported at St. Privat; and Bazaine adjourned it with a tactful intimation that a messenger was leaving shortly for Verdun and that, if his colleagues wished to send any letters, they had better write them.

The Marshal's callers were full of bright ideas for moves in all directions. Some favoured an escape towards the south by Remilly and Château-Salins. But his difficulty always was to see what they would do, if they succeeded in arriving there, and where their base would be for the next move. That was why he seemed to favour the string of secondary fortresses long the Belgian frontier by way of Montmédy and Sedan. Fortresses, even of the second order, appeared to fascinate him. For they had always played a part in classical campaigns; and he was quite determined to make war "*méthodiquement comme au XVIIᵉ siècle.*" Meanwhile he was prepared to make a move upon a modest scale. A windfall of four million rounds of ammunition, which somebody discovered in a freight-train, was most encouraging. The army's tone was better now; and he proposed to risk a limited advance towards the east in order to draw off the Germans in that direction and thus leave the way clear for Mac-Mahon to join him from the west. This operation, which Soleille and Coffinières viewed with deep misgivings, was undertaken on August 26. The Marshal was in no hurry to come on the scene; and as he left his head-quarters, he muttered that he had too little ammunition. His baggage was packed. But as it was rumoured afterwards that he had ordered dinner, it seemed unlikely that they would be leaving Metz for good that day. This half-hearted affair was fortunately interrupted by a storm of rain; and since the Germans seemed indisposed to do more than to stay where they were and Bazaine declined to launch a frontal attack in vile weather, it was suspended. But he took the opportunity of consulting his leading subordinates as to what they should do next. These meetings had been a constant feature of the French command since the outbreak of war; and there was nothing in the least unusual about Bazaine's invitation except that, through inadvertence or design, he sent Bourbaki to the wrong place.

It was just a week since St. Privat, when the Marshal assembled the collective wisdom of the Army of the Rhine. Some, like Canrobert, were his seniors, almost all his social superiors; their last meeting had been strikingly unpleasant; and he seemed a little shy of the encounter. "What are they going to say to me?" he asked his nephews more than once, as they walked their horses through the downpour on the road to the Château of Grimont. Jarras, who was not the soul of tact, answered his question by observing that, whatever any-body else might say, it was for him alone to make up his mind and to bear all responsibility. (One seems to see the reason why Bazaine contrived to see as little of Jarras as possible and preferred to work with his competent subordinate, Colonel Lewal.) It was two o'clock, when they arrived; and the in-separable Soleille and Coffinières were already waiting on the door-step. It was a pouring afternoon; and as the rain streamed down the window-panes, the troops stood waiting in the sod-den fields all round them. Bazaine explained the situation briefly, indicated that he was prepared to march on Thionville, and called upon his corps commanders to express their views. There was a fairly general uncertainty about the temper of their men, and Frossard was particularly diffident. Then the Marshal called upon Soleille, who launched into a long histori-cal analogy between their position and that of Napoleon in 1814. This seemed promising; and even if misfortune forced the country to sue for peace, he said that Metz and the army were a combination which ensured that France could never lose Lorraine. That was the bright side of Soleille's picture; but he could not conceal from his hearers that they had only enough ammunition for a single battle and that, in conse-quence, a dash for freedom was quite out of the question. It followed that they would be well-advised to stay precisely where they were. Coffinières, looking more like Vercingetorix than ever, spoke next in his familiar vein about the weakness of his forts.

The Marshal, intimating that he was not unimpressed by these opinions, called for their considered judgment. Frossard supported Soleille, with an unfavourable comment on the Army's exhausted mood which was, he thought, better suited at the moment to defence than to attack. Canrobert agreed, adding a word in favour of small-scale activities around the fortress; and Ladmirault pronounced that major operations were hardly to be thought of in the absence of sufficient ammunition. Le Bœuf indignantly denied that their unfortunate position was in any way connected with his own previous administration and stated that it was their duty to preserve the army. Just as Bazaine was preparing to adjourn the meeting on their unanimous agreement, Bourbaki arrived after a gallop through the rain from the wrong address. Informed of their decision, he promptly disagreed, indicating a vehement desire to break out to the south of Metz. He was quite unmoved by Coffinières' plea for his threatened fortress, which could not last a fortnight, if the army went away. But when Bazaine adduced the ammunition shortage, he was forced to a reluctant *non possumus*. Then, as no cavalry commanders were present, they said a few rude things about the cavalry; and their deliberations ended with the rain drumming on the windows and the halted troops outside. Nobody had mentioned Mac-Mahon; and wisdom after the event avers that if anybody had, their decision would have been entirely different. Who can say? If Mac-Mahon's whereabouts had been material to their decision, they all had tongues in their heads; and which of them was too shy to ask a question? The problem facing them that afternoon was whether the army should move north on Thionville; and as they all agreed that it was quite incapable of such an effort, it would hardly help them very much to know that Mac-Mahon was somewhere near a destination, which they could not reach. The truth was that the ammunition shortage, as presented to them by Soleille, so circumscribed the army's range of movement that it was incapable of combined strategy with anyone outside, unless their partner could force his way into the area of Metz itself. That being so, there was no more for them to do that day; and they went out into the rain.

As he rode back to headquarters, Bazaine passed a halted regiment and said, "Well, they wouldn't bite today." It was not clear if he alluded to the enemy or to his colleagues. But

there was no sense in telling the whole army of its helpless
ness; and he was right to be a little vague. In any case the day'
work had a most unhappy influence on its morale. The fals
start, followed by a halt in pouring rain and a damp return t
the place from which it had set out, was the reverse o
heartening; some of them behaved abominably; and the
found rude names for the battle of *Rentre-en-ville* and fo
Marshal '*Va-t-en z'y voir*,' by whom it had been inspired
Now the rain, grey, whispering, and pitiless, which had bee
the companion of their retreats for so long, was with ther
once again, as the disheartened army tramped back to i
sodden camps.

But the Marshal was not yet completely reconciled to
stationary role. News from the outer world appeared to shov
that Mac-Mahon was feeling for him in a northerly direction
and he resolved to try another push for Thionville. The whol
army was set in motion once again on August 31, though with
out undue haste; and the ranks began to mutter that it was
new instalment of the old story. His corps commanders wer
informed that, according to the latest information, Mac
Mahon was on his way towards them. This time Bazaine ap
peared to feel that, as at Rezonville, a demonstration of h
courage would apply the necessary stimulant; and in conse
quence the Marshal devoted more time to the encouragemen
of single units under fire than to the direction of a promp
offensive, which was not without some prospect of success
Their attack was late in starting, a circumstance which subse
quently moved Bazaine and his generals to mutual reproache
But before the light failed, it had scored a partial success a
Noisseville; and the Marshal, who exposed himself recklessly
had the satisfaction of seeing a horse killed under the prin
Jarras. In the night some of the lost ground was recovered b
the Germans, who took full advantage of French carelessnes
and when Bazaine looked out at five o'clock on the nex
morning, he found a grey wall of fog. Calmly drafting tw

telegrams for later use, of which one would inform the Emperor of a local success while the other announced that they had fallen back again on Metz, he ordered a resumption of the attack with the alternative that, if it failed, they would dig in and eventually withdraw. Their renewed offensive failed; and the whole operation cost the French 3,500 casualties.

Eighty miles away that day Mac-Mahon had blundered into the German trap at Sedan with 125,000 men. A day of agonising effort against inevitable defeat cost them 17,000 casualties and nearly 30,000 prisoners. Mac-Mahon was wounded early in the day, as guns were thudding in the morning mist; the command passed to Ducrot and finally to Wimpffen; Napoleon, who had trailed miserably in the wake of his last army, waxed his great moustache, put colour on his leaden face, and rode along the firing-line for hours, sick with pain, in search of death. It never found him. Once his gunners turned to cheer the painted Emperor, immobile on his horse among the Prussian shells. The long September day dragged on; and when everything had failed and German shells were dropping in Sedan, he sat muttering that they must stop the guns, that they must cease firing, that there must be no more bloodshed . . . and ordered somebody to hoist a white flag over Sedan. Then he wrote in his fine writing to the King of Prussia that, having failed to die at the head of his troops, there was nothing more for him to do than to give up his sword. That night the Army of Châlons surrendered in the field (as Mac-Mahon was wounded, the signature on the capitulation was Wimpffen's) with 80,000 men and 500 guns. Now there was no chance of any help for Metz.

9

The last phase could only end in one way, although they did not yet know that in Metz. But the black news came seeping through. First there was a hint of Failly's defeat at Beaumont. Then they heard the Germans cheering and began to find pieces of newspaper on trees in the front line with the first whispers of Sedan. One day the watchers on the cathedral tower saw long, dark columns moving towards Germany; and as they were too far away to make out the French red and blue, there was a rush of lively rumours that Mac-Mahon had won a battle and the enemy were in retreat, that they were moving back because the Poles had risen, that the Austrians were coming in at last. But they knew the truth, when the Germans drove five hundred French prisoners from assorted units of Mac-Mahon's army into the French lines. Unarmed and tattered, they stumbled through the autumn mist towards them waving handkerchiefs; and when they had been interrogated at the railway station in the pouring rain, Metz knew the worst.

Bazaine's first impulse was to get rid of useless mouths. Cavalry was unlikely to be of much service in a besieged fortress. Indeed, so far it had not been much use in open warfare. Besides, they had already started eating horses; and dismounted men were worse than useless. One general was told to take four regiments of cavalry and break out of Metz. But they would have to wait for better weather before making their dash for liberty; and better weather never came. For it was always raining, as the mist crept up from the Moselle to finger the tall poplars on the straight French roads that led towards the waiting Germans. They were waiting now on every side of him; and Bazaine's army backed helplessly against the ring of forts round Metz.

The Marshal in his headquarters at the trim Villa Herbin outside the town at Ban Saint-Martin was not communicative. When the faithful Willette took possession of it just after the August battles, he had notified the local manufacturer to whom it belonged that he would be proud to own a house where great events would be accomplished. But for the moment there were few events at Metz, although the outer world was anything but uneventful. For the news of Sedan had sent Paris flaming into revolution; and while the stricken Emperor trailed off into captivity, his eager subjects went roaring round the Tuileries one bright September day. A republic with Jules Favre and Gambetta for its leading ornaments proclaimed itself with General Trochu as its chosen soldier. For there was no thought of surrender, as the Empress slipped away to England and France stripped to face her enemies. At Metz the Marshal much preferred to meet his problems by himself; and when the untiring Jarras fretfully requested information as to his designs, he answered sharply that in the present circumstances he took nobody's advice. Indeed, there was not much to deliberate about, since they had decided at the Grimont conference to stay where they were. He knew there was only one way in which sieges ended, unless relief came from outside; and that, he knew now, could never come. When he had been shut up in Miliana years before, Changarnier and Mac-Mahon had come to their relief. But now Changarnier was here with him, and Mac-Mahon was somewhere on his way to Germany. He had watched from outside the slow fate of Puebla and Sebastopol; and as their long defence had been of some service (Todleben and Ortega were honoured names), that was all there now remained for them to do at Metz. There was not much to say about it; and as he said extremely little, his callers found the Marshal uncommunicative. But what was there to say? Their situation was embarrassingly simple; and if Bazaine was a sphinx, he was a sphinx without a secret.

He maintained his silence, when he walked at the head of the cortège at Manèque's funeral (and an army chaplain chanted the *Domine salvum fac imperatorem* for the last time on French territory). Several of his colleagues were anxious to ask questions; but he rode away without giving them a chance. The main thing was to find out what had been going on outside; and as the Germans were prodigal with newspapers and obligingly maintained a trickle of French prisoners who could tell him the unpleasant facts, he was soon aware of the whole uncomfortable situation. His own impression (helped by the Germans) seemed to be that France was in collapse under an insurrectionary government of dubious authority; and he imparted it one afternoon to an impressive gathering of all his corps and divisional commanders. (Had not Willette promised M. Herbin that his villa was going to see great things?) He instructed them to tell the troops to hold out for the honour of the flag, adding for their private information that supplies would last five weeks and that they must plainly wait upon events, as they could not break out of Metz without hazarding the only army in the country. They were deeply shocked; but there were no protests.

While Metz subsisted upon public readings from old newspapers by candle-light, information filtered in from the outer world; and Bazaine made an effort to get some orders from the new Minister of War of the Government of National Defence. There had always been somebody to give him orders; and that was what he wanted now. But his request got no further than the throats of two intrepid messengers, who swallowed the two tiny balls of india-rubber when a Prussian officer grew too inquisitive. Now the army was notified officially by the Marshal of the installation of the Government of National Defence in Paris and of their duty to serve their country "with the same devotion in defence of its soil against the foreigner and of social order against evil passions." This blameless sentiment was afterwards interpreted as a grave indication of reactionary purposes. But there were unhallowed elements in Paris; and if the scum had floated to the top in a swirl of insurrection, the army might have a duty to its country higher than any technical allegiance. To whom was that to be? After a moment of uncertainty, in which he seemed to contemplate a complete change of style in favour of the new republic, Bazaine retained the old Imperial forms for use in administrative documents and in his correspondence with German headquarters on the exchange of prisoners. (That came to be regarded later as a sinister attempt to cultivate the enemy, although it was also his best, perhaps his only, means of gathering intelligence about events in the outer world.) Besides, he had been discoursing to Jarras on the doctrine that the Imperial Regency was still the true government of France, duly supported by the Chambers, especially as nothing had been heard officially from the Republic. There were a few small skirmishes in front of their positions, more reminiscent of Algerian *razzias* in search of food and forage than of serious operations. But their scope was strictly limited, as Bazaine was haunted by his duty to conserve the army, "France's only army." Besides, more casualties would be a grave embarrassment, since the hospitals of Metz were full and medical supplies were running short.

Three weeks of September were behind them now, and the rain never seemed to stop. The fretted tower of the cathedral looked out across a mournful landscape of wet housetops and dripping poplars whipped by a searching wind. The Esplanade was full of tents; the Place Royale was an immense railway-siding, where long lines of coaches housed the wounded; the Red Cross flag was everywhere; and whole streets reeked of disinfectants. Life was a depressing blend of growing discomfort and shrinking rations, as horseflesh grew more unpalatable in the absence of sufficient salt to season its unpleasant sweetness; and there can never have been more discouraged listeners to

> *Les sanglots longs*
> *Des violons*
> *De l'automne.*

Their country seemed to be committed to the hopeless continuation of a war that was already lost. For Jules Favre had informed the world that France would never yield a stone of her fortresses or an inch of her territory. Such gestures might appeal to eloquent civilians. But they had few attractions for old soldiers like Bazaine, especially as the country's military fortunes now seemed to be entrusted to a junior of his named Trochu; and perhaps he spoke his mind, when he informed a major of Chasseurs that they had lost the game this time and that the thing to do was to make peace, improve themselves, and start again in two years' time.

At this point a welcome element of farce intruded on the sombre scene, when an egregious individual named Régnier emerged from a trap-door wearing a grey bowler-hat and carrying an umbrella, whose peaceable significance was emphasized by a white handkerchief tied to one end. (For, like a later statesman who also specialised in peace missions, M. Régnier entered European history with an umbrella.) The appearance of a middle-aged civilian at the French outposts in the wake of a German escort caused mild surprise, which rose at his announcement that he was on a secret mission to Marshal Bazaine. But this was nothing to the wild extravaganza of his previous adventures. A man of comfortable means, whose father-in-law appeared to own the Crystal Palace, he had long formed the habit of thinking for himself; and his reflections led him irresistibly to the conclusion that war is an evil. This being so, he took steps to stop it, if he could; and his subsequent proceedings were inspired by that happy blend of loose thinking and good intentions which is readily comprehensible to Anglo-Saxons. But French logic is less accommodating; and his baffled countrymen concluded that, if Régnier was not a German agent, he was insane.

The peace-maker, confronted with the difficulty (which Bismarck had already noticed) of finding somebody with whom the Germans could make peace and noticing that no one had yet recognised the Republic, concluded that this unpleasant duty devolved upon the Empire. True, its sole representatives at liberty were now the Empress and the Prince

Imperial, who were both at Hastings. The Regency could scarcely function, as it was not on French territory. But it occurred to the resourceful Régnier that a French warship would provide a suitable address and that, once there, Eugénie might start issuing proclamations, of which he had obligingly prepared the text. He promptly left for Hastings and assaulted the Marine Hotel, where the exiled dynasty had taken refuge. But the Empress was unresponsive; and he got no further than the Imperial entourage, which seemed to frown on his request for introductions to the captive Emperor in Germany. The prince's tutor, more impressionable, yielded to the strange caller's importunity and let his pupil write on a view of the sea-front at Hastings:

"MON CHER PAPA,
   "*Je vous envoie ces vues d'Hastings, j'espère qu'elles vous plairont.*

"LOUIS NAPOLÉON."

Armed with these odd credentials, Régnier left, as he supposed, for Wilhelmshöhe. But when a paragraph in the *Observer* caught his eye with the exciting news that Bismarck was on the point of meeting Jules Favre with a view to peace negotiations, he changed his plans and went to France instead.

His journey was adventurous. But a free use of Eugénie's name eventually got him as far as Ferrières, where the Prussian Chancellor was now installed in the Rothschilds' château. Presenting his signed photograph of the Marine Hotel, he asked Bismarck for a pass to visit Napoleon in Germany, adding in his expansive way that if the garrisons of Metz and Strasbourg were eventually forced to surrender, they would be prepared to do so in the name of the Empire rather than in that of Jules Favre's unsteady government. Bismarck took possession of the Imperial autograph and made some play with it in his discussion with the unhappy Favre as evidence that he was not his country's only spokesman. Then he re-

turned to Régnier, whose plans had changed once more. For
that versatile negotiator was now prepared to go to Metz in
order to secure that its capitulation should be made, when the
time came, in the Empire's name. This suited Bismarck, as his
object was to find, if possible, a stable party to the peace-
treaty by which he hoped to penalise the French; and his unexpected guest spent a happy night of feverish reflection, in
the course of which he formed the splendid notion that Marshal Canrobert or General Bourbaki should leave the besieged
fortress disguised as himself, stay with the Régniers at Hastings in strict seclusion except for nocturnal exercise on the
pier, and persuade the Empress to play her part in his stupen-
dous pantomine of peace. Meanwhile the noble-hearted Régnier would wait at Metz, which represented a considerable
sacrifice on his part, as an addition to his family was expected
at any moment. (The impact upon Madame Régnier of mysterious visitors with secret missions might, it seems, be disregarded.)

When this formidable dove of peace reached Metz, he
promptly saw the Marshal and exposed his latest plan, which
took the form of an evacuation of the army by German consent to some neutralised zone, where the Empress and the
Chambers might function freely with a view to making peace.
As the emissary who now confronted him had been good
enough for Bismarck, Bazaine saw no reason to doubt his
authenticity and spoke freely of the impossibility of holding
out after October 18. The programme was not unattractive,
as it would extricate the army from its present impasse, while
preserving it as a stable element in an apparently dissolving
nation, and would ultimately end the war; and the Marshal's
sole objection was to any surrender of Metz itself. He spoke
in harsh terms of the republicans—"a handful of adventurers
seeking to climb on the misfortunes of their country"—and he
was perfectly prepared to see his army used to better purpose
than Mac-Mahon's had been at Sedan in bringing peace to

France. When the unwearied autograph-collector asked him to add his signature to the Prince Imperial's under the cherished photograph of Hastings, he consented cheerfully; and on the next day he summoned Canrobert and Bourbaki to see if either of them was willing to play his part in the strange programme by consulting Eugénie in England. By this time the Marshal seemed to regard his visitor as an important member of her Household, although nobody could quite remember having seen him at the Tuileries. Canrobert declined; but the impulsive Bourbaki consented, leaving Metz unobtrusively disguised as a Red Cross doctor from Luxemburg in an extremely roomy suit belonging Bazaine with the added security of the Marshal's braces.

While Bourbaki was sped on his way to Hastings, Régnier had one more session with Bismarck at Ferrières. This time he ranged extensively over the map of Europe, allotting Germany a slice of Alsace and assigning France to a Latin *bloc* with Spain and Italy, which would leave the English isolated in their island. (In spite of his English marriage M. Régnier seemed ill-disposed towards his wife's relations.) But Bismarck was not allured by this anticipation of the New Order and had no wish for further dealings with an emissary who had no authority to speak for Bazaine and his army. The eager Bourbaki reached England; but when he found that he was not expected by the Empress or by anybody else, the ghastly outlines of the well-intentioned hoax, in which he had become involved, began to dawn upon him. The documents in Régnier's pocketbook, which he was carrying as part of the charade, turned out to be disturbingly apocalyptic; Bourbaki was overwhelmed with shame; and the gallant soldier, lured from the field of honour and unable to get back, alarmed his friends with the first of those unsuccessful attempts at suicide by which they were periodically startled. The untiring Régnier, reluctant to abandon great affairs, was still importuning Eugénie, got as far as Wilhelmshöhe (where he failed to see

Napoleon), and published a full record of his adventures in high life under the intriguing title, "*Quel est votre nom? N ou M?*" This inspired busybody was ultimately sentenced to death by his ungrateful countrymen. But as he was not in France at the time, the sentence could not be executed; and after one or two more spirited appearances on the European stage in his old manner (in the course of which he airily offered Austrian and British aid to Turkey against Russia and subsequently interviewed the Pope in order to adjust his differences with Italy) he died in a relatively modest sphere as manager of a laundry at Ramsgate. The South Coast had always been his happy hunting-ground; and this was a field in which his genius for confusion could be exercised without international consequences.

But his exploit at Metz was more than passing comedy, in which a large-hearted clown had startled everyone by turning cartwheels of officiousness across the diplomatic stage. For it seemed to show the Marshal a way out. He had no reason to doubt Régnier. All that he saw was an emissary apparently approved by Bismarck and the Regency, who spoke with great assurance and pointed to a vista of honourable service for the army under his command. Bazaine knew nothing for some time of Bismarck's refusal to have further dealings with him or of his subsequent repudiation by the Empress; and when German headquarters transmitted an enigmatic query as to whether he was willing to capitulate on Régnier's terms, he answered cautiously that he had been prepared to contemplate a surrender, from which Metz itself must be excluded, with the honours of war and that he was ready to send General Boyer with fuller information as to what had passed on the subject. There was still a flicker of inconsiderable fighting round the beleaguered fortress. But it led nowhere; and there was no human prospect of a successful outcome.

It was October now. They knew that Strasbourg had fallen; there was smallpox in the town; excited journalists filled local periodicals with wild opinions on paper of all tints and sizes; and an uncomfortable dyarchy was developing, in which Coffinières appeared to treat the town's interests as wholly separate from those of the army. When he tried to send his criticisms of Bazaine to the republican authorities at Tours by a balloon that got no further than the outposts, they were acidly returned with the Marshal's compliments. The wildest rumours circulated, Bourbaki's absence giving rise to fantastic stories that Bazaine had imprisoned him or killed him in a duel. After the first week of October it never left off raining. The whole place was a sea of mud dismally garnished with dead horses. For the busy knackers scarcely kept pace with the slow tragedy of the French cavalry. Their horse-lines were a scene of dull-eyed misery, as the bony mounts died of starvation before the slaughterers could feed them to their starving masters. There would soon be no teams to move their guns, if they should ever wish to move them. The old white horse on the Ile Chambière that everybody fed for luck could hardly drag them all by itself; and it was more obvious than ever that they had no hope of leaving Metz. The Marshal had been reading books to see how other sieges ended, to read what happened when the guns of Genoa and Danzig fell silent and Masséna and Gouvion St. Cyr had marched out between their conquerors; and he got out of the library a volume of Thiers' *Consulate and Empire* containing the depressing details of General Dupont's surrender to the Spaniards at Baylen. That was in his mind; and news that the Germans seemed to be doing well in front of Paris did little to dispel the thought.

The army saw little of the Marshal now. For he was mostly at his headquarters, although he went his rounds inconspicuously; and his seclusion drew angry comments, which grew into a legend that his time was mostly passed in playing billiards. (Bazaine and his billiards became a myth, exquisitely rendered in fiction by Alphonse Daudet, which helped his countrymen to a belief that all their failures had been due to the indifference of one man.) An indignant general recorded that he "stayed shut up in his office at Ban Saint-Martin like a Pasha in his seraglio." But what temptation was there for him to parade before his starved and sullen troops in their water-logged encampments or to encounter the reproaches of disappointed officers? Regrets were useless. He had always been a little shy of unnecessary intercourse with the fine gentlemen over whom he had been set; and as there was nothing to be done, it was less unpleasant to spend a great deal of his time in his own little circle with Boyer and Willette and his two nephews. Sometimes the monotony was broken by a deputation from the town, to which he blandly explained the difficulties of the situation. The fighting had died down round the sodden trenches, where hungry men crawled out into no-man's-land to steal potatoes; and as the date of their starvation drew slowly nearer, he circularised his generals as to the capacity of the troops under their command, enclosing a gloomy statement by Coffinières to the effect that all that now remained was five days' supply of bread and ten of wheat. Their replies were not encouraging. For while two of them seemed reconciled to a last, hopeless effort, three frankly contemplated capitulation. When they met on October 10, it was agreed once again to stay where they were and to open negotiations with a view to an evacuation upon honourable terms by agreement with the Germans. Boyer was to go to Versailles and discuss arrangements with the German high command; and Bazaine instructed him to emphasise the helpful part which the army, if maintained in being, might be called upon to play in a defeated and chaotic country. Their military role was ended; but was it treasonable to view them as the potential saviours of society?

That was the Marshal's purpose in the second week of October. The war, so far as he could judge from Metz, would soon be over. It seemed inconceivable that Paris, under a regime of pavement orators, could long resist German pressure; and when the inevitable surrender came, the country might be grateful to rely for law and order upon the disciplined force of Bazaine's army. If so, they must not be dissipated, like Mac-Mahon's unhappy host, as prisoners of war in Germany; and Boyer set off for Versailles to persuade Bismarck of the wisdom of this alternative. But were the Germans likely to see reason? True, it would be highly convenient to liberate Prince Friedrich Karl's 200,000 men round Metz for the final operations elsewhere; but the eager Prussian was excusably reluctant to miss his triumph just as the ripe fruit at Metz was on the very point of falling. A telegram from Bismarck reassured the Red Prince that Boyer's mission would not be allowed to make the slightest difference to the course of operations; and as these moved slowly towards their inevitable end, the Chancellor played a delicious game of cat and mouse. When he saw Boyer, he indicated a vague prospect of evacuation by consent, provided that his visitor was able to obtain the Empress's authority for the surrender of the Fortress or, better still, a *pronunciamiento* by Bazaine's army in favour of the fallen dynasty. (This was Régnier's plan over again, with a restored Empire to make peace with Germany and guarantee the conquerors in safe possession of their gains.) Affairs at Metz were now deteriorating rapidly in a mounting mood of hysteria; excited townsmen destroyed Imperial effigies and emblems with sweeping revolutionary gestures (Metz had always been republican); and while the Marshal played for time with vague talk about impending sorties and an unconvincing project of forthcoming operations which were judiciously postponed upon the superstitious ground that it would be unlucky to break out of Metz on the anniversary of Leipzig, impatient subalterns made wild plans for deposing him from his command and substituting the blameless Changarnier. But that veteran had no sympathy with mutineers. Besides, his Orleanist prejudices had all vanished in a new devotion to the Empire; and he sided strongly with Bazaine, who interviewed the young ringleaders almost indulgently. Indeed, Changarnier was henceforward the Marshal's closest counsellor and strongest advocate; and the old man, whom French soldiers regarded as the master of them all, was at his side until the end.

Under a low sky at Metz the rain that rained away the hopes of France fell steadily. Fog drifted over them; wind blew in chilly gusts; and water stood in pools. Boyer reported to a meeting of the high command on October 18 the state of things that he had found outside. The dark side of the picture—France prostrate in a state of anarchy without means or will to resist further—was emphasized; and as it seemed unnecessary to prolong the agony, a few French newspapers in his possession that might have shown a faint gleam of hope were not produced. In reply to Bismarck's demand for a Bonapartist declaration it was agreed that they were still the army of the Empire, to which they had all sworn allegiance. A debate ensued on their next step, Le Bœuf pleading vehemently for an immediate sortie (which he termed encouragingly *"une folie glorieuse"*), Ladmirault persisting doggedly that he would do as he was told, and all the rest electing for passivity. A further meeting on the next day heard Changarnier assert his new loyalty to the Empress Eugénie and offer to seek her co-operation in the prospective peace, if Boyer did not go; and, by seven votes to two, it was agreed to send their representative to England with the object of enlisting Eugénie's intervention with the Germans in order to obtain the evacuation of the army or, if she declined, of getting her release from their allegiance.

Was this a crime? If so, Bazaine was in good company, since Changarnier, Frossard, and Canrobert were his accomplices. True, two of them were devoted servants of the Empire; but was not the third the model of all French soldiers, whose African achievements were still one of their leading glories? Changarnier's principles had been high enough for the Prince-President to imprison him at the time of the *Coup d'état;* and they had kept the old soldier in retirement until his country was in danger. He had not always agreed with Bazaine's conduct of operations; but his exacting sense of duty had no fault to find with his proceedings at this stage. There was no mystery about Boyer's mission, which was undertaken by agreement with all the Marshal's leading colleagues. It presented the supreme advantage from his point of view that, if the Empress consented to collaborate, he would have a sovereign to give him orders. That was always a supreme need with Bazaine. For what could be more embarrassing than to command an isolated army of 150,000 men without a government? If the mission succeeded, if they won the race with time and German magnanimity conceded a reasonable peace to a restored Empire, Bazaine would be judged to have struck a good bargain for his country. But since Germans are not magnanimous and the event showed that France was no longer Bonapartist, it failed completely, leaving him to face the indignation of all French republicans and royalists. Bazaine had guessed wrong; but there is a difference between error and treason.

 Was his calculation affected by ambition? Did he aspire to play the leading part in an Imperial restoration? The role of Monk, although his name has largely been forgotten on his own side of the Channel, is strangely influential in French politics; and it could hardly fail to cross Bazaine's mind that the Marshal who commanded the only army of the Empire would be bound to play a part in the new reign. But if he was sincere in his belief that the Imperial regime was the sole alternative to anarchy, his support of it might be no more than a patriot's duty. Bazaine himself had been too long abroad to keep touch with French politics. When he returned from Mexico, he made no play with Thiers' advances; and though his contacts seemed all to be with Opposition circles, he was quite ruthless in repressing Opposition rioters in Paris and had made no effort to exploit the old popularity of 'notre glorieux Bazaine' in order to become the darling of the new republic. After Boyer left, he made a final effort to communicate with them, entrusting his request for news to six messengers. But he showed little tendency to 'play politics'. For when Bismarck invited him to make a Bonapartist pronunciamiento, he made no move. Yet he was familiar enough with Spanish military technique, as he had been a privileged spectator thirty years before of Espartero's rise to power beside a Queen-Regent; and Bazaine knew better than most men in Metz the art of winning soldiers' hearts. For he had graduated in the Legion; and he had done something of the kind in Mexico. But now he lived in obstinate seclusion behind the walls of his suburban garden, whilst angry troopers began to talk scornfully of 'Monsieur Bazaine' and disloyal staff-officers perorated inside the steamy windows of provincial cafés.

As they waited for the news to come from England, tempers rose and the strained men mistook their fancies for the facts of their intolerable situation. But Bazaine's illusions were shattered on October 24 by a telegram from Bismarck intimating that negotiations were at an end. At one instant there had even been a motion at Chislehurst of delegating the Imperial powers to Bazaine as Lieutenant-general of the Empire. But now the Germans had tired of the complicated game of diplomatic make-believe with a fallen Empire, whose sole resources consisted of a brave woman and a starving army; and events would have to take their course at Metz. The Marshal had been talking wildly to subordinates about a desperate attempt to break the German ring, taking the few guns for which they could still find teams and making no halts to pick up their wounded. There was not the vaguest notion of which way they would go, if they ever managed to reach open country; and heroic folly of this order was less calculated to find favour with his own innate caution than to impress excited officers and to keep them quiet for a few days longer. Bazaine, after all, had been a private soldier; and the price of such romantic gestures was generally paid by the ranks. But when the prospects were examined by his corps commanders, the cold shadow of reality fell across them; and they were reduced to a discussion of the terms on which they should surrender. Changarnier, "the master of us all," was delegated to see the Red Prince in a last effort to obtain a local armistice at Metz with a view to peace negotiations between the Empire and the invaders; and on the next morning he was at German headquarters. His reception was polite, but uncompromising; his alternative proposal that the army should withdraw to Algeria for internment until the war ended was dismissed; and he was coldly informed that the last word was unconditional surrender.

It was Tuesday, October 25; and that afternoon the Marshal sent General Cissey with instructions to obtain the exclusion of the town itself from the capitulation. The Germans intimated bleakly that negotiations should be carried on between the chiefs of staff; and when they showed signs of a particular interest in the fate of the French flags, Cissey was quick enough to fabricate a story that their Imperial eagles had been burnt on the proclamation of a republic. On Wednesday morning it was still raining, when eight generals and two Marshals met at Bazaine's headquarters (Willette had promised M. Herbin that his villa would see great events) and agreed that Jarras should negotiate the terms of a capitulation. It had always been a grievance with his chief of staff that Bazaine ignored him. But this time the sardonic Marshal informed his trying junior that negotiations of this character indubitably fell within his duties; and Jarras was soon driving through the sleet to interview von Stiehle. Whilst he faced an icy wall of German negatives, there was the usual confusion in Metz about the Marshal's order to destroy the flags

and a last-minute discovery of four days' rations. But Bazaine
was disinclined to prolong the agony, although the town was
feverish and the French genius for symbolic gestures had
piled flowers beneath Ney's statue in the square and was busy
winding crêpe round that of an earlier Marshal, whose pedestal proudly announced his historic resolution to make every
sacrifice rather than surrender the town entrusted to his
charge.

It was all over by Thursday evening; and on the next morning nine dejected men trooped into the Marshal's room to
hear Jarras read the terms of the capitulation, which were
gloomily approved. There was some talk afterwards about
Bazaine's order to destroy the flags; and he told someone to
remove the copy from the letterbook in case the Germans
found it and discovered that they had been deprived of their
trophies in breach of the capitulation. But fifty-three of them
were still intact at the arsenal under old Soleille's control; and
his formalism, assisted by a pious ecstasy of self-abasement,
preserved them to adorn the German triumph. The rest of
Friday was a nightmare. A proclamation by the Marshal told
his army that they were prisoners of war, insisting proudly
that he had done no more than Masséna, Kléber, and Gouvion
Saint-Cyr had been compelled to do. But these precedents
were no consolation to the haggard men in shabby uniforms;
and a few wild spirits still contemplated a dash for liberty,
if they could only find a general to lead them. But nothing
came of it; the *troueurs* got no further than making angry
speeches; and Metz fell without a gesture. A capitulation,
which gave the Germans 179,000 prisoners, more than 500
field-guns, nearly 900 guns of position, 72 wonder-working
mitrailleuses, and a virgin fortress, was the end of the last
army of the Empire; and the gaily-coloured picture that had
brightened eager eyes at Longchamps in the sunshine of 1867
lay peeling in the mud beneath a low October sky.

It was still raining. It had been raining for a fortnight; and as the Marshal turned his back on Metz that Saturday to ride into captivity, a great bell was tolling and he went out into the downpour with the broad sweep of the river and the tall cathedral tower behind him and the German lines in front. At the French outposts he gave the password, which by some ghastly mischance was '*Dumouriez*'; and Bazaine rode out of his last command with the name of a deserter on his lips. (His generals had a few days to wait, until a German train removed them to captivity, stopping obligingly to give them a full view of their men tramping the same road under guard and of their captured eagles neatly ranged in a long avenue outside German head-quarters.) He was hooted on the road by French civilians; the Red Prince kept him waiting; and after some embarrassed conversation, in which Bazaine spoke without enthusiasm of the civil population, the impossibility of fighting without food, the unhelpfulness of the Republic, and his military difficulties, he assured his host a shade gratuitously that all the surviving eagles would be surrendered. The Red Prince volunteered that if Bazaine should ever need a testimonial to his loyal conduct, his conqueror would be happy to oblige a fellow-soldier. It was agreed that he should go to Cassel, where the captive Emperor had asked for the company of his three captive Marshals (Bismarck remarked irreverently that Napoleon appeared to want a game of whist); and as he took his leave, the impassive man in French uniform impressed his host with something Polish in his look. It may have been the high cheek-bones and the narrow eyes, that told so little of his feelings. Men thought at Metz that he felt nothing. But sixteen years later he was still writing to his son on the anniversary of Rezonville that he could not sleep, because his season of black memories—August, September, and October—was back again, as Bazaine relived the slow agony of Metz.

CHAPTER V

COURT-MARTIAL

And the goat shall bear upon him all their iniquities unto a land not inhabited: and he shall let go the goat in the wilderness.

LEVITICUS XVI. 22.

I

THE war was over for Bazaine, but not for France. The German tide rolled on, flooding the whole centre of the country and reaching long fingers towards its outer edge. (St. Omer, where a small Pétain went to school, was not submerged; but the advancing flood washed the young Foch out of a Metz class-room into the blue greatcoat of a private of the Line with vague memories of an unhappy-looking Emperor.) There were still islands of resistance. Metz had held for seventy days, Strasbourg for forty-seven; and whilst impromptu armies made desperate attempts to stem the flood, Paris stood out above the dark waters of defeat for eighteen weeks, and the tricolour fluttered over Belfort until the armistice.

But the fall of Metz and the surrender of the army were an appalling shock to what remained of France. Paris got the news on the same October day that it lost Le Bourget; and Gambetta at Tours projected a sweeping excommunication in the authentic manner of the First Republic relegating unsuccessful generals to the executioner. "*Hors la loi,*" it was to have run, "*le commandant en chef de l'armée du Rhin;*

*Hors la loi les maréchaux et les généraux commandant les
corps d'armée;
Hors la loi les généraux commandant les troupes;
Hors la loi les généraux commandant d'armes spéciales . . ."*
But this spirited performance in the style of Danton was not
acceptable even from the Boanerges of the Government of
National Defence, and Gambetta was reduced to a more rea-
soned proclamation:

*"Metz a capitulé ! ! ! Le général sur qui la France comptait,
même après l'expédition du Mexique, vient d'enlever à la patrie
en danger plus de cent mille défenseurs.
Bazaine a trahi . . ."*

That was the point. It was essential, as Gambetta saw it, for
Frenchmen to believe that they had not been defeated, that
it was all due to some dark transaction between the Marshal
and the enemy, in which the Emperor had somehow been
involved. If they could only be brought to take that view,
seeing in Bazaine *"l'agent de l'homme de Sedan, le complice
de l'envahisseur,"* all would be made plain. For then France
would realise that the Empire was solely to blame for their
unhappy situation and rally cheerfully to the Republic.

It was good politics; and two of Gambetta's civilian colleagues signed the proclamation, although an admiral declined
and Thiers disapproved of the whole performance, which was
hardly calculated to inspire the French command with confidence in its new masters. This onslaught failed to make a
good impression overseas, and old Field-Marshal Sir John
Burgoyne, who had fought with Moore in Spain and served
in the Crimea with Bazaine, wrote to *The Times* in order to
express his disgust with proceedings across the Channel and
to express his respect for "a gallant fellow-soldier, whose
reputation has been assailed in so inconsiderate a manner by
political enemies." A simultaneous order of the day assured
the army that they had been betrayed. This judgment, de-

livered instantaneously on receipt of the black news from Metz, was precipitate; and when it was followed by telegraphic orders for the immediate arrest of Bazaine and his staff and for their despatch to Tours, "*sous bonne escorte*," Gambetta's southern exuberance came dangerously near to farce, as everybody knew his prisoners were all in German hands. For there were moments when *Numa Roumestan* verged on *Tartarin de Tarascon*.

But though it was impracticable to lay hands on Bazaine, there were still his female relations. The spirited Pepita had appeared in Tours some time before, resolved to join her husband at the front although she was expecting to become a mother in a few weeks. One minister invited her assistance in deciphering her husband's last despatch from Metz, as the ciphers had naturally been left in Paris. Gambetta gave her a pass, although he felt unable to go so far as a special train; and the consequent delay had postponed her departure until the fortress fell. When it began to rain proscriptions, she felt unsafe in the convent where she was staying and took refuge at the Italian legation; and her precautions were amply justified, when the police in pardonable eagerness to secure a Bazaine of some sort zealously arrested her husband's nephew's wife and children, adding his mother-in-law for good measure. But these dangerous characters were shortly authorised to leave; and Pepita, who had been surrounded by her mother from Mexico and her two small children, was soon in Brussels on her way to join her husband in captivity.

He was at Cassel now. His Emperor had greeted him with a charming note to say that it was "a true consolation in my misfortune to learn that you are near me. I should be happy to express in person my feeling for you and for the heroic army which under your command fought so many bloody battles and doggedly endured unprecedented privations." Eugénie, who had rushed over at the news from Metz, was there when he arrived; and she found time to let Pepita know how deeply she resented the imputations on Bazaine. These were growing in intensity, as excited Frenchmen echoed Gambetta's blind charge of treachery in the relief of finding somebody to blame for their defeats. The Marshal, who had drafted a brief account of his operations for the Emperor, was inclined to publish a refutation; but Canrobert wrote strongly pressing him to wait for calmer times and a more judicial atmosphere. He had already challenged Gambetta's charges, which were launched in an instant of profound despair and had been founded on the irresponsible report of a single army interpreter of dubious integrity. But as embittered prisoners of war talked freely to reporters, their feelings were relieved by imputing all their failures to Bazaine; and those of them whose politics were antagonistic to the Empire improved their prospects in the better days about to dawn by blaming a soldier of the last regime.

The charges in their richest form appeared before the end of 1870 in a long letter to a Belgian newspaper from a French prisoner at Hamburg. This composition, which was unsigned, accused the Marshal of betraying everyone in turn—the Emperor, Mac-Mahon, the Republic, and the troops under his command—for financial motives. Street arabs in Metz had enlivened the last days of the siege by singing,

> "As-tu vu Bazaine
> À la Porte des Allemands,
> Vendre la Lorraine
> Pour deux cent mille francs?"

Imputations of this character were normal in the gutter. But the anonymous letter-writer reproduced them in a grave allegation that the army had been betrayed in order to save Bazaine's "cash and plate." If so, his ill-gotten gains left singularly little trace, since the remainder of his life was passed in poverty.

Three weeks before the charge was made a letter from the Marshal told its own story:

Cassel.
2 *Novembre* 1870.

MON CHER COLONEL,

J'ai reçu ce matin l'argent que vous m'avez envoyé par un Sous-Officier d'Ordonnance, et je vous suis fort reconnaissant de l'empressement que vous avez mis; cela m'a rendu un grand service.

Recevez, Mon cher Colonel, mes sentiments affectueux.

M^{AL.} BAZAINE.

This was not the tone of a successful embezzler, although it is quite consistent with a German story that he had left a sum of 10,000 francs behind him in an inn at Pont-à-Mousson, which was afterwards returned to him. But it seems improbable that he betrayed an army and a fortress for £400; and when the war was over, he scarcely had enough to pay for his family's return to Paris.

His anonymous accuser told a sordid story of systematic treachery inspired by gross cupidity and base ambition, dwelling with gloomy pride upon the efforts of the mutineers in the last days at Metz to depose Bazaine and to break a way through the German lines. Its author was an Orleanist colonel on the staff, whose disloyalty had been conspicuous during the siege. For Comte d'Andlau, acutely conscious of his quarterings and of his military science, was a soldier of some promise whose lectures had attracted professional attention before the war. Bazaine's attainments in this field were limited; he had shown little tendency to make companions of Jarras and his learned staff officers; and d'Andlau's feelings for the Empire and for the ex-*légionnaire*, whom it had set over him, were the reverse of friendly. His bitterness now found expression in anonymous abuse through a neutral newspaper, presently elaborated in a larger work. Indignant fellow-prisoners dissented loudly from his views; and an unpleasant controversy developed, to which Bazaine contributed by publishing the text of his *Rapport sommaire*.

Pepita had joined him; and their child was born at Cassel, though her wish that he should be born on French soil was respected. For an obliging relative fetched a sack of earth from Lorraine, which was scattered underneath the German bed; and his father wistfully informed the Emperor, *"Les Prussiens ont un prisonnier de plus."* (The child, whose French nationality had been so carefully preserved, was fated to enjoy a military career as a Spanish officer, returning to serve France with distinction in 1914 and then take the wounded name of Bazaine back to Spain.)

The war was ending now, as Paris capitulated with a garrison of 400,000 men, 1,362 guns of position, and 602 field-guns in the last days of January, 1871. The terms were cruel. For France yielded Alsace (except Belfort), a great part of Lorraine including Metz, and five billions of francs, the bitter price of making war with insufficient preparation. The occupation of sixteen French departments would give security for payment; and in order that there might be no doubt as to who had won the war it was provided further that 30,000 Germans should march down the Champs Élysées and bivouac in the Place de la Concorde. As these terms were intimated to Jules Favre by Bismarck in convenient proximity to the great palace among whose mirrors the German Empire had just been proclaimed and without opportunity for free negotiation, the war ended with a *Diktat* of Versailles.

2

When peace was signed, Bazaine left for Switzerland, establishing his little family near Geneva. Things at home were still uncertain, with Paris plunging into the ten weeks' dementia

of the Commune. Thiers presided grimly over the reconquest
of the capital; and as he surveyed the soldiers qualified to
undertake the unpleasant task, his thoughts turned to Bazaine.
For he had never lost his high opinion of the Marshal; and
someone overheard his inventory of the high command. Baraguay d'Hilliers was too old; Bourbaki was convalescent from
his last attempt at suicide; Canrobert was supposed to be a
Bonapartist; and Le Bœuf was tainted with war-guilt. But
there was one soldier, *"un qui ferait parfaitement mon affaire. Malheureusement il s'appelle Bazaine."* So there was
nothing for it but Mac-Mahon.

Later in the year Bazaine applied for leave to enter France.
But General Cissey, who had served under him at Metz and
was now Minister of War, withheld it on the ground that
opinion was still too unsettled. He observed a strong revulsion
in the Marshal's favour and deprecated undue haste; Mac-
Mahon, he added, felt the same. So Bazaine stayed in Switzerland. The Spanish royal family, in exile like himself, had been
charming about offering a pair of royal godparents for the
new baby; and the christening was honoured by Queen Isabella and her small Alfonso, who gave the child his name. For
it would soon be forty years since a young captain of the
Foreign Legion had served her in the Carlist War. Not that
his establishment was equal to these royal splendours, as a
letter to his sister showed that summer:

> "I am answering in Pepita's place, because she has not much
> time for correspondence since Marie, Achille's maid, and
> Eugénie's nurse both left . . .
>
> "All my dear little folks are well, and you will find them
> grown and enchantingly lovely; this climate and the open-air
> life are doing them immense good. The Maréchale and her
> mother are very well too. As for me, the spirit wears away the
> flesh (*le moral use l'enveloppe*), and I can feel my energy grow
> less each day. My countrymen's ingratitude and the incessant
> calumnies about me are wearing me down and sapping my life.

What a poor people they are. They are told that I am rich, when I am poor. They are told that I am a dangerous political enemy, when I am more of a Republican than those who shout it from the housetops. They believe anything. What can be done? I cannot deny my humble origin; and no doubt it is because I come from the people and from the ranks that jealousy pursues me, especially since I was made a Marshal. Officers from the Special Schools cannot forgive it. If I had the means, how I would retire from the military world, where there is nothing but boasting and ambition, with principles and loyalty left in the shade.

"That is enough for to-day . . ."

It was a weary business waiting at Geneva for the tide to turn. He was sixty now. But he could not afford to leave the army; and that year he asked the Emperor, who was in England, for permission to accept a command in France, if he was offered one. Napoleon consented freely—"You will do well to accept a command since the present need is to defend society against agitators"—adding a gracious word for Pepita; and in September, 1871, Bazaine re-entered France.

But there was no command for him. He had been pressing Thiers for some time to allow him to vindicate himself by some kind of enquiry; and the question had come before the National Assembly a few months before. Changarnier took the floor to testify to Bazaine's integrity with the weight of his own unblemished record; and he was followed by the head of the French state. Speaking with the full prestige of his recent achievement in paying off the indemnity and ending the German occupation, which had just earned him the proud title of '*libérateur du territoire*,' Thiers discharged his duty "towards one who has commanded, and commanded gloriously, one of our noblest armies. Marshal Bazaine has, I am convinced, been cruelly slandered; but a government is not enough to destroy slanders. Marshal Bazaine formally demands an enquiry into events at Metz. In general I have no taste for enquiries designed to dwell upon the past and to revive strong feelings. But an enquiry designed to vindicate a noble army and to let the country know whether its commander betrayed it or not—such an enquiry, in my judgment, is an act of justice that cannot be denied to any man . . . an act of justice that cannot be denied to Marshal Bazaine. I have submitted his demand; it is for the Assembly to reply." Now Bazaine returned to face the enquiry for which he had asked; and when he called on Thiers, the little man was friendly, asking why he had been so loyal to the Empire, which had treated him so badly on his return from Mexico. The Marshal answered that his military duty had bound him to the Emperor and that the Government of National Defence never established official relations with him. Thiers, who seemed to be quite satisfied, said at parting, "You can rely on me"; and Mac-Mahon, although their meeting was a shade less cordial, appeared to be on his side as well, remarking, "I have always stood up for you here."

"And so you ought," Bazaine replied, "as you know better than anyone why we fell back on Metz."

The auguries were fair; and he received with equanimity a notice to appear before an enquiry into the capitulations of the late war, although its president was old Marshal Baraguay d'Hilliers, who had been his corps commander in the Italian campaign of 1859 and was credited by army gossip with an ancient grudge against Bazaine. A darker cloud appeared that autumn, when Colonel d'Andlau published a full-length attack. Still preferring anonymity for his campaign, he issued *Metz, Campagne et Négociations* above the modest signature of '*un Officier Supérieur de l'Armée du Rhin*' and analysed events at Metz to show that Bazaine had been uniformly false to his trust. The note of treachery was sounded at the outset and sustained throughout the narrative; and the Orleanist nobleman turned every incident to the ex-private's disadvantage, concluding with an angry question (modelled on Augustus' anguished question about Varus and his lost legions) as to what Bazaine had done with their honour. The Marshal subsequently learnt the answer, so far as d'Andlau's honour was concerned, as he lived just long enough to see his critic, now a general and senator, sentenced to five years' imprisonment for trafficking in French decorations. Indeed, Bazaine's severest critics were remarkably unfortunate in their subsequent careers. Of the intrepid *troueurs*, whose abortive mutiny at Metz was one of d'Andlau's most rewarding themes, one ringleader had already been executed by a French firing-party as a general of the Paris Commune and the other died by his own hand, while the enterprising interpreter, upon whose eloquent report Gambetta's excommunication of the Marshal had been based, was eventually sentenced to ten years' imprisonment and died in gaol.

But *Metz, Campagne et Négociations* sold like hot cakes in the later weeks of 1871 and reached its ninth edition in the next year. When Bazaine addressed a mild official protest to the Minister of War against this publication by a serving soldier, Cissey replied politely that it was quite impossible to deal with authors who omitted to reveal their names, though d'Andlau's was an open secret. Indeed, it was a consolation to large numbers of French patriots to find out that one man was responsible for the long roll of their defeats, as it was growing fashionable to blame Bazaine for Mac-Mahon's disaster at Sedan as well as for his own campaign. This view, which left other military reputations unimpaired, was a welcome tonic to the self-respect of a defeated nation. If it had all been Bazaine's fault, they had not really been defeated. True, they had not won the war. But it was comforting to feel that its unfortunate result was due to a single individual rather than to the French army and to the noble-minded Marshal who was now its leading ornament; and if that individual could safely be identified with the Empire, so much the better for republicans and royalists. It was uncertain at the moment whether France was to be a monarchy or a republic; but in either case a large body of opinion was not displeased to find a Bonapartist scapegoat. This simple act of ritual preserved the nation's faith in its own martial prowess; and as Mac-Mahon was now their leading soldier with a strong prospect of bringing off a restoration of some kind in the time-honoured role of Monk, it would be just as well to find an explanation of Sedan.

Early in 1872 Baraguay d'Hilliers' commission reported in emphatic terms that Bazaine was to blame for everything—for Mac-Mahon's march to Sedan as well as for the loss of Metz. Informed of their adverse decision, Bazaine (whose own account had just been published in *L'Armée du Rhin*) asked for a court-martial. It had been Thiers' suggestion. The little man sent for Pepita and informed her that he proposed to dismiss the proceedings in due course, adding by way of reassurance that he still regarded Bazaine as "*notre premier général.*" But while Bazaine insisted on his right to a public vindication, the Assembly took a hand and ordered an investigation into events at Metz. As there was some difficulty in finding enough Marshals to try one of their peers, the law was amended in order to enable his inferiors to try Bazaine. He had been living in the Avenue d'Iéna; but when he was notified of the impending proceedings, which were to take place at Versailles, he left Paris in May, 1872, and insisted upon placing himself under arrest at a small house in the Avenue de Picardie, while Pepita took up her residence at a convent not far away.

While the learned General Séré de Rivière proceeded with the compilation of an immense report, which ultimately ran to three hundred columns of close print, the months went by; and in March, 1873, this massive document was in the hands of the authorities. What was to happen next? Was the Marshal to be tried? That had not been Thiers' intention. But when the time came for decision, Thiers was no longer there.

BAZAINE IN DISGRACE.

(Print in author's possession)

For in May he quarrelled with the Assembly upon a larger issue and resigned, leaving the problem of Bazaine to his successor. Marshal Mac-Mahon was now President of the Republic; and Bazaine's fate was in the hands of a brother-officer, whose experiences at Wörth and Sedan might be expected to make him view defeat with an indulgent eye. But after an uncomfortable pause his Minister of War decreed that Bazaine should be tried by court-martial for premature capitulation of a fortress and surrender in the field.

These unpleasant formalities were in the hands of the new minister, General du Barail, who had held a cavalry command at Metz without much success and viewed his former chief without great relish; and there was some difficulty about constituting the tribunal. But six generals were found to try the Marshal; old General Schramm was headed off from the presidency of the court; and a strange candidate was found for this distinction. For the Duc d'Aumale, who had captured the *Smala* of Abd-el-Kader in a minor operation thirty years before, celebrated his return from exile to the French army-list by trying a French Marshal. It was an unpleasant role for a royal prince; but the young features painted by Vernet were sterner now, although twenty-two years of retirement might have made his military knowledge a trifle rusty. Edmond de Goncourt, who saw him the next year, found him *"le type du vieux colonel de cavalerie légère,"* rendered to the life with a good figure, ravaged look, bald head, grey imperial, and voice broken by a lifetime of shouting orders. Where did they propose to sit? As Aumale was living at Chantilly, the first idea was to try Bazaine close at hand at Compiègne. When the news spread, its enterprising population, deprived of their Imperial splendours, showed a strong tendency to put up prices and scared the court away. But there was always Versailles. Nothing had happened at the Grand Trianon for years, and it was decided to fit it up for the purpose and to accommodate the prisoner in the same building.

He was obstinately confident of the result. The Emperor
had written hearteningly in reply to his good wishes on the
anniversary celebrated by Bazaine two years before with a
pitiable bunch of flowers from a Metz garden. Napoleon was
at Cowes, where he had just been seeing something of some
delightful Americans named Jerome—one of them afterwards
married young Lord Randolph Churchill and had a son—and
the Imperial letter expressed total inability to understand
what the Marshal could be accused of. But that had been
more than a year ago. For seventeen long months Bazaine
lived his strange life of house-arrest at Versailles, while the
industrious de Rivière filed 2,400 documents and peered
through his glasses at 220 witnesses. Pepita brought the children; and he had his visitors—the men who still believed in
him, Queen Isabella (who came almost every week) and her
young son Alfonso, Bonapartist leaders, Archbishop Lavi-
gerie, Bishop Dupanloup, General Sherman, his lawyers,
Mornay-Soult to prepare documents for the defence, and de
Rivière to ask more questions. The house was always guarded
(they could see the soldiers' tents at the bottom of the garden), though when Pepita was taken ill, they gave him leave
to go to the convent and sit with her all day. Little Paco used
to drill the soldiers; and Pepita made brave efforts to keep
her husband cheerful. *"Allons, mon bon Willette,"* she used
to say as she arrived, *"il faut faire rire le maréchal."*

But now it was October, 1873. The Emperor had died that
year in England; the unhelpful Mac-Mahon was President of
the Republic; and there was the indictment with its three
explicit charges of capitulation at the fortress of Metz without exhausting all means of defence and doing everything
required by duty and honour, of capitulation with an army
in the field, and of negotiating with the enemy before doing
everything required by duty and honour. It was a depressing
litany; and the court-martial was due to open on October 6.
Two days earlier they drove him with the faithful Willette

past the empty fountains and the silent alleys of the park to a side-door at Trianon. This was where he was to be lodged in the wing built by the *Roi Soleil* for Monseigneur. It was sixty-two years since a child had been born at Versailles on the thirteenth of the month; and he had come back.

3

The leaves were falling; and the elegance of the Grand Trianon was never more inconsequent behind its dainty grille. For the trim colonnade between Mansart's courtyard and Le Nôtre's parterres was doing its best to look like a law-court. There were rows of seats, a large painting of the Saviour, a good deal of red cloth, and an impressive array of uniforms. His judges faced the Marshal, who was looking older than when most of them had seen him last, as he sat behind the table with his two counsel and the inseparable Willette. Perhaps it was not altogether wise to be defended by the leading criminal advocate of the day with a great reputation for emotional appeals on behalf of murderers; but Maître Lachaud had been imposed upon Bazaine by Rouher, the Bonapartist leader.

It was the first afternoon of the court-martial, and a clerk was droning out the prisoner's *État des Services*, the long record of a soldier's life that opened forty years before with his enlistment as a private, the cold inventory of his promotions, wounds, and decorations, the procession of campaigns —Africa, Crimea, Italy, Mexico. . . . They were trying forty years of French history; and somebody in court said loudly that it was the best military record of the age. Now the clerk was reading the interminable paragraphs of Séré de Rivière's report. It went on for five days with its painstaking accumulation of the case against the stolid man in the dark tunic barred with the broad, red ribbon of the Legion of Honour. His rejoinder, which took barely more than half a day to read, seemed almost meagre in comparison with accusations at least seven times as long. But perhaps the story was not quite so complicated as the prosecution seemed to think; and one phrase of Bazaine's lit up the darkness of the last phase at Metz:

> "When the final moment came and it was clear that a last effort was impossible, I sacrificed myself with a memory of my own feelings as a private in Africa forty years ago. I did not feel that I had the right to make a vain sacrifice for empty glory of those lives that were so precious to their country and their families."

Unlike the Duc d'Aumale, he had once been a private soldier; and if that was how he felt, there might have been excuses for surrendering a living army rather than a glorious cemetery. But were they likely to prevail with the stern gentlemen in front of him, who saw his duty by the clear light of wisdom after the event?

Next he was cross-examined by the Duc d'Aumale at five sittings of the court. The interrogation opened quietly. Bazaine was always unemotional; and a crowded court watched his broad back, as he faced the endless stream of questions. It was not easy to give trenchant explanations of events in the first phase of the war without grave imputations on his late sovereign and on the French army as a whole; and Bazaine was rarely trenchant. Mac-Mahon said afterwards, "Bazaine did not defend himself." For a full defence must have destroyed the faith of a defeated nation in its military leaders and annihilated the last hope of a Bonapartist restoration; and it was never made. Indeed, Pepita had a strong suspicion that his counsel sacrificed her husband's interests to those of Bonapartism. The Duc d'Aumale displayed a laudable acquaintance with the late campaign (and with Colonel d'Andlau's commentary, which had been the textbook of the prosecution). But Bazaine's replies were rarely illuminating. Even when he was questioned about his alleged irregularity in negotiating with the enemy without authority from any French government, he was almost lame:

"I think I had that right from the moment that I had no further communications with the lawful government or with the Government of National Defence. I thought that I was free. I never regarded myself as the mere commander of a fortress. As Commander-in-chief I was, by acting in that way, serving my country . . .

"There was no precedent for my situation. I had no government. I was, so to speak, my own government. There was no one to direct me. My sole director was my conscience . . .

"Military duty is binding, when there is a lawful government, when one depends on an authority which the country has recognised, but not when one is faced with a revolutionary government. I cannot admit that."

The prince uttered a sublime reproof. "There was still France," he said. It was a noble sentiment, embalming a distant recollection of one of Bugeaud's favourite stories, which he had heard the old man tell in Africa, about the day when he presented an eagle to his men after Waterloo with a proud intimation that, in spite of everything, France was still there. But however gratifying it might be for an Orleans in the ascendant to rebuke a minion of the fallen Empire, it was possible that Bazaine, who had served his country for forty years, was no less aware of it than the distinguished traveller in front of him; and, in any case, the true centre of authority in France had been by no means easy to locate in September, 1870.

He told his story without heat; and coming after the elaborate mythology of dark intrigue and sinister disloyalty accumulated round events at Metz, his evidence was something of an anti-climax. This ageing man, who sometimes seemed a little dazed, was not what they were looking for. Bazaine's demeanour was strangely unsensational; and eager readers of

Colonel d'Andlau's book, who had been expecting something more Machiavellian than a soft-spoken old gentleman adjusting his glasses to find the place in his papers, began to lose interest in the court-martial. But the show went on. It was still drawing crowded houses at Versailles (1873 was a vintage year for amateurs of trials, with the Tichborne case well into its third year at Westminster); and smart society competed with the world of the theatre for front seats. Indeed, they once collided, when a great lady rated a leading actress for appropriating the place allotted to her by the Duc d'Aumale himself. The duke, she said, should hear of it that night at dinner. But the last word was with the stage, whose representative averred with brazen cheerfulness that her side of the case would be presented to His Royal Highness still later in the evening.

The prisoner was followed by an endless line of witnesses, as Marshals tramped into the box to give warm testimonials to themselves, but rarely to each other; and spectators were regaled with Canrobert's vivacity and the solemnity of Le Bœuf. At one stage the evidence took an exciting turn, when it appeared to indicate that Mac-Mahon might actually have been responsible for his own defeat; and it was quite dramatic when Palikao crossed the court to shake Bazaine by the hand. But France had other things to think about that autumn, as everybody seemed to think the monarchy was coming back at any moment; and this prospect was infinitely more exciting than the details of unsuccessful military operations, which had gone astray three years before. These were reconstructed with immense elaboration, as officers succeeded one another in the witness-box, Marshals giving place to generals and generals in turn to staff officers and rural characters with strong provincial accents. Jarras, the trying Jarras, wept; and so did Canrobert, though that was less surprising. The court was always crowded; but now the audience was largely foreign, as the court-martial at Trianon had become one of the sights of Paris. Tourists watched the eager pantomime of humble witnesses narrating their adventure in the German lines with messages from Metz or heard the Duc d'Aumale's majestic thanks for their services to France. For he was warming to his role, discussing military matters with the full authority of twenty-two years in retirement and speaking in the name of the country to which he had so recently returned, in order that there might be no excuse for anyone to fail to notice that France had a soldier prince.

The evidence dragged on for seven weeks; and as the end approached, newspaper reports began to lengthen once again and public interest returned. Now every figure in the story (except the elusive Régnier) had passed across the screen, re-enacting in slow motion all that they had done in those tragic weeks of 1870; and the interminable record was enriched by the testimony of 365 witnesses. They had been sitting since the first week of October. It was December now; the leaves had fallen; and the trees were bare in the long alleys of the park outside. The prosecutor was reading them a speech (attributed by some to a less military hand); and as there was a certain spaciousness about most things connected with the trial, he went on reading for three days.

This composition opened with a sweeping compliment to the defeated army, whose "officers and men invariably did their duty," and to the President of the Republic, whose disaster at Sedan was gracefully explained away by a statement that "in his anxiety to save the army of Metz Marshal Mac-Mahon became the victim of his own chivalrous devotion." (There was no allusion to his earlier defeat at Wörth, because no ingenuity had yet suggested any means by which it could be plausibly attributed to anybody else.) The honour of the army and its leading ornament being thus preserved, the speaker launched into his long denunciation of Bazaine. His earlier career appeared to give few openings; but the prosecutor turned a scornful eye upon his long experience in the

Bureau arabe, where deceit and subtlety flourished in "the practice of the crooked methods of native politics." This was unkind to the impulsive Bourbaki, who had been trained in the same school, no less than to the knightly Lamoricière, the unblemished Chanzy, and his own Minister of War, General du Barail, who had all passed through the *Bureau arabe* without visible effects. The familiar case unfolded slowly, as the hours crept by. But it was interesting to observe that nothing verging upon treachery was now alleged against Bazaine and all the cruder imputations of financial motives had completely vanished. His misconduct was attributed to "personal ambition," to a criminal attempt to choose a form of government for France before the nation had made up its mind. As France had not yet made a final choice three years after the event and time at Metz was strictly limited, there might be some excuse for his precipitation. But as his choice had plainly been the Empire, he could not expect a royal prince presiding in a court appointed by the Republic to applaud it.

It was not easy for Bazaine to listen to the prosecutor's virulence. Sometimes his face was covered. But his hands were working; and when they swept the court at night, they found that he had lacerated the arms of his chair and ripped the carpet at his feet. The strain eased a little, as his advocate launched into a four days' reply. The sun was shining and the hall was packed to hear Maître Lachaud's celebrated eloquence. His exordium revived old voices of the dead—praise from the austere Cavaignac and Crimean laurels awarded by Pélissier, gracious words from Maximilian and calm letters from Charlotte in her retirement beyond the reach of pain. But the great advocate was singularly tactless, when he was tempted to reply to a French school-mistress, who swore that she had overheard some German generals suggesting (at the tops of their voices, it would appear, and in French) that it would be a good idea to bribe Bazaine. For Maître Lachaud responded with a testimonial to his client's character from

Prince Friedrich Karl. Nothing was less calculated to endear him to a French tribunal; and the endless waves of Lachaud's eloquence broke against an iron coast.

He finished before midday on December 10. But though the court rose for two hours and a half, no member of the public left his seat. They were still there to hear the prosecutor's brief reply and Lachaud's closing speech, a swift, emotional affair of broken tones and slightly lachrymose appeals. It was after four o'clock on the winter afternoon, when Aumale asked the Marshal if he had anything to add; and as Bazaine rose, they could see the great *plaque* of the Legion of Honour gleaming on his breast. "I wear," he said, "two words: *'Honneur et Patrie.'* They have guided me through all my military life. I have never failed them either at Metz or elsewhere in the forty-two years that I have loyally served France. I swear it here before Christ." Then they led him off, while the court retired.

There were long silences that night at dinner with Princess Mathilde. Everyone was wondering about Bazaine; and afterwards she kept asking anybody who came in for news. When it grew unbearable, she sent young Gautier to find out at the club. Four hours later they returned and sentenced the prisoner to death with degradation from his rank. He was not in court. For ritual required him to wait outside; and he was somewhere upstairs with his family, when a whisper of "*À mort*" from Willette told him the worst. (Young Gautier passed Edmond de Goncourt, who was just leaving the princess, with a muttered, "*Condamné à mort à l'unanimité!*") He went down into a lamplit room, where twelve soldiers of the Line were waiting with some officers. There were four Bouchers on the wall, whose voluptuous grace contrasted oddly with the heavy uniforms and the twelve rifles. He asked where he was to stand; and somebody read out the sentence. The Marshal said he was quite ready. But they told him that he had twenty-four hours to appeal. That night he wrote to

Lachaud, thanking him for all that he had done and declining to make any further move.

But the decision was not left to him. For Aumale and the court had accompanied their sentence with a strong appeal for mercy, recalling all the difficulties inherited by Bazaine at the outset of the campaign, his long service, and his invariable gallantry under fire. Feeling that the victim had suffered quite enough, they shrank from the legal consequences of their own judgment and left it to Mac-Mahon. That Roman warrior, who had already considered the possibilities with his ministers, insisted on imprisonment for life, although his colleagues would have preferred banishment. Late that night Pepita with some encouragement from Bishop Dupanloup, who had been pleading with Mac-Mahon, stormed the President's official residence, asking Mac-Mahon if he proposed to have her husband shot and departing like a whirlwind when he promised a reprieve.

The next day passed; the lamps were lit once more at Trianon; and at midnight someone knocked at Bazaine's door. As the time for his appeal had now expired, he asked the visitor if he had come to tell him the time and place of execution. But he was informed that his old comrade had commuted the sentence to imprisonment for twenty years (he would be sixty-three in a few weeks) without the odious formality of public degradation. Was there a touch of the old irony in his letter to Mac-Mahon expressing a polite fear that the President had let his feelings run away with him?

4

At dusk on Christmas day a closed carriage left Versailles; the night train for Marseilles was stopped at a wayside station; and Bazaine with his little boy was on the way to his island prison. The last fortnight it had rained condolences—a gracious telegram from the Empress Eugénie, a visit from

Queen Isabella and her daughter, warm tributes from dignitaries of the Empire, and a comforting assertion of his innocence from the Bishop of Verdun. A Versailles priest had seen him regularly during the trial; and Pepita moved the fearless Dupanloup to wire to Mac-Mahon on his behalf. But nothing less than imprisonment would satisfy the President's stern sense of duty; and the train rattled southward through the winter night.

When they reached Antibes, an angry mob was yelling, "*A l'eau le bourreau!*" But it was dark, and the hotel omnibus eluded them by driving round another way to the little harbour. Bazaine was soon on board a tug and steaming through the night towards an island looming right ahead. For the rocky Lérins lay off the coast halfway between Cap d'Antibes and Cannes; and there was a convenient prison on the largest island of the group. The little citadel of Ile Ste. Marguerite, begun by Richelieu and improved by Vauban, had opened its career two centuries before by lodging the Man in the Iron Mask for a few years of his long imprisonment. But Bazaine's accommodation was less severe, since he occupied two rooms in a building on the battlements. Willette was always with him, and Pepita brought the younger children. They made a strange little home on the lonely rock. He had ordered pink cretonne for her room; and the dining-room was blue. All day long he wrote or read or watched the children playing croquet or paced the terrace or gave lessons to his little boy.

He had his callers, when General Castagny ate a meal whose vileness lived in his memory; and one day a visitor out of the distant past arrived, when Captain Doineau came to see him. His life had been strangely lacking in excitement since his conviction for the murder of the Agha of the Beni-Snouss on the road outside Tlemcen nearly twenty years before. His reprieve owed something to Bazaine's intervention. But the gas-works at Monte Carlo were a poor substitute for his military career; and when the war broke out, his offer to

serve in the French army had been declined. Disliking the
idea of joining Garibaldi's foreign auxiliaries, he had cam-
paigned under a false name with some distinction as a *franc-
tireur*; and this veteran sat talking to his old commander with
Madame Bazaine and the children on the Ile Ste. Marguerite.
It was pleasant to talk over old times in Algeria; but Doineau
could divine the profound unhappiness of the man to whom
he owed his freedom.

For prison life was growing quite intolerable to Bazaine.
The view was exquisite; Golfe Jouan sparkled in the sun; the
distant coast displayed its charms, as winter turned to spring
and spring deeped into summer. But landscape was no substitute for life. He was unaccustomed to inaction; and the yoke
lay heavy on him, as the patient Willette attended to his little
garden (with less attention to his tomatoes than to clearing an
old passage through to battlements) and the two men bent
over their strange experiments in tailoring their precious uniforms. Besides, he had expected to be treated as a military
prisoner; and it was unbearable to find that he was something
in the nature of a convict and that every line he wrote was
scrutinised by a prison official. There were even ugly hints of
cropped hair and convict dress. It was past mid-summer now;
and at his next visit Doineau found him quite determined to
escape. Bazaine's notion was a dash for the mainland, followed
by a precarious journey over the frontier. Two English girls,
who used to sail about the bay and sent him sweets for his
little boy, had offered to assist. For what could be more
romantic than to rescue a French prisoner from a lonely
island? It was quite like *Monte Cristo*; and Miss Charlotte
Campbell, who always wore her blue dress for these exciting
expeditions, thrilled at the thought. But the old campaigner
preferred Doineau, Pepita, and Willette as conspirators, and
something better was devised.

She left the island with the children and made a last attempt
to melt Mac-Mahon into granting a release. When this failed

in an angry interview, Pepita went to work. Leaving the children in Belgium, she went off to Genoa with a spirited young cousin from Mexico. The youthful couple (she was only twenty-six), assuming a sonorous Spanish title, hired a small steamer for a pleasure cruise in the imposing character of a Castilian duke and duchess. One steamer in particular had caught her fancy, since it was named *Elba*, a good omen for escaping prisoners. But it was otherwise engaged, and she had to put up with another vessel. A telegram from Genoa warned Doineau, who went across to tell Bazaine that all was ready for the next Sunday night. The prisoner appeared to hesitate, as his part of the programme included the descent of a high cliff and there was some doubt about the rope. Bazaine had never been a coward; but he was a heavy man, and rock-climbing at sixty-three was something of an undertaking. After hearing Mass, however, he made up his mind; and they all waited for the night of August 9.

The night was cloudy; the *Barone Ricasoli* was anchored in Golfe Jouan, where that charming couple, the Duke and Duchess of Revilla, had gone ashore on the odd pretext of picking up an old manservant; and they were engaged in a protracted argument on the Croizette at Cannes with a reluctant boatman, who was unwilling to believe that the hour was suitable for two foreigners to think of going for a row. Doineau, a master of the alibi, was just asking somebody at Nice to have an ice with him in the Café Américain. On the island they had finished dinner; and Willette, who was understood to be going home for good on the next day, was listening to a desultory conversation between Bazaine and the prison governor on the safe subject of astronomy. The prisoner was most informing about meteorites, telling the governor that there were a lot of them about at this time of year and adding helpfully that, if he looked that night, he would see a particularly large one in flight. Then they parted for the night. The wind was rising, and the rowing-boat from Cannes was on its way (Pepita had taken the wise precaution of bringing a waterproof). In half an hour a sentry would come on duty, and then they would be locked in as usual. But before he came, the two men had slipped out of the building and hidden on the terrace. The rope which they had fabricated by tying together all the cords off all their luggage, was produced; and this life-line was looped round Bazaine with some assistance from a croquet-hoop. Then he started down the cliff, leaving Willette to look after the other end, which was secured to an iron bar and passed through an ancient gargoyle on the battlements in close proximity to which Willette had practised the more significant parts of his horticulture. It was a formidable journey for a bulky man of sixty-three on a rough night. A youth with whom the authorities experimented later over the same course in broad daylight was badly scared and slightly damaged; and it was small wonder that Bazaine was bruised and shaken, when he reached the bottom. Pepita watched the swaying body, as it crept towards them down the cliff. Once he seemed to vanish; and the scared woman, thinking he was lost, cried, "*Se matô*." But Bazaine was down at last. One of them struck a match to show him where the boat was waiting; he struck another in reply; and they dragged him into safety in the boat.

It had been a crowded evening; and sometime after midnight the sleeping captain of the *Barone Ricasoli* was roused by his young patrons (now accompanied by their faithful Pedro) with peremptory orders to head for Genoa at once. Behind them in the darkness of Golfe Jouan an inquisitive boatman had rowed out from Cannes to raise some kind of alarm. But all was quiet on the Ile Ste. Marguerite; and next morning, as they steamed into Italian waters, Willette left the island and took the early train to Paris. Nothing stirred in Bazaine's quarters, until they took his letters in and found that he was gone. Two hours later he stepped ashore in Italy, a free man.

BAZAINE'S PRISON.

(From a photograph in the author's possession)

An angry government showered prosecutions left and right. Attempts were later made to hint that his indulgent gaolers, acting on official orders, had let him walk down an easy slope through a gate that was deliberately left unlocked. But such artifices were not in Mac-Mahon's character; and there was a determined effort to convict somebody for the escape. Willette and Doineau were the leading culprits. But the scandalous activities of Bazaine's English neighbours drew suspicion upon all pairs of blonde young ladies with English accents on French territory; and "An Angry Husband" had occasion to address a letter to *The Times* that month complaining of discourtesy by French gendarmes so far afield as Calais.

When the case was heard at Grasse, Willette was defended by Maître Lachaud and Doineau faced a French tribunal for the second time in that adventurous career. Both men were convicted and sentenced to a few months' imprisonment; and Doineau vanished into a silence which remained unbroken for thirty years, until he walked into the chambers of a Paris lawyer, who had lately published a study of the case of the Lyons Mail highly favourable to the hitherto misunderstood Lesurques, with the suggestion that its author should perform a corresponding office for himself.

CHAPTER VI

DIMINUENDO

He hates him much
That would upon the rack of this rough world
Stretch him out longer.

KING LEAR.

WHEN Bazaine walked ashore at Genoa on August 10, 1874, he was a free man again at sixty-three. But what was he to do with his freedom? It was just eight months since a French court-martial had sentenced him to death, and he could never enter France again until the Empire came to its own and rewarded its much-enduring servant. That was, to say the least, a possibility in 1874; and his first move was to pay his respects in Switzerland to Eugénie and the slim young man whom the faithful knew as Napoleon IV. The prince was playing croquet when they arrived and ran to call his mother, who was charming to Pepita. "*Mais, ma petite maré-chale,*" she said rather ruefully, "*l'histoire s'occupera de vous avec avantage; vous avez été encore la plus heureuse.*" For Bazaine moved in higher spheres than most escaping prisoners. Hostile French observers were exasperated by the stately courtesy of his expression of regret that circumstances had compelled him to pass through the military district commanded by Prince Humbert of Italy without a formal call; and when this was followed by visits to exiled royalty, their abuse grew almost shrill.

His first stop, after Italy and Switzerland, was at Cologne.

Then he was off to Spa to see the children; and for some weeks he alternated between Germany and Belgium. A letter to the Minister of the Interior was dated from Cologne and explained lucidly that nobody had been to blame for his escape except his own relations; and in the first week of September he was at Liège, composing a long letter to Mr. James Gordon Bennett for publication in the New York *Herald*. This was a more serious attempt to state his case than any made by the impassive prisoner at Trianon. For he permitted himself a genial reminder to Mac-Mahon that Alsace had been lost at Wörth; Aumale was more roughly handled than he had ever been in the elaborate courtesy of their exchanges in court; and his irony returned in an allusion to mutes with bow-strings or hara-kiri as the lot of unsuccessful generals. He even approached a true diagnosis of the causes of the French defeat, when he wrote that "African victories had been taken too seriously." As for himself, a skilful touch of advocacy commended him to Mr. Gordon Bennett's Transatlantic readers by reminding them that he had found a wife in the New World and alluding gracefully to the precedent of General Lee as a model for defeated soldiers, although he added hopefully that his own military career was not yet over.

But where was that to be? He was in London for a short time that year, staying with the Hayters at 14, Harewood Square, N.W. They were old connections, as it was nearly twenty years since he had asked his present host to visit him at his headquarters after Solferino; and this link with the painter of "The Trial of Queen Caroline" seemed quite appropriate. For if Sir George had lived, what a crowded canvas he could have made of the court-martial. Bazaine's stay in England was inconspicuous, although he had received a rapturous communication after his escape from one of his young ladies of Golfe Jouan, romantically signed "*La Robe bleue* (Charlotte Campbell)" and expressing her parents' hope to receive the Marshal and his family at 15, Kildare Terrace,

Westbourne Grove. A member of Eugénie's little Household
called at Harewood Square. But though he remained a faithful
Bonapartist, Bazaine left England. It was already rumoured
that he was to command one side or the other in the eternal
Spanish civil war. For that undying conflict had broken out
again; and now the Carlists were assailing an insecure republic.
Spain, at any rate, appeared to meet the case. He spoke the
language; it would suit Pepita; and when Queen Isabella's
son was proclaimed king, he moved to Spain. For a month
after Alfonso XII arrived at Barcelona in January, 1875, Bazaine appeared at Santander; and by midsummer he was in
Madrid.

Life was not easy, though the French Government had
paid the costs of the court-martial, for which he was liable.
But this generosity was easily explained, as he had no assets
in France and few elsewhere. The new King of Spain had
visited him before his trial at Versailles, and Bazaine was received at Court until the French ambassador complained
officially. His family was at full strength in their Spanish
home with Pepita and Pepita's mother and the children and
their faithful Mexican nurse, although they seemed to find
Madrid rather chillier than Mexico. He still remembered
Bonapartist anniversaries, sending a birthday letter to the
Prince Imperial by Mr. Hayter.

> Madrid.
> *9th March*, '76.

My very dear Angelo,

Will you be good enough to post the enclosed letter to the
Prince Imperial? I am writing to him for his birthday, which is
March 16. If you have occasion to call there, you should ask to
see Comte Clary; and as you come from me, he would present
you to the Prince, who is most affable. Comte Clary came to
your house when you were giving me such affectionate hospi-
tality.

My children ought to write to yours to thank them for their kind message. But they have had frightful colds for over a month, because the winter has been most severe for Madrid.

The Maréchale has had bronchitis for the same time, and so has her mother. So the house is a hospital.

As for myself, I am pretty well, although my wounds with old age coming on fast give me a good deal of pain.

Good-bye, my dear Angelo. Pray give a message to your admirable wife and beg her to excuse the Maréchale's laziness in not writing. Both of you believe in my very sincere affection.

Your brother and friend,

M^{al.} BAZAINE.

Kisses from us all to your two big boys, of whom I am very fond, because they work hard and obey their father and mother. God bless them.

Three years later he still remembered the Prince Imperial's birthday, as the anniversary came round again; and in writing to a member of the Imperial circle in England he surveyed without enthusiasm the spectacle of France under the Third Republic.

Madrid.

11th March, '79.

My Dear Count and Friend,

Have your plans changed? When is your trip to Spain to be? For I still hope to shake your hand here, though business remains dull and nervous as long as the civil war goes on; and the latter shows no sign of ending quickly. But there are army contracts, which they say are highly profitable; there is also a prospect of financial deals, as both the Royal Government and the Republicans will shortly be on the rocks . . .

Please give Clary the enclosed letter of congratulation for the Prince Imperial.

Give me news of the national *fête* on the 16th, because we know nothing of events abroad.

What a mess the Government of our country is in. I hope
they are beginning to understand the conduct of the loyal
'modern Bayard,' the defeated hero; and what a gang of crooks
our parliamentarians are! When is the clean sweep coming (*à
quand le coup de balai*)? I am all ready for it.

Good-bye. My respects to Comtesse de la Chapelle, greet-
ings from the Maréchale, and a very affectionate hand-shake
for you from your devoted

M^{al.} BAZAINE.

His bitter fling at Mac-Mahon, unlovingly portrayed as "*loyal
Bayard Moderne*" and "*l'illustre vaincu*," was underlined in
red pencil. For it was not easy to watch life go by from
lodgings in Madrid.

The days passed slowly. It would soon be ten years since
his conviction, and he was getting on for seventy. Now there
were no more birthday letters for the Prince Imperial, as Zulu
assegais had ended the reign that never started. But Bazaine
was working at his book, the book that was to make it all so
clear and set him right at last. Besides, he had his little family
and wrote charming letters to the smaller boy, who was at
school in France in charge of his uncle Dominique, giving him
all the news from home and quantities of good advice about
his duty to his uncle who was now, "as our sublime Religion
defines it," in his father's place, and about his first communion,
when they would all be praying for him in Madrid. The
elder boy was in charge of a French *abbé* at the Escorial; the
girl was at a convent; and grandmamma was generally ill. It
was an uneventful scene, and his own memories of prison life
on the Ile Ste. Marguerite—"*volière politique, pleine de
parfums et d'oiseaux*"—were sometimes almost tender now.

His book, *Épisodes de la Guerre de 1870 et le Blocus de
Metz*, appeared in 1883 with a singularly touching dedication
to one old friend, by whom he had never been forgotten:

A
SA MAJESTÉ LA REINE
ISABELLE II

MADAME,

Votre Majesté m'ayant témoigné, dans les mauvais comme dans les bons jours, sa constante bienveillance, je la supplie d'agréer la dédicace de ce livre militaire, dont le but est de démontrer que le soldat qui avait servi la cause de Votre Majesté, pendant sa minorité, est resté digne de sa royale sympathie.

Son très humble et très dévoué serviteur,
FRANCOIS ACHILLE BAZAINE,
Ex-fusilier au 37e de Ligne,
Ex-officier supérieur au service de l'Espagne,
Ex-Maréchal de France,
Réfugié en Espagne depuis 1874.

The whole unhappy story was set out in detail and without bitterness; and he closed with a good Frenchman's prayer for his country, which responded with abuse. But Archibald Forbes, who had been with the Germans outside Metz, published a commentary that almost satisfied him.

As the years went by, a lonely figure was still slipping through side-streets in Madrid. They were miserably poor. His elder boy was now a non-commissioned officer in the Spanish Guards. The heat that year was very trying (it was 1886, and Bazaine was seventy-five); and as the breathless August days stole on, he wrote to his small son in France that he was sleeping badly, as his "season of black memories"—the three months of Metz—was with him once again.

But he endured; and in the next year a demented commercial traveller from La Rochelle with an obsession about Metz earned a long sentence from a Spanish court by a cowardly attempt to murder him. The indignant patriot knifed the old man in the face. He could still write, though.

Madrid.
6th *January*, 1888.

DEAR COUNT AND FRIEND,

I have your affectionate letter of December 31, and I thank you sincerely. My best wishes for the recovery of your health, without which there can be no inner happiness.

My nephew Clapeyron has given you the extract from my army record made by the Ministry of War. It must be incomplete, like everything which comes out of that factory of papers, all more or less careless according to the nature of the official copyist. I have just sent him some documents relating to the capture of Kinburn.

Comte Kératry was my orderly officer in Mexico; and as I had no fault to find with him, I have always defended him and given strong support when he was attacked. Kindly assure him that I bear him no ill-will for his rather risky statement to the commission of the Chamber on the Government of National Defence, which MM. St. Marc Girardin and Daru used against me.

The past is dead, as the *Arabs* say, and all is forgotten. Give him a sincere handshake from me in token of my friendship . . .

M^AL. BAZAINE.

He had always relished Arab proverbs; and now the past was dead indeed. He still lingered for a few months longer in Madrid. But it had never suited Pepita; and she was in Mexico, when the end came that autumn on September 23, 1888. For this time he was spared a part of his "*trimestre de* souvenirs noirs, *août, septembre, octobre,* 70." A little group of Spaniards, a French priest, and his boys followed a dead Marshal to the foreign cemetery. They said it was his heart.

CHAPTER VII

VIDI

Regardez la trouée des Vosges.
GAMBETTA.

FRANCE after the war of 1870 was a defeated nation. But any undue sense of inferiority was averted by a convenient decision that it had all been someone else's fault. Republicans and royalists attributed it to the Empire; conservatives inclined to find fault with the ill-regulated impulses of the Government of National Defence; and practically everybody blamed Bazaine. The main thing, as they were now confronted with the armed might of Germany, was to rearm themselves; and if that was to be done, the first essential was to preserve the nation's faith in the French army and its present leaders. This was not easy, as large portions of the army had not behaved too well, and there was hardly one of its present leaders who had not a major defeat to his credit. But defeated nations (as Germany and Europe were to learn two generations later) are unusually credulous about the cause of their defeat; and the French managed to retain their faith in the army and even to elect President of the Republic the only Marshal who had been defeated more often than Bazaine.

The acclamation of Mac-Mahon as '*soldat sans peur et sans reproche*' was, in some ways, the strangest part of the whole business. No one was more typical of the Algerian practitioners whose complete inadequacy for European warfare had been demonstrated all the way from Wörth to Sedan.

But French opinion insisted upon rallying round this emblem
of defeat with Micawber-like determination. Indeed, the same
decade witnessed an expression of the same feeling in art,
where Alphonse de Neuville's canvases harped almost mor-
bidly on the nostalgia of failure, with French casualties huddled in the snow or wild-eyed men firing their last shot at overwhelming German odds from upper windows. (It was his
Dernières Cartouches that launched the painter's popularity.)
True, he sometimes permitted a knot of *franc-tireurs* to in-
terrogate a sullen German. But his favourite emotion was pity
for his own defeated countrymen, for the brave hostages
under grim Teutonic guard or the young Frenchman dropping to a German bullet. Detaille, although his mood was less
dejected, struck the same note with his despairing huddle of
Cuirassiers shot to pieces in a village street at Mac-Mahon's
first defeat; and it was strange to find that synonym for
Wörth and Sedan as the first President of the Third Republic.

France chose to recuperate under the Marshal for stronger
reasons than the mere accident of politics which rendered him
acceptable to all conservatives. His wife, a fervent royalist,
might dutifully murmur *"Nous ne sommes ici que pour tenir
la place."* But he showed no tendency to give it up when
challenged by his lawful king; and Henri V departed sorrow-
fully, muttering that he had taken Mac-Mahon for a Constable
of France and found a police inspector. It was growing
obvious that, in his own opinion, he was there on his own
merits. His initial manifesto, invoking God, the army, and
all honest folk, was the sincere expression of a point of view.
In this philosophy religion, the armed forces, and an upper
class of undefined proportions were to combine for the pres-
ervation of *"l'ordre moral,"* which bore a strong resemblance
to Bazaine's notorious announcement that the Army of the
Rhine existed to defend "social order against evil passions."
But the atmosphere of 1873 was more favourable to such
aspirations than it had been three years before; and the Mar-

shal was assisted by a vast increase of piety, by which the
national catastrophe had been followed. Calamities often
engender a mood of somewhat exaggerated penitence; and the
Marshal's France was nothing if not penitential. There was a
rage for public pilgrimages; Chartres saw a long procession
including 140 Deputies; France was publicly dedicated to the
Sacré Cœur; and as the great basilica began to tower over
Paris, the Pope expressed his strong distaste for the French
Revolution and a corresponding joy in observing the return
of France to faith. This seemed a worthier employment of
Montmartre than for the beginnings of the Commune of the
mayoralty of young Georges Clemenceau; and French politics
passed momentarily under the control of the *bien-pensants*
and their aged military nominee. Public life was full of dukes,
dukes of all shapes and sizes, of old creations and of new,
dukes with names that echoed the Ancien Regime, the First
Empire and the Second, the stern days of Napoleon and the
comfortable era of Louis Philippe, dukes with mutton-chop
whiskers like de Broglie or the splendid weeping Dundrearies
of d'Audiffret Pasquier, dukes with titles ranging from
Decazes to Magenta.

The foremost of them all, a Second Empire title super-
imposed upon the old *noblesse* and crowned with the highest
office of the Third Republic, presided in the Élysée. He was
not clever. Somebody had said that his first act upon assuming
office was to ask for a copy of the rules; and disrespectful
Bonapartists, remembering their Shakespeare, called him '*Mac-
bête.*' For his repartee was rarely brisk; discretion often confined his conversation to the weather; and his meagre utterances
were lovingly embroidered by the legend which recalled
that his sole comment on a Presidential visit to flood
victims had been to the effect that there was a great deal of
water or, when visiting a fever hospital, '*Ah, la fièvre
typhoïde, je l'ai eue; on en meurt ou on en reste idiot.*' But

the tendency remained to celebrate this steadfast figure as '*le Bayard des temps modernes*'; and if the little rhymes about

> *Notre Bayard couvert de gloire,*
> *Notre chef, illustre vaincu* . . .

occasionally had disrespectful endings, large numbers of French provincials, who had been badly scared by the Parisian excesses of the Commune and found Gambetta and his friends only one degree less alarming, clung to the Marshal.

The shadow of this venerable effigy hung over France, as she recovered from defeat and young Philippe Pétain was growing up. If men's ambitions are often fixed upon the type admired by the world in which they come of age, the figure of Mac-Mahon, the *illustre vaincu*, could not be overlooked by the Dominicans' young pupil in their college at Arcueil. He had gone to school at St. Omer in the big bare buildings of the Collège St. Bertin, where his sole recorded utterance was a blameless ambition to grow up to be a lieutenant of Chasseurs; and he went on to the Dominicans at Arcueil, until he passed into St. Cyr. For the examination, which had proved too much for Bazaine at the Polytechnique, was no obstacle to Pétain at St. Cyr; and as his military education opened, the fluffy beard of Continental adolescence vanished, though he retained a large moustache. He was just twenty; it was 1876; and for two years he wore the dainty, plumed shako and white gloves of the *premier bataillon de France*, until he emerged as *sous-lieutenant* in the 24th Chasseurs.

The sober years that followed 1870 had made great changes in the army. Military thought is frequently accelerated by defeat. Guibert and du Teil, stimulated by the reverses of Louis XV, had furnished many of the ideas with which the armies of the First Republic and Napoleon overran the continent; the Boer War did wonders for the military mind of Britain; and Cissey and du Barail now presided at the Ministry of War over a period of intelligent activity. Liability to military service became universal; and the disappearance of the Imperial Guard facilitated an approach to uniformity. There were no more *corps d'élite*, although the Zouaves survived and the *Chasseurs à pied* still wore their dark uniforms and marched to the quickstep of *Sidi-Brahim*. A chastened strategy, deprived of the frontier defences formerly supplied by Metz, Strasburg, and the Rhine, proceeded to create an artificial frontier. This was largely due to General de Rivière, the learned sapper whose ingenuity had played so large a part in Bazaine's prosecution; and it consisted of a chain of fortresses and single forts designed to cover the interior of France against a German thrust, affording absolute protection to vital areas and canalising the invasion in directions where it could be disposed of by the defending forces. This modest aspiration was completely satisfied by the event, since German strategy in 1914 made no serious attempt to penetrate the permanent defences of the French frontier between Verdun and Belfort and preferred to risk a vast outflanking movement through Belgium.

In 1878 the new forts were rising on the bare hills above Verdun, and a subaltern was on his way to join the 24th Chasseurs at Villefranche. Young Pétain had never been so far from home before. His school at St. Omer was only a few miles from his village; and the Dominican college was just outside Paris. Even the examination for St. Cyr had only taken him to Nancy. But now the south was waiting for him. It was strange for a slow-spoken young man from Flanders to find himself among bright-eyed, dark-haired men with names like Marius and Numa, who talked with every feature of their faces and insisted upon seeing prospects of unlimited magnificence, which his chilly northern vision told him were not there at all. He found them entertaining and retained a lifelong taste for funny stories about the *Midi* and its ludicrous inhabitants. (Strange that his little kingdom, when he made himself a sort of king, consisted largely of the *Midi*.) The *sous-lieutenant* in his dark tunic and blue *képi* stopped to look at Lyons and Marseilles; his large, fair moustache was seen on the Canebière; and he even strolled round Nice before reporting to his unit at Villefranche. Then regimental life absorbed him, until he went off for a course near Lyons, worked uncommonly hard, learnt enduring lessons about fire-power, and became a remarkably good shot. His thoughts were simple; for his highest aspiration, placed on record in a confession-book at this stage of his career, was limited to the routine desire, *"Mourir pour mon pays."*

Hardened by five years of strenuous existence with the 24th on the Riviera, punctuated by mountain exercises in the coast range, he joined the 3rd Chasseurs as a lieutenant in 1884. He would soon be thirty; his moustache was even longer now; and he was stationed at Besançon. These were the rousing years when Paris packed the Alcazar to hear Paulus sing *En revenant de la Revue;* and as they reached the rousing chorus, everybody felt that the French army was looking up at last behind a handsome general on a black horse. For the bearded Boulanger was Minister of War.

This decorative figure, actuated by a laudable desire to give the public what it wanted, had served with moderate distinction in North Africa and the siege of Paris and possessed an unusual instinct for patriotic gestures. His aptitude had been expressed in firmness with Italian residents in Tunis and in vigorous complaints at the White House because the tricolours displayed at the centenary of Yorktown were not large enough. Such gifts must plainly not be wasted; and as Minister of War he seemed capable of standing up to Germany. As that was all the public wanted, there were cheering crowds along the road from Longchamps after the review. For their confidence was coming back; and *'not' brav' général Boulanger'* was the living symbol of its return. Had he not taken a strong line about a frontier incident, to say nothing of renaming large numbers of provincial barracks after national heroes and painting tricolour stripes on all French sentry-boxes? His politics might be a shade tangential, since at the moment he was ardently republican (Clemenceau amiably called him 'Augereau'), sternly relegating Aumale and the other princes to outer darkness once again. This phase was followed by a highly questionable period of groping for support among wealthy royalists in order (it might be supposed) to replace the Third Republic with something more august. But it was Boulanger's merit that he gave the French something which they had not known since 1870. For he gave them something to cheer; and more than once the Third Republic rocked a little on its base, as the Paris streets bawled:

> *C'est Boulang', Boulang', Boulange,*
> *C'est Boulanger qu'il nous faut,*
> *Ho! Ho! Ho! Ho!*

He never nerved himself to take the plunge; and the experiment collapsed a few years later, after a few heartening disorders on the Paris boulevards and his ignominious defeat in a duel by an elderly civilian, terminating in the warrior's departure with a charming (though consumptive) blonde to Brussels, followed by a life of comfortable exile in Portland Place and the Channel Islands and his suicide at her grave in a Belgian cemetery. This was a miserable exit for his country's *jeune premier*. Perhaps the general had been too handsome after all.

But he had shown that the Republic might not be France's fate for ever. It was passing through a sordid phase of minor scandals, in which public men (including d'Andlau, the sternest of Bazaine's accusers) were found in association with a feminine underworld for the ignoble purpose of trafficking in decorations; and as civilian politicians sank in the scale, the army held its head a little higher. For Boulanger had taught it, as old Changarnier said, to wear its *képi* on one side. These excitements were a long way from a lieutenant of Chasseurs at Besançon, although a greasy-looking boy outside a butcher's shop at Chateldon was not far off. But Lieutenant Pétain had not yet made Pierre Laval's acquaintance. His next move was to the *École Supérieure de Guerre*, where the best military minds of France professed the higher mysteries, for a two years' course. (Lewal, whom Bazaine had found the least unhelpful of Jarras' staff officers, was its first commandant.) Promoted captain in 1890, he was on the staff at Marseilles and savoured once again the glorious absurdity of southerners. Their mood was not infectious, though, since his corps commander, reporting upon Captain Pétain, found him "silent, cold, calm, disinclined to precipitate decisions, and always acting on his orders." But he was soon back with the Chasseurs, going to the 29th at Vincennes in 1892. His politics were still obscure, though when a private in his company, absent without leave, turned out to have gone to Paris for the purpose of delivering a speech in the Chamber, the soldier-Deputy was sternly dealt with by Captain Pétain, in whose view military discipline appeared to come before democratic institutions. The two were shortly in collision. For soon afterwards Captain Pétain's interlude of regimental life at Vincennes ended with his appointment to the staff of the Military Governor of Paris; and it was not long before Captain Dreyfus was convicted of espionage.

The conviction was eccentric, as it rested largely upon documents so secret that they were not shown to the defence. But they were good enough for the court-martial; and while Captain Pétain sat amongst official files at a stuffy office in the Place Vendôme, the dismal ritual of degradation in a barrack-square ended the career of Alfred Dreyfus, who was shipped off to French Guiana. That was in 1894, and nobody except his family minded very much. The world went on; a new Military Governor of Paris made Captain Pétain his assistant; and when they left the rabbit-warren in the Place Vendôme for better premises, the captain organised their new office at the Invalides. (His contribution to administrative life was soundly made, because his system for the office of the Military Governor survived two wars—until, in fact, the Military Governor of Paris was a German.)

Pétain was over forty now, a captain with a large moustache who worked all day at an office table where nothing seemed to happen. But not far away there was an unpleasant stir at the Ministry of War, where it was dawning upon someone that there had been something very wrong about the Dreyfus case, because the handwriting of the fatal letter to Colonel von Schwarzkoppen was uncomfortably like Major Esterhazy's. This was highly inconvenient, as the General Staff was thoroughly committed to the view of Dreyfus' guilt; and Colonel Picquart's doubts were promptly set at rest by his despatch to the most dangerous part of southern Tunisia. The case was not particularly important in itself, as the military secrets in which Colonel von Schwarzkoppen's correspondent appeared to be trafficking were not of the first order. But the high command had jumped with premature agility to the conclusion that Dreyfus, who was not particularly liked and incidentally a Jew, was the culprit; and it was most desirable, unless their hold on public confidence was to be seriously impaired, that their conclusions should be left undisturbed.

In the last decade of the Nineteenth Century the army occupied an exceptional position in French public life. For politics and politicians were in some discredit owing to the simple appetites revealed by large numbers of public figures in relation to the finance, publicity, legislative facilities, and even construction of the Panama Canal by a French company. This enterprise, commended to the nation by the heroic optimism of de Lesseps, penetrated a rank undergrowth of graft at home almost as slowly as it worked its way through the impenetrable jungle of Colombia; and as French opinion awoke to the unpleasant reality of yellow fever on the Isthmus, it began to realise that public life in France was almost as unhealthy. It was not unduly shocked by the discovery, as politics had long been viewed rather as an exciting (and not ill-rewarded) branch of sport than as a form of government. But it was gravely disconcerting to those thoughtful Britons, who admire only those French politicians who resemble British statesmen and compose judicious surveys of French institutions that sometimes read like the slightly bilious verdict of a disappointed Bryce, as they scanned the unprepossessing vista of the Third Republic for a French replica of Mr. Gladstone. For the personnel of French politics had been unnaturally depleted by a strong tendency to disqualify the aristocracy; and since democracy had failed to throw up a sufficiency of talent, the void was filled by large numbers of nonentities. Their glaring mediocrity inspired Gambetta's scornful comment on the '*sous-vétérinaires*,' who gave up to their country's ills the talents meant for those of horses; and the electorate, which had never thought very much of its representatives, thought less of them than ever. Within this narrow circle politics were still highly acrimonious, because (in the words of one observer) "it is to the French that Frenchmen display animosity more savage, more incessant, and more inequitable than to people of any other race." But in the nation at large there was a spreading tendency to say, "*Je ne m'occupe pas de politique, Monsieur.*" An indifferent electorate appeared to want little more than representation without taxation; and one enquiring stranger, diagnosing the strange "*nostalgie du pouvoir fort*" left behind by long centuries of monarchy and Empire, prophesied that "the day will come when no power will prevent France from hailing a head of her choice. Whether he will bear the name of a once reigning dynasty, or whether he will be a statesman to inspire victory, or a soldier to achieve it, the next generation will know."

The main thing was victory; and as the only victory that mattered was one over the Germans, the army had become an almost sacred instrument of national resurgence. When civilian politics were slightly nauseating and the Third Republic not particularly sacrosanct, large sections of the nation clung to the army; and its high reputation had to be maintained at all cost—even at the cost of some injustice to one unhappy individual on an island off the coast of French Guiana. But this was not so easy as it looked with growing numbers of officious individuals demanding reconsideration of the Dreyfus case, because the *bordereau* was in someone else's handwriting. On the rising uproar disinterested men united with the victim's angry relatives, politicians eager to make a come-back, enterprising journalists, and Émile Zola. The novelist had already included in his vast canvas on the adventures of a French family under the Second Empire an uncomfortably accurate portrayal in *La Débacle* of Mac-Mahon's army at Sedan; and as its military characters were mainly of a low order of intelligence, the two sons of General Margueritte, who fell with the Chasseurs d'Afrique at Floing, were tempted to reply with a book about Bazaine's army at Metz, entitled *Le Désastre* and representing almost all French soldiers (except the Marshal) as beings of a lofty type. When the growing controversy about Dreyfus raised doubts as to the army's judicial qualities, Zola approached the problem without romantic prejudices, stating his adverse conclusions with joyous emphasis in an open letter to the President, for which Clemenceau suggested the inspired title, "*J'accuse.*" The public was invited to believe that the high command had used unpardonable methods to conceal the awkward truth that Dreyfus was innocent; and those to whom authority was uncongenial agreed. Their ranks included politicians of the Left and progressive literary men, while the contrary opinion was stoutly held by devotees of military and religious discipline. Indeed, the schism seemed to lie between those sections of society which could read and write and those which found it preferable to watch and pray.

241

France was in two minds about it. There were even soldiers who agreed with Colonel Picquart that Dreyfus was innocent although he was a Jew. But it was scarcely likely that an officer on General Zurlinden's staff at the Invalides was so unorthodox. A friend of Pétain's has recorded the existence of "une parfaite entente" with his chief, Zurlinden; and as the general was a staunch anti-Dreyfusard, the inference as to his subordinate's opinions is plain. The army's case continued to be urged with emphasis; and, like so many unsuccessful conquerors, it was still winning battles, when the war was evidently lost. Esterhazy was acquitted; Zola was condemned; and Picquart was imprisoned. But the revelation that large portions of the army's case had rested upon simple forgery was disconcerting; and though these fabrications might have been inspired by the highest motives, the world outside a narrow circle often fails to relish the combination of deep piety with crime. Besides, if the generals were going to be quite so stupid in the field as they appeared to be in court, the prospects of the next campaign were hardly promising; and it was greatly to be hoped that the *Deuxième Bureau* was better at military intelligence than it had been at forgery.

While these thunders rolled overhead, Pétain reverted to a regiment once more, joining the 8th Chasseurs at Amiens. The brigadier was Bonnal, who had been one of his teachers at the *École de Guerre* ten years before and now found in his pupil a rare blend of "*les qualités de vigueur, de caractère, de décision et d'intelligence dans la juste proportion désirable chez un futur grand chef.*" But this paragon, at forty-three, was still a captain, although a course with the balloons at Meudon had added to his repertoire the strange accomplishments of *officier d'aérostier;* and before the year was out, he was promoted *Chef de bataillon.* It was 1900 now; he knew some German, a little English, and a great deal about his own profession including an acquaintance with the ground on which the war of 1870 had been lost; and that year he was

sent to make trouble at the Châlons school of musketry, whose
teachers were officially suspected of talking nonsense. These
suspicions were correct; and when *Commandant* Pétain re-
futed the prevailing heresy with a vigorous exposition of his
favourite theme, the merits of well-directed fire-power, he
was hurriedly invited to name another post of his own choice.
Selecting a Line regiment in Paris, he spent a few months
with the 5th. This time his path almost crossed Laval's, as
that unattractive adolescent (who answered freely to the
name of 'Jamaica'), after an apprenticeship spent dodging
round the tables of his father's café with a tray of glasses, had
taken his degree in Paris and was now an ornament of the
lower levels of French pedagogy. Their interests were widely
different, though, since young Laval's military service was
shortly curtailed upon medical grounds and his political
opinions were of an extreme character. Such luxuries were
not for middle-aged *Commandants* of the Line; and Pétain
was never reckless.

His next avatar was a spell of teaching under Bonnal and
Lanrezac at the *École de Guerre*, where he did well and was
offered the command of the Châlons school of musketry.
But he declined, objecting that if he went, he would be junior
in rank to his own subordinates; and even an immediate offer
of the rank of lieutenant-colonel failed to move the cautious
major. So he reverted to regimental life once more and passed
1903 among the red trousers of the 104th of the Line. But he
was soon back at the *École de Guerre*, propagating views upon
fire-discipline on which he was becoming a leading authority.
He was a chilly teacher (they called him '*Précis-le-sec*'),
who never wasted words and corrected their exercises with
a turn of irony; and a commandant who failed to appreciate
his angular subordinate relegated him to regimental life again.
As he had asked to be sent to the Eastern frontier, they sent
him just the other way to the 118th of the Line at Quimper.
He was a lieutenant-colonel now, past fifty, and condemned

to a term of drilling *piou-pious* at an uninteresting garrison in Brittany. But Maunoury brought him back to the *École de Guerre;* and this time he got his head.

His passion for fire-power impelled him to seek means of co-ordinating infantry operations with the guns behind them. For the cautious Pétain disliked the notion of launching infantry attacks without sufficient artillery preparation. This challenged both the strong autonomy of gunners and the current tendency to hold that the whole duty of French infantry was to charge anything in front of them without the least regard to what it was. (A touching faith in the *furia francese* had become almost universal since the defeats of their stationary masses in 1870.) A bold experiment directed by Percin and Pétain at the autumn manœuvres resulted in official acceptance of this new association of the two arms in 1910. Henceforward infantry might hope for some share in the direction of its artillery support; and Pétain's cherished repertory of fire-power had received a formidable addition. Flushed with this success, his teaching tended still more to emphasise the strength of the defensive, a cautious attitude epitomised by one pupil as "*la crainte salutaire que l'on doit avoir des feux de l'adversaire.*" This timid doctrine, entirely contrary to that prevailing in the army, did not deter a pupil named de Gaulle, whom he impressed immensely, from applying for attachment to Pétain's unit, when he left the *École de Guerre;* nor did it deprive the teacher of Foch's good opinion. But though the new commandant reported warmly on his subordinate's high character and clear intelligence, commending his grasp of tactics, he proposed that these qualities should be recognised by the command of an infantry regiment. This was conferred on him in 1911; and the *Ecole de Guerre* knew him no more.

The cautious teacher left the classroom now for good, apart from a few lectures to the cavalry at Saumur. On the whole he had not made much impression except on a few individuals like young de Gaulle. (Another of his pupils, a curly-haired young Spanish officer, named Franco, seemed rather to have impressed his teacher.) The views that he expressed were most unlikely to obtain acceptance in army circles, which were universally committed to an almost evangelical belief in the offensive. Observing that the defeated armies of 1870 had invariably stood on the defensive and that Napoleon's victories were always won on the offensive, French military thought concluded that the only way to win was to attack. This frame of mind dwelt lovingly upon the bayonet and bravely ignored the growing power of the machine-gun to interpose impenetrable curtains of fire between the bayonet and its objective. It even modified the cautious strategy of the defended frontier, replacing de Rivière's fortress barrier with the heroic absurdities of 'Plan XVII', which contemplated an immediate rush of French armies into German territory without regard either to the disparity of numbers or to the prepared defences of the points selected for attack. A feeling grew that one decisive battle in Lorraine (or, if the Germans were unchivalrous enough to violate Belgian neutrality, in the Ardennes) would settle everything; and it was largely to be won by charging with the bayonet in red *képis* and blue greatcoats. This was not quite how recent actions in South Africa and Manchuria had been conducted by the British and the Japanese. But it was the way that France proposed to win the war on lines differing almost equally from modern warfare and from Colonel Pétain's cautionary teaching.

France was calmer now. Though politics were still acrimonious, a fair number of public men in almost every party admitted that their country's claims might in certain circumstances be superior to party vengeances, and the French army waited soberly for the shock of European war. This time they had prepared an instrument designed for fighting Germany; and though their uniforms were garish and automatic weapons almost totally ignored, they had an admirable field-gun. True, the balance of man-power was seriously adverse, as a population of 40,000,000 now confronted one of 65,000,000; and the thrifty families of the Third Republic could not hope to face 9,750,000 adult Germans with more than 5,940,000 Frenchmen. The days of single-handed combat between France and Germany were plainly over; and French policy was now dependent upon France's alliances. But as Germany could always be depended on to make friends for France, the Franco-Russian combination was almost a generation old; and the more recent *Entente* with Great Britain seemed to be reliable. This grouping of the Powers meant that in the event of war Russia would engage the Germans on the eastern front, whilst a British Expeditionary Force would make a contribution of some kind in France or Belgium. It was 1911; and that summer a German gunboat went to Agadir. This challenge to French claims in Africa brought Europe to the edge of war. It was plain that German appetites were growing dangerously large again. A period of apprehension, the same uneasy interval by which a German act of violence is normally preceded, sobered eager politicians; and the uncomfortable world of 1912 and 1913 waited to see when the war would come.

Pétain, a colonel now, commanded the 33rd of the Line at Arras in his own unattractive north; and for three long years this painstaking officer discharged his regimental duties. The colonel was ubiquitous, and his paternalism positively found a way of accelerating the laggards' return from week-end leave by writing to their families himself. He was well thought of; a course at the *Centre des Hautes Études Militaires* marked him for a command (Lieutenant-colonel Weygand, of the 5th Hussars, was there a little later); and early in 1914 he positively found himself commanding a whole brigade at his native St. Omer.

The wheel had come full-circle. He was fifty-eight, and he would be retiring soon. Big, bald-headed Colonel Pétain with his chilly manner and his large moustache was near the end of his career. It had not been particularly distinguished. Perhaps his obsession about fire-power had kept him back in a generation which believed implicity in the *offensive à outrance*. Other men of the same age had gone a good deal further. Franchet d'Espérey was to have an army corps and Humbert, who was six years younger, a division, while Pétain commanded a brigade like Mangin, ten years his junior. Lyautey, who was only two years older, ruled all Morocco; and Joffre, who was to command them all, was no more than sixty-two. Their lives had been more interesting, too. For while Pétain was lecturing on tactics or drilling infantry in dull provincial garrisons, many of his brother-officers had seen the world and even met the English. Madagascar, Senegal, Tonkin, and the empty sunshine of Morocco had all heard French bugles; and Mangin had seen the palms of the White Nile wave their stiff hosannas, as Major Marchand hoisted the tricolour at Fashoda. But Colonel Pétain, who had not yet heard a shot fired in anger, never went overseas in his slow progress through the army-list. His provinciality was quite intact. If there was anything to see outside France, he had not seen it; and he had few memories to take with him to the small house outside St. Omer, which he had chosen for his retirement.

That would be coming soon; and when it came, he would live there alone, since his enthusiasm for the family was a plant of later growth. An elderly bachelor with a big moustache and a frosty manner, Colonel Pétain waited for his pension at fifty-eight. But life was not yet over for the bald colonel at St. Omer.

CHAPTER VIII

VICI

C'est à Verdun qu'avec une fermeté tranquille la France lui a répondu; "On ne passe pas."

POINCARÉ.

I

WAR came in August, 1914, just forty-four years after Sedan; and once again it was the Germans' gift to Europe. This time a murder in the Balkans encouraged the empty-headed Austrians to seek a stern vengeance and an inexpensive triumph from a small Slav kingdom in the happy certainty that Germany would stand behind them. Russia, which had been humiliated recently when the Japs and the revolution of 1905 left her in no condition to reply to a similar aggression in the Balkans on the part of the Teutonic twins, was reluctant to permit this degradation of a poor relation; France was bound by her alliance to march with Russia, if Germany supported Austria; and as the Germans chose to out-manœuvre the French armies by fetching a wide circuit across Belgium, this violation of a harmless neutral, whose immunity was guaranteed by treaty, left Great Britain with no alternative to war. That fatal chain of circumstance, originating in an Austro-German initiative and enlarged by a German military plan, dragged Europe into war. Peace had been precarious for some time under the successive shocks of Kaiser Wilhelm's impulsive diplomacy, which indicated artlessly that peace was only tolerable so long as Germany

248

could get its way. This time the road was plainly barred. For Russia was in no mood to tolerate the execution of Serbia; and Great Britain insisted sharply that a German march through Belgium was a breach of public law which Germany, no less than Britain, had guaranteed. But as German strategy is rarely impeded by a German signature and the British took a more pedantic view of treaty obligations, Reichskanzler von Bethmann-Hollweg was left deploring the exaggerated scruples of a nation that proposed to go to war "just for a word—'neutrality'—just for a scrap of paper."

The first blow fell on the French. This time they mobilised efficiently; 4,278 trains brought nearly 3,000,000 men into position; and the game was ready to begin. Five French armies lay along the frontier; and every Frenchman was at his post. General Joffre was at headquarters with a smooth, chubby little staff officer named Gamelin, who had worked under him since 1906; Foch was a corps commander in Lorraine; Colonel Pétain and his infantry brigade were somewhere in the north; and Laval, who was now a deputy and had made quite a name by appearing for trade unions in police-court cases, was on the Sûreté's list of undesirables qualified by their disloyal views for immediate arrest on the outbreak of war. Dreyfus and du Paty de Clam both marched in the same ranks; and Bazaine's son had left his Spanish uniform to join his father's old service.

As Colonel Pétain's first experience of active service opened, he found the 4th Brigade in Lanrezac's Fifth Army on the left of the French line behind the Belgian frontier. Presently the strange prescriptions of 'Plan XVII,' by which it was decreed that French armies should attack the Germans all along the line, launched them into Belgium; and as the Germans had the same idea, the colonel marched against the stream of a depressing exodus of Belgian refugees. He met the Germans on the Meuse south of Dinant and made strong defensive preparations to hold them off with wire, trenches, and artillery support, a saner method than the wasted gallantry of cheers, bayonets, white gloves, and waving swords, with which another school of French military thought was decimating French battalions in Lorraine. But as the French thrusts were uniformly unsuccessful (for the hard facts of war were strangely unlike 'Plan XVII') and the German wheel through Belgium began to overlap Lanrezac's unguarded left, the 4th Brigade was withdrawn. His men tramped down the dusty roads with their faces towards France again; and Colonel Pétain marched with his rear battalion.

Their situation was unpleasant, since the Germans were acting in the most unexpected way. Instead of waiting for the French attacks and yielding gracefully, they were shattering the *offensive à outrance* with machine-gun fire and developing a disconcerting movement of their own through Belgium. Its range and weight were still obscure; and the Fifth Army had nothing to confront it with except their own resources and the problematical assistance of the British, who were just arriving on their left. This was viewed with some scepticism, as Lanrezac's chief of staff greeted their ally's first spokesman, a former French military attaché in London, without geniality. "Well, here you are," he said, "it is just about time. If we are beaten, it will be thanks to you." The same unhappy tone prevailed in even higher quarters, since Lanrezac's first meeting with Sir John French was conspicuously unsuccessful. For the trim Field-Marshal found little to admire in a bulky Frenchman with a ragged moustache and a pair of pince-nez hooked over one ear, who spoke no English; and as Sir John did not speak French, their intercourse was fragmentary. Even the assistance of interpreters failed to bridge the gap, as when Sir John (armed with the right phrase by a respectful bystander) enquired, "*Mon général, est-ce-que les Allemands vont traverser la Meuse à Hoy?*" this innocent enquiry, with its well-meant approximation to the name of Huy, elicited no more from Lanrezac than the tart answer, "*Pourquoi sont-ils arrivés? Mais pour pêcher dans la rivière.*" Irony is frequently misplaced in official intercourse; and the sally, which left a British Field-Marshal under the impression that a foreigner was being funny in a language he could not understand, was a poor beginning for Anglo-French co-operation in the field. French and Lanrezac continued in this key; the Field-Marshal's call was not returned; and the French general whose army was in immediate contact with the British Expeditionary Force concluded sombrely that "our military relations with the British would be anything but easy in spite of undeniable good-will on both sides; we did not speak the same language, and moreover we had different ideas of war."

It was plain that Lanrezac viewed his British allies with profound misgivings; and these unflattering opinions were quite unconcealed from those around him, as one observer at his headquarters notes that "every officer on his staff knew that neither the British, nor the Belgians for that matter, found favour in his eyes. He was apt to lump them in with his own Reserve Divisions as being all equally useless. During the whole period of his command he never saw a British unit." The Fifth Army, it would seem, in which Pétain commanded a brigade, was not a school of Anglophil opinions. Lanrezac was a distinguished teacher, under whom he had served at the *École de Guerre*; and if the headmaster had his prejudices, one of his favourite subordinates might share them. (Pétain told a British soldier later in the war that they were supposed in the French army to be ignorant of the *grande guerre*.) It is clear that there was a close bond between the two men, as Lanrezac in recommending him nearly three years afterwards for a post he had declined himself remarked of Pétain, "He is one of my own children, and I can answer for him." The parent, it is plain, was a stout Anglophobe; and it is at least possible that Pétain learned his inability to love the British at Lanrezac's knee.

Retreat is a hard school of war; and after a disastrous experiment in the offensive at Charleroi the Fifth Army was in full retreat. Always a pessimist, Lanrezac had found reality exceeding his gloomiest anticipations and drew off his shattered forces into France, while the British on his left eluded von Kluck's embrace at Mons and kept pace with the French withdrawal. Pétain's brigade, which had been in reserve, was quite intact and helped to cover the retreat of the Fifth Army. The stand at Guise, unsupported by the British, was an uncomfortable experience hardly calculated to increase the Brigadier's regard for his allies; and two days later on August 31 Colonel Pétain was promoted *Général de brigade* and transferred to command the 6th Division. There was no time to celebrate his elevation with a new uniform. But somewhere along their line of march an elderly spinster found some stars for his tunic on a deceased relative's old uniform in an upstairs cupboard. The general's *képi* with gold oak leaves would have to wait, as General Pétain's more immediate business was to take over his command. The 6th Division was one of Lanrezac's retreating units; and one evening their new commander found them tramping wearily along a dusty road. They had been roughly handled; large numbers had thrown away their packs; and he sat his horse at the crossroads to watch the jaded men go by. The staff found him a little chilling; but he pulled the troops together, and they were equal to an effort, when the tide of their retreat turned at the Marne. That day (it was September 6) French strategy redeemed the follies of 'Plan XVII' by improvising victory over the advancing Germans; and Pétain's division went in to attack in front of Montceau-les-Provins. He launched them after judicious artillery preparation. But when the infantry hung back under a storm of German shells, Pétain walked slowly forward with his staff into the front line. The sight of a still figure steadied the advancing troops, and their attack developed with success.

The beaten Germans fell back towards the Aisne; and
eager strategists at headquarters began to count the days before they would be arriving on the Rhine, Joffre's chief of
staff giving them three weeks and Henry Wilson, more con-
servative, declaring for a month. But the Germans were still
fifty miles inside the French frontier, to say nothing of the
whole width of Belgium; and presently the French advance
was checked by a line of strong positions. The pursuit was
over. Although they did not know it, it was over for four
years; and while more ardent spirits soared generously across
the map of Western Europe, the realistic Pétain settled down
to the defensive. Here was the logical conclusion of his unwearied faith in fire-power; and as the autumn days went by,
he organised his sector of the front with a solidity that was
quite novel in 1914. When the Germans lunged again, the
6th Division held them off; and General Pétain earned a
mention for "his tenacity, steadiness under fire, unfailing foresight, continual intervention at awkward moments," resulting
in a defensive victory over a fortnight of German attacks. He
was beginning to be recognised; his methods were discussed;
and as his sparing use of men, combined with careful artillery
preparation, seemed to yield satisfactory results, he was now
a coming man. For he had noticed rather earlier than most
of his profession that siege-warfare was the order of the day.

This discovery was shortly recognised by his promotion to
the rank of *Général de division*, the Legion of Honour, and
elevation to the XXXIII Army corps. A corps commander
now, he found himself in front of Arras on ground over
which he had trained his infantry regiment in time of peace.
It was October; and Maudhuy's Tenth Army, of which his
corps formed part, was engaged in a spasmodic series of
attacks under the general direction of Foch, the *bouillant
Achille* of French strategy, whose thoughts, gestures, speech,
and vivid pantomime ran wholly on the offensive. Pétain did
all that was required of him, although his more passive predi-

lections appeared in careful papers on defensive organisation, cross-fire, strong-points in villages, and camouflage. The trenches in his sector grew deeper, as wire started to proliferate in front of them; and while communication-trenches crept towards them from the rear, there were even traces of a second line. General Pétain, it was plain, had settled into his positions and was unlikely to be leaving them for some time. But the French command was not yet reconciled to this uneventful form of war; and just after Christmas they attacked again. In front of Pétain the Germans held their ground, and the mid-winter mud of Artois checked a French advance. After the first day the General went to headquarters and insisted that the attack must be broken off. For Pétain was quite unsentimental. He had already evacuated French villages whose occupation seemed to call for an excessive price in human lives; and he preferred to admit failure at the outset rather than to risk more casualties. Was he a pessimist? A lucid vision of the obstacles confronting him often sobered his decisions; and such sobriety was badly needed by the French command in 1914. Other men of more heroic moods had failed. The first month of war had shattered French illusions; and blasted reputations lay as thick as fallen leaves that autumn. But Pétain's had steadily advanced. A brigadier in August, he was a corps commander by October. It was swift promotion in eleven weeks; and three months of war had quite made up for the slow progress of his early years. For the General was barely fifty-nine; and that, by French standards, was comparatively young.

2

The shock had been severe. In the first movement of the war France was decisively defeated at Morhange, the Semoy, and Charleroi, although an anxious public was not permitted to know very much until long afterwards (and the names are still comparatively unfamiliar). But they could hardly fail to notice that the French armies were in full retreat or that the Germans were within forty miles of Paris. It was evident that something had gone very wrong, that events on the frontier entirely stultified French military ideas, and their plan of campaign had completely failed. The President's post-bag began to fill with voices of dark foreboding, as large numbers of priests and women importuned him to dedicate his country to the Sacré Cœur. Some of them were touching in their sincerity; but there were others who impressed M. Poincaré as being more political in the sources of their inspiration, which had moved the writers to "represent our reverses as God's just punishment of the Republic." Such letters, although outnumbered by his other correspondents of a manlier tone, continued to arrive at the Élysée; and the President began to wonder whether national unity, embodied with such care that month in M. Viviani's all-party administration, was to be endangered. Were there really Frenchmen who would bow the head beneath calamity in an unhappy mysticism of defeat? In this uncomfortable mood the Government left Paris for the south; and while pietists exhaled their melancholy resignation and the high command (where Colonel Gamelin was serving his apprenticeship) exuded a fatuous optimism, they crowded into their provincial quarters at Bordeaux. More than once in recent history French self-control has failed before the sumptuous cuisine of Languedoc; and on the very day that Joffre's weary men were gathering for a decisive spring at the advancing Germans on the Marne somebody complained to the President that this was hardly the time for ministers to show themselves with charming guests in Bordeaux restaurants. (The comfortable grotto of the *Chapon Fin*, where the tragedians of 1940 subsequently sought refreshment, appears to have an irresistible attraction at moments of national calamity.) True, the Minister of the Interior, who had omitted to arrest Laval and subsequently showed a misplaced tenderness for disloyal friends of M. Caillaux, explained with some embarrassment that, if he had been seen one Sunday in an official automobile with large quantities of flowers, his health had lately been far from satisfactory, entailing a short visit to the seaside, and that the floral tributes were entirely due to the enthusiasm of his local supporters.

But this time Bordeaux was not permitted to decide the fate of France. A stouter generation held the reins. For Maginot was still a sergeant; Gamelin was running errands at headquarters for old Joffre; Weygand, a dapper colonel of Hussars, had just been attached to General Foch; and Laval was lying low. The sky was dark; but Poincaré watched the horizon; Clemenceau was there to find fault with everyone; and Joffre with the lantern-jawed Galliéni, achieving an unlikely victory between them on the Marne, brought France safely into 1915.

The war had not been lost. But with the Germans firmly lodged in a long line across a dozen French departments that slanted from the Swiss frontier to the Belgian coast it was far from won. A gloomy bishop in Algeria still preached that France was paying for her sins and had deserved the war. But his mood was not infectious, since the Republic was admirably served by generals of deep religious faith; and its adversaries had not yet brought themselves to prefer their country's enemies to its form of government. For Charles Maurras, who purveyed extreme ideas to the Right, assured the President that year: "*Mon point de vue est d'opposant, mais d'opposant national avant tout. Mon seul désir étant de servir le mieux possible . . .*" In 1915 the Opposition of the Third Republic still had a conscience; and as it was a French conscience, the world was spared the unpleasing spectacle of later years, in which some Frenchmen were found prepared to buy a party triumph with a national defeat. But that was still a quarter of a century away. Treason was not yet regarded as an elevated form of public duty. Life was simpler in 1915, when men reasoned that France was in danger and that the first task confronting every Frenchman was to deal faithfully with the invader.

Pétain's problem with his XXXIII Corps was to see what could be done in Artois. Fresh offensives were in the air; and his cautious temper called loudly for an overwhelming mass of munitions. Where other corps commanders asked for 5,000 grenades, Pétain demanded 50,000; and the General was often seen on lonely walks, head down, as he attempted to find an answer to the riddle of the war in 1915. A lifetime of theory (one derisive general had asked him at an awkward moment before Guise, "Well, *Monsieur le Professeur à l'École de Guerre*, what do you think of this movement?"), followed by four months of highly disconcerting practice, had left him with a great deal to think about; and he liked time for thought. Not that the solitary walker was always silent. For he had a caustic tongue, which had been freely used upon his pupils; and sometimes it ran away with him. He might not have Lanrezac's scholastic trick of wearing pince-nez draped over one ear. But schoolmasters are often privileged to use strong language before audiences that cannot answer back; and Pétain's gift of irony was occasionally unrestrained. It was even whispered that the President of the Republic, who was developing a tendency to pay visits to the front in a striking costume of his own invention, consisting of an Inverness cape, knickerbockers, and a yachting-cap, was slightly disconcerted to be informed, in reply to a polite enquiry as to General Pétain's view of the situation, that nobody was better placed than the President himself to be aware that France was neither led nor governed. This was not how the Chief Executive was normally addressed by generals.

"*Vous plaisantez, mon général*," returned that ruffled dignitary.

"*Mais pas du tout*," said the big man in the blue uniform. If that was the nature of their first encounter, Poincaré was not unfavourably impressed, as his diary records the meeting with a tribute to Pétain's intelligence and lucidity. His portrait of the General was almost flattering—"tall, well built, and smartly turned out, he explained his dispositions with luminous simplicity, but was severely free from all illusions." His views, as might have been expected, were rather adverse to the offensive favoured by the more dashing d'Urbal. For d'Urbal was a cavalryman, while Pétain was a foot-soldier in process of developing a gunner's outlook.

But corps commanders could not be choosers; and on May 9 his carefully prepared attack was launched in the direction of Souchez. The whole thing had been meticulously organised. They said he had laid every gun himself; and he had certainly gone round all his batteries to watch each piece register on its appointed target. The assaulting infantry had been nursed with care, since Pétain was lavish with leave in Amiens and had even introduced the innovation of theatrical performances not far from the front line. Groomed to a hair, the XXXIII Corps broke through the German line, capturing 3,000 prisoners, six guns, and twenty-five machine-guns and advancing at least two miles. Judged by the scale and pace of operations in the trench-warfare of 1915, this was sensational. Indeed, the pace of their attack outran the possibility of reinforcing them; and the decisive moment passed. For the nearest French reserves were more than seven miles away. One unkind critic at headquarters hinted that Pétain had been too far behind his troops to exploit his own success; and the high command was eager for a further thrust. As Foch ingeminated energetic counsels and Joffre even ordered up the cavalry for the long-awaited charge that was to take them right back to the frontier, Pétain was rewarded with a step in the Legion of Honour and incited to go forward once again. But he was modestly convinced that his remaining duty was to hold the ground which he had gained, until the troops on either side came up with him. The days went by; the

French attack began to slacken; and as it died away in June, Pétain's success at Vimy remained its brightest spot. For his initial achievement had shown what could be done with careful preparation; and the skilled practitioner was rewarded by promotion to command the Second Army in Champagne, leaving his old corps to Fayolle.

The President was still impressed with his "calm, power, and lucidity," noting deep reserves of feeling somewhere underneath that frigid exterior. It was just a year since he had been responsible for a single brigade; and now he was in command of thirteen divisions. What was he to do with them? His own preference at this stage was for a sparing use of men, since Pétain had now arrived at a conviction that the appointed instrument of victory was attrition and that the war would be won by the side which could bring up the last reserves. If that were so, French man-power would have to be conserved. But the high command thought otherwise, proposing to win the war by an irresistible attack in 1915 and bringing Pétain to Champagne as the ablest practitioner of the offensive. But though his preparation was more methodical than ever, the results were disappointing. Once he postponed the attack in order to prepare still further; but when it was launched in the last week of September after a bombardment of three days, the gains were meagre in proportion to the vast expenditure of life and ammunition; and Pétain, never guilty of undue optimism, broke it off before his superiors authorised him. A large bag of 25,000 German prisoners was no compensation for the heavy casualties and a growing sense that the invader could not be successfully ejected by assault. The great attack had failed; and Pétain was quick to draw the moral, prescribing a war of attrition, to be conducted by a succession of strictly limited offensives and depending for its eventual success on guns rather than on rifles. For he had come to see the war in terms of artillery. There were, in his sober view, no short cuts to victory; and early in 1916 he was

in control of four army corps for training in the new forms
of war imposed by modern weapons in the light of seventeen painful and instructive months. But one dark February
morning a 14-inch shell burst in the Bishop's Palace, as the
German guns opened on Verdun.

3

The defence of Verdun, which a world held its breath to
watch in the first half of 1916, was not quite what it seemed.
Before the war, when the frontier was guarded by the defensive system created by General Séré de Rivière, Verdun
had been a first-class fortress. Just opposite to Metz, it barred
the road across the Meuse which a German invasion might
naturally be expected to follow; and the great circle of its
forts, which broke the sky-line of the bare slopes on both
sides of the river, was the country's first line of defence.
France seemed to depend for her continued safety on the guns
of Verdun and the rest of her imposing line of fixed defences,
which ran through Toul and Épinal to Belfort. But when
French strategy abandoned the defensive and 'Plan XVII'
replaced the fortress barrier with advancing lines of flesh and
blood, the strong places of the Eastern frontier were relegated
to a secondary role; and when the German plan, with an
admission of their formidable character, elected to omit them
from the zone of active operations and to attack through Belgium, the significance of Verdun was almost gone. The war
was now a duel fought from two confronting lines of trenches
along a continuous front from the North Sea to Switzerland,
in which the great fortress on the Meuse hardly signified.
True, the front passed a few miles to the north of it before
turning south towards the Swiss frontier. But there was no
reason to suppose that the forts of Verdun would be called
upon to play a part in active operations. Forts, indeed, were
in discredit since the swift collapse of the forts at Liège before

the heavy Skoda howitzers brought against them in 1914. European governments had poured millions in the past half-century into these enormous masses of steel and concrete with their heavy guns in revolving cupolas; but if Brialmont's masterpiece of fortification had only lasted for twelve days in Belgium, it might be doubted how much longer Séré de Rivière's creations would be able to hold out in France. For modern war appeared to have passed into a new phase, in which forts were largely meaningless and the last word was now a line of muddy trenches. Yielding to this feeling in 1915, the French high command dismantled all its forts and removed the guns, which were transferred to the field-armies; and it resulted that, when Verdun was attacked in the next year, it was no longer a fortress.

As the march of progress is noticeably circular, it was discovered at a later stage that the forts would have been extremely useful after all. (A corresponding impulse had led war-correspondents in 1914 to deride the helmets of French Dragoons as a picturesque survival of the Middle Ages and subsequently moved all belligerents to equip their troops with steel helmets; and the wheel came full-circle, as spectators, who had been officially regaled at the Military Tournament in London a few weeks before the war with the quaint spectacle of soldiers throwing hand-grenades in the old-fashioned uniforms appropriate to this historic exercise, learned that the grenade had just been rediscovered to be a vital part of modern infantry equipment.) But when the Germans launched their great attack on Verdun, a ring of empty forts surmounted the bare hillsides above the little town. Its real defences lay further off, where the trench-line made a great angle on the north and east of Verdun; and the place itself was no more a fortress than the Bishop's Palace, which received the first shell of the bombardment and had been a museum for some years, was a sacred edifice.

It is not easy to say why the Germans chose this relatively

unimportant point on the long front for their offensive. It was arguable that in French hands it was a menace to their railway communications with Germany and to the iron district of Lorraine; but the argument is unconvincing in view of the existing lines of railway, which would always enable them to bring up more reserves against a French attack from Verdun than the French could possibly put in. If it was not much use to the French, what results did a victory at Verdun promise the Germans? It was von Falkenhayn's idea; and his explanation was that an attack on a historic fortress would infallibly draw French reserves to its defence in such quantities that French man-power would be irreparably weakened by the effort to retain Verdun. German estimates of French psychology are often sound. Bismarck had not misjudged the effect of the Ems telegram on French opinion in 1870. When Verdun was threatened, they acted largely as Falkenhayn had predicted; and Germans read the mind of France in 1940 more accurately than her allies. Indeed, the outcome largely justified Falkenhayn's conception. For French casualties at Verdun between February and June, 1916, outnumbered those of the enemy by three to two, amounting to 460,000 men against a German total of 278,000. If the French succeeded in holding Verdun, they lost something far more irreplaceable upon the naked slopes above a town of no particular significance; and to this extent the German move succeeded.

But that, in Pétain's view, was not the whole of Falkenhayn's objective. It seems unlikely that Verdun was selected in the hope of a mere break-through, since a success of this character would have had far greater effect at some point nearer Paris, which was 140 miles away. Pétain's opinion, in the narrative which he published in 1929 (with a graceful tribute to the "soldierly sincerity" of the Crown Prince and a curt dismissal of Britain's war-effort in 1916 with a sour reference to the postponement of conscription and practically none at all to her war-industries), was that Falkenhayn was after bigger game. For if the attack on Verdun succeeded in drawing large French forces into a German trap on the Meuse, it might be Sedan over again a little higher up that fatal river. This, in Pétain's belief, was the full German purpose, though all that the world could see was a blind onslaught on Verdun.

It opened in the last week of February with an intense bombardment, which put two million shells into a narrow area north of the town; and in the winter dusk waves of German infantry climbed out of their trenches and stormed the battered French positions. In the first three days they bit deeply into the French line, and on the fourth General de Langle de Cary ordered an extensive withdrawal north and east of Verdun. That day (it was February 24) Castelnau, Joffre's second-in-command, was on his way to Verdun, and Pétain was ordered to report at Chantilly, whilst his staff was sent east in the direction of the threatened fortress. On the next morning he saw Joffre, who told him that he would be in charge of Verdun, adding in his comfortable way, "Well, my friend, now you are easy in your mind." There have been more reassuring situations than the Verdun command on February 25, 1916. But if Pétain had been worrying about the German progress or his own future, he knew now precisely where he was. It had been Castelnau's idea to send Pétain to Verdun. But it did not come as a complete surprise, since that methodical commander had already sent the head of his own Intelligence to find out what was going on there.

He started off that morning and spent a chilly day of motoring halfway across France on freezing roads. It was dark, when he reached headquarters at Souilly behind Verdun; and as there was some doubt as to exactly what had happened in the last few hours, he pushed on to find out. The news he met at Dugny was highly disagreeable, since the German tide was still running strongly and had passed the empty fort of

Douaumont that day. A little before midnight he was back at Souilly, where Castelnau confirmed him in command of the Second Army with orders to "stop the enemy's attack north of Verdun"; and a few minutes later he was telephoning to his corps commanders from an empty room in the dark Hôtel de Ville. That night his chief of staff arrived and pasted up a large map, on which Pétain chalked the line that was to be held. Then he dictated orders to his new command; and General Pétain's first night at Verdun was over.

In the next few days he gripped the situation firmly, creating a hard core of resistance round Verdun and re-establishing the forts "as the chief bulwarks of the system of defence." Pétain was deeply impressed with the high military value of steel and concrete, which his predecessors had cheerfully discarded; and that lesson stayed with him for life. For the infantryman was quite the gunner now; and his invariable opening at their daily conference was, "What have your batteries been doing? We will discuss other points later." What Pétain wanted was "bursts of concentrated fire which really constituted independent operations, carefully prepared beforehand, and which, without causing us any losses, inflicted loss on the enemy." That was his system. But how was their ammunition to be brought up, and how were 436,600 men and 136,000 animals to be supplied with every road to Verdun under German fire except one local tramway and the road from Bar-le-Duc? Here was a problem (which a sudden thaw did nothing to improve) admirably suited for solution by his methodical approach; and presently the slender track of the *Petit Meusien* was carrying traffic far beyond the wildest dreams of its designers, whilst he organised civil and military labour gangs to quarry road-metal from local quarries for the maintenance and enlargement of the vital highway, and a system of motor convoys passed over it with reinforcements and supplies, and improvised plants made new tyres for the groaning lorries. An endless line of *camions*, four to the minute, toiled up the road to Verdun; and in eight days between February 27 and March 6 the threatened place received 25,000 tons of freight and 190,000 men. All this traffic passed along the 'Sacred Way,' which Pétain had created; and it was more than a sentimental monument to those who passed up it to the sacrifice, since his application of the mechanics of modern transport to a military problem had saved Verdun.

The threat was fainter now, although his gentle pessimism hardly permitted him to share the confidence about the future which was growing general in March. Joffre seemed almost too hopeful with his proud announcement that the defenders "will be among those of whom it shall be said: 'They held the gate of Verdun against the Germans' "; and when the President of the Republic paid him a visit, Pétain felt that M. Poincaré was a little disappointed with his defensive mood. The General had a bad cold that day; and Poincaré recorded the tempered optimism of his feeling that Verdun could be held, although they might have to yield more ground. Indeed, a few days later it appeared at the Élysée that Pétain was a shade too passive, though Colonel Repington, who visited him in the last week of March, was much attracted by the quiet bearing of the tall soldier with the big moustache. He diagnosed "a soldier before all, and one with strong will and decide opinions," and was much edified at lunch by his host's exposition of his faith that "artillery now conquers a position and the infantry occupies it. So he had gone all out for the guns." Pétain was inordinately civil to an influential military critic, congratulating Repington upon his writings and acknowledging the official use which he had made of a recent article. His claws were sheathed that day, although "he was very critical of Lord K."; and he was anxious to impress his guest from London that the battle for Verdun was not yet over.

The long struggle swayed round the naked uplands of Mort-Homme; and in April German pressure rose to a crescendo, eliciting from Pétain his first public hint of victory in an order of the day that ended on the unfamiliar and rousing note of "*Courage . . . on les aura!*" The battered line still held, and the French high command was eager to recover some of the lost ground. The well-timed retirement of de Langle created a vacancy in the august command of an Army Group; and Joffre, a little chilled by Pétain's persistent caution, seized the opportunity to elevate his unadventurous subordinate. For the General was still frankly pessimistic about the prospects of an Allied offensive; and if there had to be one, he preferred to leave it to the English on the Somme. Now it was May; and Pétain had exchanged immediate responsibility for Verdun (which passed to General Nivelle) for a more general supervision as commander of the Central Army Group, writing almost ruefully to Painlevé that he regarded this promotion as a dismissal. But, dismissed or not, public opinion insisted on regarding him as the saviour of Verdun, although Nivelle had now replaced him, uttering the splendid negation, "*Ils ne passeront pas.*" Pétain was still opposed to any energetic counter-offensive. But he had withstood the German onslaught; and his figure lived in the nation's memory as a tall, white-faced man standing on the steps outside his headquarters at Souilly to watch an endless line of men go up the 'Sacred Way' to Verdun.

Back at Bar-le-Duc, he was in control of fifty-two divisions, of which twenty-four were always in front of Verdun. His outlook was not cheerful, as he wrote in May that "we are wearing ourselves out slowly and surely; so are the Germans; but as they have more reserves they will come out on top unless the Allies intervene." An unsuccessful push for Douaumont by Mangin hardly raised his spirits; and in June he telegraphed headquarters that he could not hold Verdun with the troops under his command, unless the British advanced the date of their offensive. (He was almost complimentary about the British now, sending polite messages to

Repington about the possibility of combined Franco-British
divisions and telling somebody that if he had only had a
British division, he could have held the Bois d'Avocourt.)
Joffre was complaining bitterly that "Pétain had scared everyone again" and did his best to stiffen his discouraged subordinate, recording one conversation which "made me afraid that
Pétain had let the enemy impress him once again." For the
imperturbable old soldier at Chantilly, who had lived
through darker days in 1914, was losing patience with his
nervous colleague. A loss of ground in front of Verdun
plunged him into gloom at midsummer, though Poincaré
found him confident and highly critical of Joffre. But when
the Commander-in-chief visited him in July at his new headquarters, Joffre was "impressed with his pessimism, and
shortly afterwards there was further evidence of this frame
of mind."

There was always something low-toned about Pétain's outlook; and perhaps his experiences at Verdun were not calculated to enliven him. For he had watched seventy-eight
divisions pass up the 'Sacred Way' and through the grinding
mill of sacrifice. As the strain relaxed in the later months of
1916 with enormous British casualties on the Somme and
a consequent decline of German interest in Verdun, his mood
grew easier and he was even reconciled to a resumption of the
offensive. Forts Douaumont and Vaux were brilliantly recovered by Mangin and Nivelle under his superior command; but
though the latter carried off the laurels of a swift attack,
Pétain remained the hero of the long defence.

4

As France looked towards 1917, the man of promise (he
was just turned sixty) paused in his swift ascent. Brigade,
division, corps in 1914, Army in 1915, Army Group in 1916—
Pétain's progress had been rapid and uninterrupted; and a still

higher vista opened in the last weeks of the year, as the search began for something more adventurous than the static qualities of Joffre in supreme command. The possibilities were limited; and they were reduced still further by the strange prejudices of French politics. For a shrewd British ambassador reported to Sir Douglas Haig that "Foch is objected to because he has a Jesuit brother, Pétain because he was brought up by the Dominicans, and Castelnau still more because he goes to Mass." The taboos of the Chamber of Deputies were awkward and, so far as Pétain was concerned, unjust. True, he had been educated by the Dominicans at Arcueil. But the depth of the impression left upon their pupil is open to some doubt, since he confessed to Repington at Bar-le-Duc in April, 1917, that his unpopularity with politicians could hardly be on spiritual grounds. "No," said General Pétain, "I am certainly a Catholic and respect my faith, but I am not *pratiquant*, and have not been to Mass for thirty years." (He was at some pains to cultivate the good opinion of the influential Englishman; and his religious fervour, like his enthusiasm for the family, would appear to be a plant of somewhat later growth.) But he was a lively talker, inclining to be blasphemous about the high command. For somebody had asked him whether he agreed with the three essential qualities of a successful French general:

"*Avoir du cran;*
"*Avoir du courage à prendre des risques illimités,*
"*Avoir une confiance aveugle dans le G.Q.G.*"

"*Oui,*" answered Pétain wickedly, "*je suis d'accord. Mais je mettrai la dernière clause entre les deux autres par peur qu'elle n'échappe.*"

His unguarded tongue had even gone so far as to cast doubts upon the supreme wisdom of French politicians, as he was reported to have said that Joffre's successor would be well-advised not only to claim control of all French reserves, but also to demand that Parliament should be prorogued until the war was over. He was careful to explain to Repington that it was a joke. But politicians could not be expected to see jokes of this character, although they might be acceptable to the military correspondent of *The Times*. French Deputies were always on the watch for unconstitutional leanings on the part of generals. Boulanger's career had been a warning; the Dreyfus case had revealed a military caste that seemed to be prepared to govern France by the unaided wisdom of the General Staff; and it could hardly be forgotten that Pétain had served harmoniously under General Zurlinden, a staunch anti-Dreyfusard. He may have been joking in 1917; but the jest was quite enough to startle politicians who were looking for an eligible Commander-in-chief, since it would be just as well to find one in whom military talents were combined with a belief in the institutions of the Third Republic. Besides, his subsequent career appears to indicate that in suggesting the elimination of a legislature General Pétain was saying exactly what he meant.

His respect for politicians was not increased by a feeling that his *boutade* had, as he told Repington, "established a blue funk of me in Parliament." But there were other reasons for preferring a more enterprising successor to Joffre for the campaign of 1917. Pétain's slightly pessimistic mood had already attracted notice; the President was finding him a trifle negative; and French strategy appeared to call for something livelier than a general who still favoured a continuance of the defensive. Opinion had been much impressed by the dash and effectiveness of General Nivelle's recovery of Douaumont; and that feeling was not confined to excitable civilians, since Mangin's order of the day proclaimed unqualified faith in this new star in the military firmament with its hopeful affirmation: "*Nous tenons la méthode et nous avons le Chef. C'est la certitude du succès.*" Besides, the favoured candidate was a Protestant; and the Reformed religion held no terrors for the Third Republic. He even had an English mother and was believed to speak the language of his allies, although this was a minor point. If the war was to be won by a great offensive in 1917, Nivelle appeared to be the man to do it; and his appointment was universally acclaimed, while Joffre faded into retirement with a Marshal's *bâton* and the memory of Gamelin's embarrassed plea not to "be too hard on those with a career to make," who had deserted their old chief.

But as the date approached, the symphony was marred by other notes. The war was now in its third year; and Frenchmen had begun to feel the strain. They were not superhuman; and when the shocks of 1914 were followed by the dragging disappointments of the next two years, the strain began to tell. France was not entirely populated by heroic figures ingeminating '*Courage, on les aura*' and '*Ils ne passeront pas*' or by indomitable *poilus* in shell-holes with their gay '*Pourvu que les civils tiennent.*' Even the army was not unshaken by its experiences. They had few illusions left; leave had been irregular; and although they had money to spend, there was not much on which to spend it except wine. Discipline began to suffer; and there were disturbing indications that subversive literature was circulating widely among the troops. Nivelle demanded strong action against pacifist activities and more production from French labour in establishments engaged on national work. For strange figures were abroad. The bald head of M. Joseph Caillaux gleamed in the most unlikely places; an equivocal pasha named Bolo frequented German agents in Switzerland; Socialist zealots fortified their faith in world-revolution by trips to Lenin; odd characters produced still odder newspapers, whose readers filled their regimental officers with anxiety or impeded the war-effort by an outbreak of strikes; and this carnival of enlightenment proceeded without much interference from M. Malvy, who was still Minister of the Interior. Laval, who was getting on and would be moving to a house of some pretensions in the Avenue du Bois de Boulogne that year (the careful Auvergnat secured a highly favourable lease by reason of the risk of air-raids and eventually bought it cheap), moved in the inner circles of revolutionary Socialism, paid the bill when Trotsky took coffee with a few of his colleagues, and made rousing speeches to his working-class constituents in which the President of the Republic was unpatriotically termed *"Poincaré-la-guerre."*

The war, it seemed, was not to Laval's liking; and in the early months of 1917 a good many Frenchmen agreed with him. As the date of Nivelle's offensive drew nearer, confidence in its success began to waver. There was a change of government; a new Minister of War began to hear the most disturbing things about the prospects of the spring campaign; and the enemy transformed the war-map by their spontaneous withdrawal to the Hindenburg Line. Nivelle's subordinates gave free expression to their misgivings, and Pétain was invited by the Minister of War to meet the new Premier at dinner. The former, an able mathematician named Painlevé, was greatly attracted by the General's systematic approach to military problems. But M. Ribot, the Prime Minister, was an old Radical; and a politician had once been warned by Sarrail that General Pétain *"n'est pas des notres."* Although he found the General "extremely intelligent, more intelligent than Nivelle," he was not entirely captivated, as Pétain's tongue was too sharp and his *"esprit critique"* was not wholly reassuring. This private interview was followed by a formal meeting of the high command, at which the President of the Republic found Pétain *"de tous le moins optimiste."* His view was lucidly expressed:

"Are we strong enough for an offensive against the enemy's first line?—Yes.

"Are we strong enough to press the operation further?—No."

This could hardly be misunderstood; and the unhappy Nivelle, whose authority was gravely impaired by such deliberations, promptly resigned. But his resignation was not accepted; Pétain urged the lamentable consequences of a change in the command at this moment; lunch was served; and a hasty unanimity confirmed the forthcoming offensive.

When it was launched in April, preceded by the British thrust at Vimy Ridge, it was a brilliant failure which advanced less than two miles, took 21,000 prisoners and 183 guns, and lost 100,000 men. This was hardly calculated to reassure an anxious nation; and as the French tide beat vainly against the Chemin des Dames, the star of General Nivelle was setting. Attack had plainly failed; and the next thing to do was to call in the high-priest of defence. On April 29 Pétain was offered and refused the post of Commander-in-chief. But though he declined to command the armies in the field, he consented to become Chief of the General Staff at the Ministry of War; and for a fortnight he presided over an unhappy whirl of disputing generals. Colonel Repington, who saw him at this stage, found him "as calm and inscrutable as ever." Nivelle, who was still titular *generalissimo*, was present and plainly dominated by his colleague—"it was like pupil and master." But when their conversation left the war, Pétain (who was just sixty-one) gave an exposition of his views on marriage. He was still, he said, a bachelor. But he was fond of children; and when the war was over, he felt that he would have to choose between suicide and marriage. As for the children, his notion would be to adopt some of about five or six. The war, it seemed, was quickening (in theory, at least) his feeling for the family.

But when Nivelle left them, graver matters were discussed; and Pétain cross-examined his English visitor about the British generals and ministers with whom he might be called upon to work, if he succeeded Nivelle in supreme command. A warning from Repington that he was regarded in some quarters as a pacifist excited him to an indignant lecture on his warrecord; and he expounded his faith in limited offensives. He was highly complimentary about British troops (this was not quite the language he had lately used, when he shocked Henry Wilson by arguing that three German divisions of nine battalions were equal to four French or British of thirteen) and expressed a hope "that the British people appreciated him and would soon learn to know him better," ensuring Colonel Repington's continued advocacy by a further tribute to his journalism. The dose gave satisfactory results, as shortly afterwards his visitor "cabled to London a warm eulogy of Pétain which duly appeared in *The Times*, and I wrote to Lloyd George, Sir W(illiam) R(obertson), and Geoffrey Robinson to counteract the anti-Pétain cabal." But the unbelievers were not yet wholly converted, Henry Wilson continuing to argue that Pétain's programme was "squat, do little and have small losses . . . and that 'squat' was fatal." Haig, however, found him "most clear headed and easy to discuss things with," as well as "businesslike, knowledgeable and brief of speech." The recalcitrant, it seemed, was Robertson, whom Pétain disarmed at the next inter-Allied conference by a blunt statement that he knew the stories current about him, followed by a recital of his war-record and terminating with a sharp enquiry "whether any one else had undertaken more resolute attacks, and whether he deserved the sneers of being called a pacifist."

It cannot have been easy for a man of his reserve to plead with foreigners. But he told Repington that "he had, in effect, found that the British had a *prévention* against him," which he did his best to dissipate. He was plainly to succeed Nivelle, and Allied harmony was indispensable. But the incalculable British were still something of an obstacle, since even after he had captivated their soldiers, the War Cabinet seemed to hold out against him. For there was talk of a telegram from London opposing his appointment. Colonel Repington heard something of it in Paris; and it was known to the French, since Painlevé, recounting his campaign in favour of Pétain's promotion to supreme command, "spoke with some warmth of the 'horrible despatch' which our War Cabinet had sent on this subject." If that were so, the incident was hardly calculated to deepen Pétain's affection for the British.

He was still pessimistic about French man-power. Indeed, his pessimism ranged still further, since the day after his appointment as Commander-in-chief of the French armies, with Foch as Chief of the General Staff, he startled Henry Wilson by announcing that "if Russia ran out then we might have to make peace." It was plain that the new generalissimo would not err on the side of overconfidence. But grounds for confidence were not unduly prominent in May, 1917. For the spring offensive was a failure; on the eastern front Russia was subsiding into revolution; and the French army had begun to mutiny.

Few episodes in history are more obscure than the French mutinies of 1917. Indeed, fuller knowledge might have spared the world some of its surprise at the French collapse in 1940, for which 1917 was in many ways a dress-rehearsal. But at the time wise strategy dictated a complete suppression of the fact that the French army was so demoralised as to be incapable of active operations; the fact itself was concealed from the British Cabinet, although Pétain disclosed it in the strictest confidence to Haig; and French patriotism has excusably shown little tendency to revive the unhappy story.

The facts were lamentably simple. The explosive elements already present in the early months of 1917 were detonated by the failure of Nivelle's offensive with some assistance from the news of the Russian revolution. It started in the last days of April, when a battalion refused to go back to the trenches. Order was restored; but the infection spread, and there was a rapid increase of desertion and insubordination. The modest figure of 509 deserters in 1914 rose in 1917 to 21,174; and large numbers of men, who stayed with the colours, indulged in noisy demonstrations of their refusal to attack the enemy. Leaflets appeared ingeminating '*À bas la guerre*' and the more dangerous incitement, '*Mort aux responsables*'; officers were stoned; there was a growing tendency to sing the *Internationale*; and leave-trains left a broad wake of disloyalty behind them. A mob of soldiers marched through a town with loud imitations of a flock of sheep to signify their destination for the slaughter-house; and the premonitory symptoms of disintegration appeared on every side. The Russian army had already liquefied into a grey surge of public meetings; and the French army seemed to be going the same way. More than a hundred units were affected; less than half the divisions in the French army were uncontaminated; the disorder ranged as far behind the line as Bordeaux and Nantes; and at one moment there were believed to be no more than two sound divisions between Soissons and Paris. Two battalions, indeed, proposed to march on Paris in order to demand "Peace and the Russian Revolution."

This was the army over which Pétain was now summoned to preside; and as he frequently foresaw the worst, he was well qualified to deal with it. Though Henry Wilson was still calling him "a pacifist general," his suppression of pacifist literature was ruthless and complete. Laval, who went so far as to inform the Chamber that "a wind of peace is sweeping through the country," invoked the healing powers of a forthcoming gathering of international Socialists at Stockholm. But as their points of view were not yet harmonised in 1917, Pétain insisted sternly that no Frenchman should be permitted to attend. He was still pressing ministers to deal more firmly with pacifist propaganda; and he applied himself unsparingly to healing the sick army. A stern decree enabled him to confirm all death-sentences without recourse to the President. But he was sparing of the rod; and there were less than sixty executions in all. He was careful to keep undesirables away from Paris and even sought to influence the press in order to secure sound reading for his patients.

But he was the best agent of his own propaganda. All through that anxious summer, while the British bore the burden of the war in Flanders, his car drove up and down the front and a big man looked the troops squarely in the eye. He met audiences of all ranks and, abstaining from heroics, told them their duty and where the fault appeared to lie. The level voice informed them without artifice; and when he had finished, there were often tears. But he did not deal exclusively in blame, since he was lavish with decorations; regimental colours received fresh honours; and this judicious blend of reward and punishment restored the nervous balance of the shaken army. Leave was better organised; modest comforts were provided at railway stations; food was improved; wine was restricted; savings were encouraged; and even sport received his blessing. For his object was to cure a case of nerves. Was he not '*le médecin de l'armée*'? Presently the convalescents were equal to a minor operation at La Malmaison (it was October now), in which they inflicted 40,000 casualties, capturing nearly 12,000 prisoners and 200 German guns, at a cost of 14,000 killed and wounded. Their trouble, it appeared, was yielding to Pétain's treatment, and the French army was on the road to recovery. But his own outlook was profoundly affected by the experience. For when Pétain reached the summit of a French soldier's career, he commanded a defeated army.

5

It was unlikely that the new Commander-in-chief of the French armies would be particularly enterprising in 1917 or, for that matter, in 1918 either. Two facts, apart from the French mutinies, created a new situation. For the United States had come into the war; and Soviet Russia, in whom enthusiasm for a Second Front was still unborn, went out.

This meant that the Germans would shortly be at liberty to concentrate their whole weight on the front which Pétain shared with Haig. At the moment 177 Allied divisions faced 155 German divisions from the North Sea to Switzerland; but the balance would be gravely altered by the arrival of 50 German divisions from the eastern front. In these disturbing circumstances Pétain's predilection for a defensive attitude was powerfully reinforced; and the burden of his song became, '*Il faut attendre les Américains.*'

This was no surprise, as his collaborators had long known what to expect from Pétain. When he met Lloyd George that spring, he challenged the Prime Minister almost jocosely, saying "I suppose you think I can't fight."

"No, General," was the reply, "with your record I could not make that mistake, but I am certain that for some reason or other you won't fight."

The Prime Minister's impression was of "an able man and a good soldier . . . careful and cautious to the confines of timidity." There was no denying his achievement in averting the worst consequences of the mutinies with a deft alternation of strong sedatives and mild stimulants administered by "a head nurse in a home for cases of shell-shock." But the time might come when something more was called for; and how far could they expect it from Pétain?

More professional observers were favourably impressed, Repington savouring the big maps upon his wall and his "acute, pungent, and penetrating remarks," though General Maurice was inclined to grumble that he never took privates by the ear and called them '*mon enfant*' in the Napoleonic fashion favoured by old Joffre and relished by French soldiers. But he liked Pétain; and so did Haig, who said he was "a splendid fellow." Sir Douglas found it an immense relief to do business with a foreigner so admirably free from foreign eloquence. Frenchmen, as he once remarked, were funny fellows. But he could see that Pétain was not quite so funny as the rest, finding him "straightforward and clear in his views, and most businesslike." They got on extremely well; and, as the Scotsman told Poincaré that summer, *"Nous ne parlons ensemble ni français ni anglais; nous parlons militaire, et nous nous entendons."*

Pétain's own countrymen were sometimes less appreciative of these Anglo-Saxon virtues, which they found a trifle chilling. But Clemenceau told someone that he was the right man for this phase of the war; and that summer the battered Citadel of Verdun saw him decorated with the Grand Cross of the Legion of Honour. He went about his business methodically, nursing the convalescent army and defining its new programme from his room at Compiègne. It was laid down in lucid terms that they were not to attempt anything in the nature of a break-through; and he told the President that there were neither men, guns, nor planes enough for a French offensive. (More sensible than Haig of the new factor of air-power, he announced that year that "aviation dominates war," a highly creditable statement for any general in 1917.) His main idea was to get the British to occupy a longer front, and though they were not always as amenable as he could wish, he got on a good deal better with Haig than with the less manageable Pershing. For Pétain's difficulties with the American command were just beginning. He had a teacher's outlook; his own army was sent back to school that year in training-camps, where the new principles of his sometimes derided *'bouquin rouge'* were patiently absorbed; and when he encountered a reluctant pupil from America, he was sometimes overcome by a schoolmaster's impatience.

Mr. Lloyd George, profoundly sceptical about costly and prolonged offensives in the Flanders mud, was a ready convert to his point of view; and Pétain reciprocated by a liberal outlook on Allied operations in Italy. When his method seemed to yield satisfactory results from strictly limited attacks, the British Cabinet enquired politely (and without undue regard for its own soldiers' feelings) for General Pétain's recipe for winning battles without losses, and was candidly informed that his successes had been rendered possible by the magnitude of British efforts elsewhere (Pétain was more gracious now) and that his purpose had not been to fight, but to organise his army. His guiding principle was that "the American contribution is not likely to carry much weight in the battle before 1919, and until that date the Franco-British troops must be handled with such prudence as to leave the slightest possible role to be played by chance." Pétain had never favoured taking chances; and though Foch chafed at the restraint, his hand lay heavy on French strategy. For there was general acceptance of his view that no action should be initiated by the Allies that might have the effect of rendering 1918 a year of destiny.

While Pétain nursed the last army of France, the country turned to its last minister. For the wastage among French politicians in the Palais Bourbon had been no less severe than among French effectives at Verdun; and that autumn, all imaginable permutations of public figures having exhausted the contrasting charms of every other combination, France passed into the strong hands of Georges Clemenceau. Deep in the jungle of French politics, this formidable septuagenarian had stalked his quarry for a generation. His claws had mauled every administration of the last thirty years except his own; and his passion for his country was only equalled by his distaste for practically all its public men. In his fierce simplicity he was not unlike a character from Victor Hugo; in his principles he was undeniably the last of the Jacobins; and in his ability to animate a fainting nation he showed that democracy, unlike dictatorship, can rally from defeat. Forty years before his vote had been cast against the surrender of Alsace-Lorraine; and the lost provinces were always in his mind. His single aim was now to win the war; and he believed in victory because, as he said afterwards, there had to be a victory. Ruling without noticeable colleagues, he dragged his country out of the uncertainties of 1917. French defeatism was grasped with an ungentle hand. Malvy and Caillaux were arrested; Bolo was shot; and as the *poilus* met their new Prime Minister, the front line learned to know a muddy figure with a large moustache, fierce eyebrows, and a battered hat.

An exacting master, he was not dissatisfied with Pétain, who was more manageable than Foch and less clerical in his affiliations. He judged the General to be *"le meilleur de nos chefs, quoique avec des partis pris de complaisance et de camaraderie, des idées quelquefois un peu fausses, quelquefois de fâcheuses paroles de pessimisme et de découragement."* This was in November, 1917, when such limitations did not greatly matter. With the war in an inactive phase Pétain's pessimism could not do much harm; and Clemenceau was quite prepared to accept his defensive strategy, although he soon began to find him *"trop négatif, trop timide."* An interminable argument proceeded about the constitution of an Anglo-French reserve to take the strain of the next German thrust; and in spite of differences about the length of front entrusted to the British, Haig seemed to find Pétain's opinions more congenial than those of his own Prime Minister. Both soldiers agreed that they got on so well together that no further co-ordination by a supreme commander was necessary; and the Allied reserve with its uncomfortable hint of an Allied generalissimo, who might be neither Haig nor Pétain, was not permitted to materialise. Early in 1918 there was a feeling that the British line had been stretched a little further than was altogether safe. Officers began to tell Clemenceau that Pétain's views erred on the defensive side: and he struck the President as being much too gloomy about the prospects of the next campaign. For he had been saying that if it lasted more than a month, his man-power would be exhausted, although he told somebody a few days later that if they only had gas, there might be a chance of holding on. But German troop-trains had been rolling westwards across Europe; the collapse of Russia had set free 1,000,000 men and 3,000 guns; and in the darkness before a March dawn the barrage shut down on the British lines, as Mr. Churchill watched the flaming line of German batteries and returned reluctantly to Whitehall, leaving behind him the crash and glare of Ludendorff's supreme offensive.

6

The March offensive of 1918, by which the Germans came within measurable distance of winning the war a few months before a March dawn the barrage shut down on the British supreme commander. Shattering General Gough's Fifth Army, it tore a great rent in the British line and threatened to reach Amiens and separate the French from their allies. If they were parted, if Haig's army was herded north towards the Channel ports while Pétain withdrew southwards to cover Paris, Ludendorff could deal with them in detail and the war would be over in a few weeks. On the third day of the attack, when the British had already lost 100,000 men and 500 guns, the French commander saw Haig at his headquarters and "seems most anxious to do all he can to support me and agrees that the only principle which should guide us in our movements is to keep the two armies in touch." But Pétain's respect for this principle was somewhat theoretical, since his reply to Haig's request for the concentration of strong French reserves in the neighbourhood of Amiens was a statement that, whilst he was anxious to do all he could in Haig's support, he was expecting an attack upon his own positions in Champagne. This was not encouraging, though Pétain seemed to be clear that they must keep together at all costs and suggested that Haig should even uncover the Channel ports in order to do so. But encouragement was never Pétain's forte. That morning he had warned Clemenceau and Poincaré that things were "not merely serious, but grave."

The next day was Sunday, and Haig "attended the Church of Scotland at 9.30 a.m. The Rev. Mr. Black of Edinburgh preached an excellent sermon, indicating why we can and should rely on the gospel of Christ to guide us in the present and future." But when the calm Scot saw Pétain late that night (it was March 24), he found the French commander "very much upset, almost unbalanced and most anxious." He seemed to have a notion that the British meant to fall back to the sea, leaving him to cover Paris; and he had been telling Clemenceau that, if he was beaten, it would be their allies' fault. Haig's explanation of what he really meant to do could hardly fail to dissipate this false impression. But when Haig pressed him once again for strong French reinforcements round Amiens, he replied that although the British army was unfortunately situated, he was still expecting to be attacked in Champagne and did not believe that the main German blow had yet fallen. He added that such French reserves as were concentrating at Montdidier had been ordered to fall back on Beauvais and to cover Paris in the event of further German progress. That withdrawal would leave the British flank uncovered and separate the Allied armies; and Pétain's intention was quite unconcealed in the orders in which it was defined with his accustomed lucidity:

> "Before everything to keep the French Armies together as one solid whole; in particular, not to allow the G.A.R. (*Groupe d'armées de réserve*) to be cut off from the rest of our forces. Secondly, if it is possible, to maintain liaison with the British forces."

The order of his preference was ominous; and it was plain that Franco-British military unity was no longer his guiding principle. He made no mystery of his intentions, handing Haig a copy of the order. Haig asked him bluntly "if he meant to abandon my right flank." Pétain nodded, adding, "It is the only thing possible, if the enemy compel the Allies to fall back still further." Now Haig knew precisely where he was, with an army in retreat and an ally whose primary concern appeared to be to cover Paris, whilst acquiescing in a military situation that would isolate the British and leave them to be driven back on Boulogne and Calais—and Dunkirk.

Haig's revulsion was immediate. This was what had come of his honeymoon with Pétain. But the days of speaking *"militaire"* together were over now; and after midnight he was telegraphing London for the Chief of the Imperial General Staff and the Secretary of State for War "to come to France at once in order to arrange that General Foch or some other determined general, who would fight, should be given supreme control of the operations in France." For Pétain was a broken reed. Clemenceau was complaining loudly to the President of his exaggerated pessimism and scoffed at his perpetual apprehensions of an attack in Champagne. The British had completely lost faith in him. Lord Milner, who had come over from the War Office, was urging Clemenceau that under no circumstances must Pétain be appointed to supreme command; there was to be an Allied conference on these grave topics; and on March 26 carloads of exalted personages were bowling down the road to Doullens in the spring sunshine. German shells were dropping not far off; and as they waited for the British to make up their minds inside the Mairie, the French leaders walked up and down the little garden. Clemenceau was cracking jokes, but broke off to tell Poincaré regretfully that Pétain had ordered a retreat towards the south, leaving the British to fall back towards the sea alone. Foch confirmed this depressing news and expressed strong disapproval, delivering a spirited harangue to a little audience of four civilians. Clemenceau was visibly impressed by this exposition of a more courageous strategy and took the President aside.

"Pétain," he said, "is intolerable with his pessimism. Would you believe it, he said something to me which I would not tell any other living being. This is what he said: 'The Germans are going to defeat the English in the field, and then they are going to defeat us.' Should a general talk or even think like that?"

Foch was still haranguing them upon his programme of fighting in front of Amiens, in Amiens, and behind Amiens. Then they went into the conference, where Pétain favoured them with his customary exposition of the worst, adding a genial comparison of Gough's Fifth Army to the Italians after Caporetto. Since issuing his fatal order he had moved his headquarters from Compiègne to Chantilly, nearer to Paris and further from the German threat to Amiens. He gave the observant Milner "an impression of coldness and circumspection, like a man playing for safety"; but to Haig "Pétain had a terrible look. He had the appearance of a commander who has lost his nerve." As the discussion opened, Henry Wilson "fell out with Pétain for contemplating a retreat." Then Milner made a sign to Clemenceau, and Haig joined them behind Poincaré's chair. Milner spoke without enthusiasm of Pétain, under whom he was not disposed to place the British forces. But he felt that something might be done with Foch. (A few minutes earlier Haig had greeted an outburst by Foch against retreat by saying, "If General Foch will consent to give me his advice, I will gladly follow it.") Haig's view was that the main thing was to put someone in control of Pétain; and they all agreed to appoint Foch, who was explaining to the President in lively pantomime the way to stop the Germans, as co-ordinator of the operations of the Allied armies on the western front.

That decision gave Pétain a superior; and they spoke freely of his defects now, Joffre telling someone that he had "shown the same faults as when he wanted to abandon Verdun" and Clemenceau informing Haig that he was "a very nervous man." The old Prime Minister was scathing when he reported to his colleagues, telling them that "Pétain, who always looks on the worst side of things with some reason, but sometimes overlooks the good side rather too much, had been giving extraordinary orders. He foresaw the worst and contemplated withdrawals, of which it was dangerous to show the troops a possibility." That night a minister complained to Poincaré that Pétain was a defeatist and had said to him a few days earlier that it was time to negotiate for peace. But happily for France there were stronger wills than Pétain's in March, 1918. Joffre said that he lacked character; and Haig's impression was that "at times his nerve seems to have gone—and he imagines that he is to be attacked in force." But now his plans were scrutinised with care; and when Clemenceau wished to fortify Foch's position, a new conference was held to strengthen the Allied command. The Prime Minister's idea was "principally to allow Foch to coerce Pétain"; and Foch explained that he required "the power of creating action. For this reason the text of the Doullens arrangement was insufficient, and should be made to include 'power for the infusion of an idea of action'." Mr. Lloyd George and the Americans warmly supported him; and Foch emerged from the Beauvais conference on April 3 with "the strategic direction of military operations." Pétain made some difficulty about signing the document, until Clemenceau formally requested him to do so. It was not surprising, since by its terms he receded one stage further from responsible command of the French armies. For it was undeniable that in the testing days of 1918 Pétain had been tried and found wanting; and as the British had been the first to find him wanting, he was unlikely to remember them with gratitude.

7

As the war went on, its mounting symphony marched to a firmer beat than Pétain's; and in the closing months Foch held the *bâton*, while Pétain performed as a mere instrumentalist. True, his instrument was still the French army on the western front. But his performances upon it were confined to the execution of someone else's compositions; and if they were often hardly to his taste, the most that he could do was to play a little behind the beat. Foch was satisfied with his subordinate, reporting to the President that "in the second rank, as an executant, Pétain is perfect, but that he shrinks from responsibility and is unfit to be Commander-in-chief." His language was still pessimistic. But that did not greatly matter now, as Allied operations took their tone from Foch; and Pétain's opinions were a distinctly secondary consideration. His abdication was appreciated, the President observing, "*C'est un beau caractère.*" This was reported to Pétain, who was quite grateful for the intimation of Poincaré's good opinion. Haig was so far melted as to contemplate the possibility of Anthoine or Pétain as Foch's successor in case of accidents; and Clemenceau defended him from critics, telling the President that Pétain was the complement of Foch and including him in a vindication of the high command before a nervous Chamber, which heard the old man praise "*des chefs, de bons chefs, de grands chefs*" and fling into the face of the advancing Germans his challenging "*Je me bats devant Paris, je me bats dans Paris, je me bats derrière Paris.*"

That tone came from the barricades and from the indomitable Foch. But Pétain never caught it. At the end of May a gleam of patriotic eloquence inspired his order of the day, "*Debout, les héros de la Marne!*" But on the same day Clemenceau found him "very gloomy" and contemplating the evacuation of Paris; and the Prime Minister, admitting that he had his faults and was better in the second place than in the first, insisted that "*le plus défensif de nos chefs*" was perfect where he was. Foch's feeling was that he needed support and encouragement; and Weygand, who ran Foch's errands, had been sent to administer the necessary stimulant. It was a strange position for a Commander-in-chief; and the removal of his valued Anthoine, because Foch could not get on with him, was a blow to Pétain. But he continued to do his duty; and after midsummer, when Foch was made a Marshal, he was awarded the *Médaille militaire*. Pétain was positively cheerful; tea, cakes, and sandwiches were served after the ceremony; and the President found him "radiant, extremely confident," and even indulging in a touch of his old sarcasm about Pershing, whom Foch was finding no easier to get on with. He was still apt to question the sufficiency of his resources. But his genius for defence, which had been displayed that summer in Champagne, was less needed now, as the Allied armies edged forward in the last offensive.

Colonel Repington saw him again that autumn in his headquarters at Provins. They were fourteen at lunch; and Pétain was on his highest horse—"Freezing formality as usual. Pétain inspires terror except among a few of his old hands. He reminds me of the average Royal Personage, who is one person in company and another when alone. The penalty of grandeur I suppose . . . As usual no one addressed Pétain unless he first addressed them, and only one person spoke at a time." But Repington managed to say the right thing at lunch by praising Gouraud's success in Champagne, which had all been Pétain's doing; though someone else, who tried to lure their host into an indiscretion about Foch, had no success. For after the old story about a doctor who apologised to his patient after an operation for forgetting to put back his brain, receiving the reply that it did not matter, as he was a general, a daring guest enquired, "What about a Marshal?" "He," said their alarming host, "is an omnipotent being above criticism"; and the subject dropped in a royal silence. For his tongue was more guarded now; and his own equivocal position was shrouded in impenetrable dignity.

But after lunch he was eloquent upon his loyalty to Foch (although his appreciation did not extend to Weygand) and fairly complimentary about the Americans, urging his British visitor to do his best for him with Pershing. Repington judged him to be innocent of the arts of publicity, because the only photograph that he could find of Pétain showed him scowling at the camera; but he had quite failed to notice Pétain's artful courtship of himself. The French commander was still soberly anticipating a campaign of 1919. But events were too swift for him; and in October he was discussing the terms of a victorious armistice, stipulating for the immediate withdrawal of the Germans to their own country without a gun or a tank, the surrender of 5,000 locomotives and 100,000 trucks, and the occupation of a zone east of the Rhine. At one Allied meeting Haig heard Pétain talking "of taking a huge indemnity from Germany, so large that she will never be able to pay it. Meantime, French troops will hold the left bank of the Rhine as a pledge." He was not there to savour the splendid drama of Foch's railway-carriage at Retondes, when four drooping Germans capitulated to a French marshal and a British admiral just after five o'clock on a November morning. But on the day French bugles sounded down the road to Metz for the first time since Bazaine's had died away Pétain was in command. He told the President of the Republic afterwards that their reception in the new quarters of the city had been a little chilly; but the old town, where the Lorrainers lived, had cheered them wildly, until he passed into the shadow of the great cathedral, whose despairing bell had tolled for the surrender forty-seven years before, to hear a *Te Deum*. The cold man had been moved by the experience. That week Foch slipped into Metz with the faithful Weygand and, dodging the official cars, strolled round the snowy streets smoking his pipe to find his first tobacconist's and to see the pedestals of unlovely German monuments summarily deprived of their Teutonic heroes.

One Sunday morning in December the President's train drew into Metz with Clemenceau and the attendant Mandel, Lord Derby, the United States ambassador, and a galaxy of civil dignitaries. They had left Paris overnight; and by morn-

PETAIN IN GOOD COMPANY.

The Marshal gets his baton before Marshals Joffre and Foch, Field-Marshal
Haig, and Generals Pershing and Weygand, Metz, December, 1918.

(Imperial War Museum photo)

ing the Moselle was sliding past the carriage windows. Beyond Ars, where angry villagers had stoned Bazaine, they crossed the river, as the line turned east for Metz, leaving behind them a bare upland where the road from Gravelotte drove towards Rezonville and Marsla-Tour. History was in reverse that day. For the great German railway-station echoed to the *Marseillaise;* small girls in short Lorraine petticoats presented bouquets; and Foch led the way to Kaiser Wilhelm's waiting-room. Then they drove out into the town, Poincaré bare-headed and Clemenceau with his hat almost straight, side by side in an open carriage full of flowers. More flowers arrived at intervals, as small Lorrainers climbed all over them demanding to be kissed; and when they reached the Esplanade, Pétain was waiting for them with a guard of honour where Bazaine's tents had stood. The stands were bright with tricolours and full of cheering people; and presently the tall man in the light-blue uniform was listening to Poincaré's official eulogy in front of Haig, Pershing, Weygand, Foch, and Joffre in his old dark tunic. Then the smiling President handed him a Marshal's *bâton;* and as Marshal Pétain grasped it in a gloved hand on the Esplanade of Metz, the unhappy ghost of the Army of the Rhine was laid.

CHAPTER IX

VICHY

O drapeau de Wagram! ô pays de Voltaire!
Puissance, liberté, vieil honneur militaire,
Principes, droits, pensées, ils font en ce moment
De toute cette gloire un vaste abaissement.

Les Châtiments.

I

THE war was over; and this time France was indubitably
on the winning side. But the mood of 1919 was disinclined to speculate as to how or by whom it had been won. As
it had been fought in France and largely by French soldiers,
French logic concluded that it was a French victory. True,
there had been Allies. But Foch had shown them all the way;
and if there had been anxious moments, the vicissitudes and
failures were all forgotten now. For a great pile of broken
German guns stood in the shadow of the Arc de Triomphe,
guarded by French mounted sentries and crowned by the
exultant fighting-cock of the Third Republic.

They were in triumphal mood. It was not too triumphal
for them to deny themselves the pleasures of politics and to
reject Clemenceau, when they elected a new President a few
months later. But every French soldier shared the glory. Foch
was pre-eminent. There had been no mention of Pétain in the
Chamber's tribute to the two saviours of their country. But it
was not long before Lloyd George was telling somebody that
Clemenceau was waiting for a chance to get rid of Foch and

to replace him with Pétain. The old man had always found him less troublesome than Foch, though Pétain was disinclined to lend himself to the manœuvre. For the Commander-in-chief occupied his pedestal at Chantilly with careful dignity, keeping clear of Paris, taking part in no public festivities, and asking no Deputies to dine except official guests. This caution kept his name out of the papers and preserved his status. He was busy with the narrative of French operations in the war and the regulations of the post-war army. For if Foch stood for their past achievement, Pétain (at sixty-three) appeared to represent the future of the French army.

This was recognised by his selection as Vice-President of the *Conseil supérieur de la Guerre;* and when M. Maginot added his appointment to be Inspector-General of the Army, the old teacher was installed as headmaster. He had no thought of retirement. For the war had not disagreed with him; and a country doctor, who examined him soon afterwards at a health-resort in Savoy, pronounced a highly reassuring verdict.

"*Tout cela,*" said the physician, "*est parfait. On voit bien que vous n'avez pas fait la guerre. Quel nom?*"

"*Maréchal Pétain.*"

This vigorous old gentleman, who rode at half-past six each morning, proceeded to assert his youth by appearing in the unexpected role of bridegroom. For one afternoon in 1920 readers of the evening papers were intrigued to learn that "Marshal Pétain has become engaged to Mme. Hardon. The ceremony, which will be very quiet, will take place shortly in Paris." Indeed, it was so quiet that it had already taken place, *The Times* recording it with rare discretion:

"Very quietly—almost secretly—Marshal Pétain was married yesterday to Madame Hardon. The greatest care had been taken to keep the ceremony private, and the public was reading a

discreetly worded announcement of 'the forthcoming marriage' in the evening papers yesterday, some hours after the
marriage had taken place. The Marshal's witness was his old
comrade in arms, General Fayolle.

"The marriage is said to be the happy ending of a very old
romance, as Marshal Pétain's friendship with his wife dates back
to the days before her first marriage."

If the romance was very old, so was the bridegroom, who
was sixty-four; and Paris was not told whether the bride's
first marriage had been dissolved by death or by divorce. But
he had always said that he would have to marry or to commit
suicide; and the last alternative was now happily averted.

The next thing was to find a home; and one was ready-
made. The little house outside St. Omer, in which he had
once contemplated spending his retirement, was quite forgotten now. That might suit a colonel of the Line. But it would
never do for a Marshal; and he was already the owner of a
small property between Antibes and Cagnes. The coast was
charming; and in clear weather there was an admirable view
of Bazaine's island prison from the point beyond Antibes.

He was hard at work in his Paris office on the post-war
problems of the French army, for which Marshal Pétain remained officially responsible until he was turned seventy-five.
Youth is rarely served in the French high command; and the
price of victory is often paid in the next generation by those
communities which leave their veterans in charge. Wellington had endowed his countrymen with an army capable of
winning Waterloo (should the necessity recur), which remained equal to doing so for the next forty years and failed
wretchedly in the Crimea, because it was no longer 1815.
For time does not stand still in military matters; and when
Marshal Pétain provided France with a complete solution of
the military problems of 1918, it proved quite irrelevant in
1940, because defeated nations are less sentimental and the
Germans, while venerating Hindenburg as a patriotic effigy,

had left von Seeckt and a younger generation of soldiers and airmen to remake the German army.

Pétain's work was conscientious; and he left his office to inspect the army of occupation on the Rhine and in the Ruhr, toured North Africa, and followed the manœuvres of 1929 and 1930. He was progressive about aviation, although he resisted the creation of an independent Air Ministry. But their major problem was the defence of the new Eastern frontier. For it began to dawn on them in 1921 that Germany would not be disarmed forever; and when the question was raised, Pétain favoured a solution fully sanctioned by the past, advocating the construction of a solid line of continuous defences on the model of the Hindenburg Line. He always said that he had no imagination. But he had an excellent memory; and if the Germans attacked them once again, this seemed the way to go on with the war from the point at which they had left off in 1918. Military opinion was not unanimous, since other soldiers preferred a defensive system less obviously modelled on the Great Wall of China. But there was no urgency about it in 1922, and a commission was appointed. Meanwhile, a grave deterioration in the national finances rendered the cost of public works on such a scale prohibitive; and for a time the whole question was left in abeyance.

At this stage events in Africa called the Marshal to a new field of endeavour. Abd-el-Krim, ex-Cadi of Melilla, had enjoyed a European training, some acquaintance with the Germans, and familiarity with the arts of war and government as practised in the Spanish Zone of Morocco. He observed with particular interest a war-time insurrection engineered by a grandson of Abd-el-Kader and, returning to his native Riff, raised the hill-country against the Spaniards. When a large Spanish army commanded by a dashing general attempted the simple operation of traversing the Riff, it was impressively defeated with the loss of ten or twelve thousand lives, all its artillery, and large quantities of small-arms; and Silvestre's reverse at Anual shared the ill-omened notoriety of Baratieri's at Adowa. The annihilation of an army in the field (which might have been expected to impair public faith in the intelligence of generals) led, by a somewhat unexpected sequence, to the elevation of General Primo de Rivera to supreme authority in Spain. For the Spanish mind occasionally works by contraries. A native rising, in which the aborigines were well supplied with machine-guns and field telephones, was an unpleasant novelty; and Abd-el-Krim was shortly in control of the whole mountain system lying between the Spanish and French Zones. But the new Abd-el-Kader's ambitions extended still further, threatening important points in French Morocco. This was more serious; and Marshal Lyautey began to call for reinforcements. The solution appeared to be a joint Franco-Spanish operation against Abd-el-Krim on a considerable scale; and in 1925 Pétain was put in charge. He flew from Toulouse to Rabat with General Georges, surveyed the situation on the spot, and returned by way of Tetuan, where he conferred with Primo de Rivera. Strong reinforcements began to appear; and Lyautey's feelings seemed unhurt by this intervention of another soldier in the field which he had made his own for so long. But when Pétain reappeared to take command (after an enthusiastic meeting *en route* with the Spanish dictator at Algeciras), things did not go so well. It was galling for Lyautey to be superseded in his own viceroyalty by a novice in colonial affairs; and shortly afterwards the great administrator of Morocco resigned. On the day that he parted from weeping multitudes on the waterfront of Casablanca Pétain was too busy at the front to see him off. But if he failed to get on with Lyautey, he was on the best of terms with Primo de Rivera.

The joint operation proceeded smoothly; and before the end of 1925 the Marshal was free to return to France. Early in the new year he made a stately progress to Madrid, where he was received with warm attentions by the dictator and his royal master. It was his first experience (at seventy) of the great world outside France; and what he saw was most instructive, since he was able to observe a military man in supreme control of Spain. Pétain was banqueted and decorated in the intervals of outlining the course of future operations in the Riff, which ended before midsummer with the surrender of Abd-el-Krim. Eighty years before his predecessor had surrendered to Bazaine; and when the new Abd-el-Kader gave himself up, the witnesses were no less ominous. For though Lieutenant-Colonel Giraud was on duty, his brigadier that day was Colonel Corap.

Pétain's good relations with the Spaniards persisted; and in the next year he was the leading delegate at a Franco-Spanish conference in Paris, followed by a state visit of Primo de Rivera. The two soldiers stood side by side at the Arc de Triomphe, as Giraud took his native infantry past at the salute; and Pétain remained a name to conjure with in Spanish military circles. But he had graver things to think about in 1927. For the problem of the Eastern frontier was drifting steadily towards solution. A commission had reported in favour of elaborate concrete constructions; and that summer the Marshal toured the frontier, studying the ground in detail. A lifelong faith in fire-power inclined him to believe in the inevitable prevalence of fixed defences over anything that could be brought against them; and he had been deeply impressed with the solidity of the old forts at Verdun, to which he published a reasoned tribute in 1929. Others might prefer defence in depth or a system of defended areas, each sufficiently extensive to contain its own aerodromes. Indeed, the last solution was urged on him by a young subordinate named de Gaulle; and the old man admitted to him that it was the best. But the General Staff preferred the Engineers' proposal; and Pétain at seventy-three lacked energy and inclination to resist. Besides, the war of 1918 had been fought on a continuous front; and what was there to show that the next war

was going to be any different? Early in 1930 M. Maginot induced the Chamber to vote the necessary money; and General
Belhague became the latter-day Séré de Rivière of a new
Eastern frontier. But every plan was passed by Marshal
Pétain; he corrected details of construction in the light of his
own knowledge of the ground; and when a grateful country
named this masterpiece of the defensive art after M. Maginot,
it should in justice have borne Pétain's name.

The Maginot Line was the old man's legacy to France; and
if it was a shade behind times, this was scarcely to be
wondered at, since he was seventy-four. The thick crust of
his experience in the last war was penetrated with some difficulty by new ideas. Indeed, one of his collaborators had said
of Pétain that he "died in 1925"; and his contribution to the
emergency of 1940 was a full equipment for the military
situation of 1918.

As the hillsides of Lorraine were drilled and tunnelled
into new shapes, his term of office as Inspector-General of the
Army was drawing to a close; and in 1931 he resigned the
succession to General Weygand, the veteran of seventy-four
being relieved by a mere lad of sixty-four. For more than a
century the French have shown a marked preference for
generals (and leading ladies) of advanced years. It was four
generations since the flaming youth of the First Republic
and Empire had raced to victory across a continent behind the
Emperor of forty and his young captains; and the same
loyalty, which had kept them faithful through uncounted
years to Sarah Bernhardt and Cécile Sorel, still ensured their
unquestioning devotion to the oldest generals that France
could find. The last whisper of 1918 had not died away with
Pétain, since there was still Weygand, the faithful Weygand,
who always knew where Foch could find his papers, interpreted his aphorisms into practicable terms, and was believed
to have made a useful contribution when the Bolshevik

advance on Warsaw came to a standstill; and this dapper little figure came on guard, as Pétain passed into retirement.

A trusted servant of the Third Republic, the Marshal had worked comfortably under a long line of ministers. The old faces changed, as Poincaré and Briand gave way to Herriot and Daladier; and strange figures began to reappear in public life, when Caillaux was readmitted to office and returned to Paris on Laval's arm. For times were changing, and the suspects of 1917 were now their country's guides. Laval was sliding imperceptibly towards the Right; his clientèle was more financial now; he reached the Senate; and in 1931, when Pétain ceased to be head of the French army, his Prime Minister was Pierre Laval. The Marshal served them all impartially; and, so far as anyone could see, he had no fault to find with the Third Republic.

2

Relieved at seventy-four from his duties as Inspector-General of the Army, the Marshal showed no tendency to seek repose. For he was promptly reappointed Inspector-General of Air Defence, a new post which moved his office and his staff a little higher up the street and left him with immense, if slightly undefined, responsibilities. He had always taken an enlightened view of the air arm; and a few months later he was reporting to Laval on the necessity for centralising the high command of the land and air forces in view of the new fact that war was now three-dimensional. Laval responded by appointing Pétain to co-ordinate air, army, navy, and civil defence; and in the latter part of 1931 his aptitude for facing the worst found congenial employment in a series of provincial conferences, at which he enlightened local authorities on the unpleasant realities of air warfare. At the same time he pressed for the formation of a single Ministry of Defence. But the wheel of politics revolved once more, removing Laval; and when their first collaboration ended, the Marshal's allegiance was transferred to a new Prime Minister.

There was a tendency to overlook him now; and as the fighting services resumed their former independence, Pétain looked back almost wistfully to the days when he had been appreciated by Laval and practically employed as chief of staff to an unborn Ministry of Defence. They had visited the United States together in the fall of 1931. The team appeared to be harmonious; and it was not without significance that Pétain and Laval had discovered once another. After Laval's departure in the next year the Marshal was still full of ideas on the reorganisation of the high command in order to accommodate the air arm, favouring Weygand with his opinions. But nobody paid much attention, until his old friend Painlevé returned to office under M. Herriot, when Pétain found himself appointed to a new Council of Defence. The burden of his song was now the need for a single generalissimo with power over all three services. But he was careful to explain that this would have to be someone else; and when Pierre Cot urged him to accept the post in 1933, the Marshal answered that he was too old. His influence was still exercised in the direction of a unified command; he was writing prefaces to books upon air warfare on the 'total' lines announced by the Italian General Douhet; and M. Daladier had the benefit of his advice, as the roulette of politics spun merrily and eager amateurs enjoyed the carnival of mud-throwing that followed the prosecution and death of a shady character named Stavisky. This speculator seemed to have secured some measure of protection in official circles; and though the range of his political affiliations was infinitely smaller than those uncovered in the case of Panama, the hunt for them appeared to promise good sport to such critics of the Third Republic as preferred to think the worst of public men. Presently muck-raking was followed by disorder in the Paris streets, which added a few touches to their long tradition from the new technique of rioting in special party costumes inaugurated by the latest practitioners in Italy and Germany. The tumult rose to a crescendo in February, 1934. Shots were fired in the Place de la Concorde, as a processional attack upon the Chamber clashed with the police; M. Daladier resigned; and a new ministry was formed to save society under an ex-President of the Republic.

M. Doumergue approached the Marshal and was told that the best thing would be to make him Minister of State with authority over the three fighting services. But when he made a lower bid, offering the Ministry of War alone, Pétain accepted after some pressure from Weygand. His sole condition was that there should be no further reductions of the army; and the new minister austerely informed the press that he had joined the government because he had been told that the nation needed him, adding that he had never indulged in politics and that he did not propose to do so now.

For nine months longer, from February to November, 1934, the Marshal was responsible for the French army as Minister of War. The situation was alarming, as the Germans were rearming fast; and the disparity of numbers between the rival armies would be gravely accentuated by the smaller yield of French recruits born in the lean years of the last war. But whilst he was in office, Pétain made no move to repair this deficiency by the unpopular measure of reintroducing a longer term of military service, although he subsequently advocated it from the security of private life. He had always liked to face the worst; but whilst he was in office, political discretion was too strong for him. His cautious mood preferred a succession of half-measures; and numerical inferiority remained the lot of the French army. Nor did the Marshal evince the slightest sympathy with the opinions published that year by his young collaborator, de Gaulle, who seemed to think that tanks had restored mobility to modern warfare; and when Pétain left the Ministry of War, French equipment was much as he had found it nine months earlier. His administration was uneventful. He kept a careful eye on school-teachers with subversive views and a brisk handshake for provincial commanders, who were asked to stay to lunch. He was learning to be tactful with politicians (including M. Caillaux), and the Chamber heard him in a respectful silence. But he was more at ease in the Senate, although he never cared for meetings of the Cabinet. It struck him as a waste of time to seek unanimity about the right thing to do. For his favourite reading—Vauban, Bossuet, La Bruyère, La Rochefoucauld—all came from the age of Louis XIV; and the Grand Siècle had rarely troubled with a search for unanimity. Neither, for that matter, had his friend General Primo de Rivera in Spain, although the latter's gallant effort to stabilise his country had now been overtaken by a republic.

But his official life was not passed entirely at his desk in the Rue St. Dominique, where General Gamelin came every afternoon and General Weygand called once a week. Sometimes he visited the works in progress on the frontier; and sometimes he favoured provincial audiences with the platitudes appropriate to Service gatherings or the inauguration of war memorials, alluding enviously to the discipline prevailing in adjacent countries. When he spoke of education, he emphasised the need for inculcating martial virtues. Once, indeed, in a tribute to Lyautey he pronounced a strange excommunication of intelligence: "France has greater need of toil and conscience and self-denial than of ideas. Men are too often divided by ideas, whilst they are united by endeavour." The silent harmony of drilled communities was plainly calling to Pétain in 1934; and when the King of Jugoslavia was murdered at Marseilles that year, the Marshal went to Belgrade for the funeral and enjoyed two hours' conversation with a stout young man, who made a deep impression on him. For Hermann Goering, who had burnt the Reichstag a few months before, held similar opinions upon the undesirability of too many ideas; and his aged interlocutor was already taking to the Germans. They had the martial virtues; they were most respectful; and when they came to Paris, they always made a point of calling on the hero of Verdun.

He was beginning to have views outside the narrow circle of his own official business; and while they were reconstructing the administration on the death of his old friend Barthou (which brought Laval to the Quai d'Orsay as his successor), the Marshal insisted sternly on the elimination of a colleague suspected of undue tenderness for Stavisky's associates. But his new instinct for politics had few opportunities under M. Doumergue, whose government shortly disappeared; and as the Marshal declined to serve under M. Flandin, he reverted to private life.

3

A little late in life the veteran was reaching the most interesting stage of his political development. He was not far off eighty, when the world began to hear of his opinions for the first time. But though they had not been unduly prominent hitherto, there was a strong consistency about them. When the Dreyfus case divided France upon a simple choice between uniformed authority and the Rights (as they were termed) of Man, Captain Pétain's sympathy with General Zurlinden had aligned him with the anti-Dreyfusards. Their doctrine tended to exalt discipline above free institutions; and this tendency recurred in General Pétain, when he shocked the President of the Republic early in the war by informing him that France was neither led nor governed. A similar opinion underlay his daring observation that a Commander-in-chief would be well advised to prorogue Parliament for the duration of the war; and there was no reason to suppose that Marshal Pétain had changed his attitude. Indeed, there was a good deal in the world of 1934 to strengthen it. For a tide was running against liberty, as the Nineteenth Century had understood it. Fascism in Italy, Nazism in Germany, and the military experiment of his friend, Primo de Rivera in Spain had all proceeded on a blunt denial of the principles embodied in the Third Republic; and its critics, upon whom kaleidoscopic Parliamentary politics had begun to pall, turned eagerly towards the simpler discipline of these more up-to-date communities. True, Spain had relapsed into a semblance of democracy. But Germany and Italy were an inspiring spectacle for disciplinarians. An old soldier might be excused for preferring the parade-ground to the public meeting as a form of government; and it was not surprising that a Marshal of seventy-eight found his sympathies inclining further and further to the Right. He knew more than most men about the disintegration of the French army in the mutinies of 1917; and he was professionally bound to favour any move in the direction of national discipline.

These views had informed his utterances as Minister of War, which dwelt upon the duty of the citizen to serve the state and tended to exalt the peasant virtues. A war memorial at Verdun even heard from him a mild French version of the *Führerprinzip*, which aligned every German behind his Leader:

> "A Frenchman does not fight without his leaders. He wants them with him. At every moment of the fight he looks to them, he judges them, he awaits their order, their example, their support . . ."

This was not quite the full, deep-chested note of latter-day autocracy. But it was something; and the agreeable confusion of French politics in 1935 was diversified by a pamphlet entitled (with a variation on the old theme of General Boulanger), "*C'est Pétain qu'il nous faut.*" This contained an outline of something authoritarian by which the Third Republic might be replaced, although the author was careful to point out that "in peace-time it is not possible to upset a regime by a *coup d'état*, unless that regime is acquiescent and has no supporting elements in the armed forces, in the civil service or among the population. Only in war-time and especially in a moment of defeat, when every citizen is armed, can the operation succeed." Would they find the requisite support in time of peace? That seemed possible, since extremists of the Right were already creating a *Comité Social d'Action Révolutionnaire* and the vague, hooded figures of the *Cagoulards*, who combined high principles with underground activities in a French Ku Klux Klan, whispered that they could count upon a Marshal. Or would they have to wait until there was a war? And if it came, were they quite sure that there would be a moment of defeat?

The Marshal, who was generally careful to keep his name out of the papers, even intervened in the election of 1936, when France went to the polls to choose between the solid Left and the assorted voices of the Right, where the apprehensions of big business mingled with the shrill Fascist utterance of Colonel de la Rocque's *Croix de Feu*. The Marshal issued an appeal for "National Reconciliation," which an English journalist found "full of *Croix de Feu* terminology." But nobody paid much attention; the *Croix de Feu* fell flatter than usual; and in spite of Pétain's unsolicited advice France preferred the Popular Front with M. Léon Blum. This was not encouraging; and while the French proceeded to solve their problems in their own way, Marshal Pétain subsided once again. A mood of mild despair seemed to possess him; and in the next year he was telling somebody that he had never thought that France could fall so low—"Mind you, I do not think that she is finished. But how much effort will be needed to restore her? That is what many people are asking; but if the *many* were *all*, salvation would be simple." But France in 1937 was not totalitarian.

His interests, apart from war and politics, were limited. He had been a member of the *Institut* since 1919; but his sole contribution was a discourse (in secret session) on the mutinies

of 1917. When he joined the Academy in 1931, his distinguished pallor and light-blue uniform were much admired,
and he contributed a somewhat guarded eulogy of Foch.
Occasionally seen at literary gatherings, he had friends who
could read and write—and even draw, since he was intimate
with Forain, a sturdy anti-Dreyfusard, who shared his poor
opinion of contemporary politicians. But he limited his own
output to grave pronouncements in the *Revue des Deux
Mondes* on army matters and national education. Now he had
been seeing a little more of the world outside his country.
There were tours to French Africa and Switzerland; a royal
wedding took him to Italy; a military funeral took him there
a second time; and when Pilsudski died, he went to Cracow.
The respectful Goering was in Poland, too. Laval, Prime
Minister again, returning from his visit to Moscow to sign
the Franco-Soviet Pact, was there as well; and when the
watchful politician saw how Goering saluted Pétain, he could
see the Marshal's value. Pétain and Goering returned to Germany together. The strange pair went for a long walk in
Berlin; and their conversation cannot have been difficult, as
Pétain told a journalist that year that European peace was
impracticable until they brought Germany into the peace
system, and he made a warm public reference in the next year
to Franco-German reconciliation. (Laval's agile mind was
leaping in the same direction; but by that time his preliminary
effort at a deal with Italy had succumbed to British prejudices.) Pétain's travels had even ranged as far as the United
States in 1931, when he spent a crowded fortnight in official
celebrations of the 150th anniversary of Yorktown. Follow-
ing in Boulanger's footsteps, he surveyed the scene of Franco-
American victory over British arms, visited Annapolis and
West Point, paid homage at Mount Vernon, and gratified
innumerable banquets with his dignified impersonation of
French military glory. It was an immense success; and M.
Laval, who was there at the same time, found him a pictur-

esque adjunct to his talks with Mr. Hoover on the more mundane subject of war debts. The discerning President told Borah of his "appreciation of Laval's frankness and direct-ness"; and his mission was appreciably enhanced by Pétain's decorative quality, which might come in again one day.

But he was disinclined to cultivate his personal publicity at home, dealing sternly with press photographers and pro-hibiting the erection of a statue at Verdun in his own lifetime. His role of Elder Statesman (he had always said that a Com-mander-in-chief should be a statesman) was performed in other ways. He had already indicated his preferences in politics; and he was still the national consultant on military affairs, continuing to sit on the Committee of National De-fence under Léon Blum and Daladier. But his guidance was occasionally offered to a wider public; and when General Chauvineau examined the exciting question, *"Une Invasion est-elle encore possible?"* in 1939, his work was honoured by a preface from the Marshal's pen. The General, who taught at the *École de Guerre,* was untouched by de Gaulle's excit-ing doctrines, holding stoutly that the war of movement was extinct. Arguing that siege-warfare, as conducted under Louis XIV and M. Poincaré, was the normal form of war and that Napoleon had been an improper interruption of its stately evolution, he reached the strange conclusion that the increased speed of modern movement would inevitably militate in favour of the defence. He was not greatly impressed with the utility of tanks, holding that they were entirely useless without infantry and enquiring gravely what could be effected by a raid of tanks. (That was discovered by his countrymen a little later.) His preference was for a new and inexpensive use of concrete in defences; and there would be ample time to put it to the test, since he was sure that Ger-many would not be dangerous until 1945.

This thoughtful composition was adorned with sixteen pages of the Marshal's prose, commending it to French readers. The old enthusiast for the defensive lovingly enumerated the increasing perils of attack in modern war, dwelt upon the author's doctrine that fronts should be continuous upon the spacious lines prevailing in the static warfare of 1915–18, and concluded that "the views of General Chauvineau on the opening of land operations are full of wisdom." Then he proceeded to state a doctrine of his own, announcing with authority that "the continuous front is a fact which it is rash to disregard" and frowning upon "certain tendencies to resume the doctrine of the war of movement at the beginning of hostilities according to the ideas prevailing before 1914." His cautious notion was to avoid defeat rather than to win victory. That was somehow to come afterwards, when the defending armies went over to the offensive. But he had no good word to say for de Gaulle's armoured "*armée de métier*." In the first phase of a war, as foreseen by Pétain, France would stand obstinately on the defensive along a continuous front running the whole length of the frontier; and if the enemy ignored the rules, so much the worse. This was Pétain's military testament, executed in 1938; and as the Maginot Line had been his legacy to France, here was the codicil.

4

The road to Vichy started from Madrid; and when the Marshal went to Spain in March, 1939, as ambassador to General Franco at the end of one more Spanish civil war, he approached the starting-point. The victor owed his success to overwhelming German and Italian aid; and though the policy of non-intervention, by which France and Great Britain remained spectators of the lively intervention practised by General Franco's more enterprising friends, had been an invention of M. Léon Blum, the *Caudillo* was ungrateful to the French. But it was hoped that an eminent ambassador might restore France to his affections. True, he had only sent to Paris a Señor Lequerica, who had been mayor of Bilbao and was connected with a Spanish newspaper that loved the Germans and reviled the French. But France proposed to turn the other cheek. Who could be more eminent than Marshal Pétain, who had defended Verdun and helped Primo de Rivera to subdue the Riff? Besides, General Franco had been one of the Marshal's pupils at the *École de Guerre* and might, it was hoped, appreciate the compliment.

The aged emblem of goodwill, selected by MM. Daladier and Bonnet for this conciliatory purpose, left his train at Hendaye and met a group of smiling Spaniards in the middle of the frontier bridge across the Bidassoa before an interested crowd. They were most obliging; but they kept him waiting for a week in the French embassy at San Sebastian before General Franco was ready to receive the new ambassador. Alacrity had never been a Spanish failing; and though spring weather in the Pyrenees was apt to be severe, it is not easy to believe that snow had interrupted all communication between the north and Burgos. Perhaps dictators liked to keep their aged callers waiting; or perhaps the delay was connected with the awkward question of some Spanish warships which had taken refuge at Bizerta. At any rate, the ships were given up, and the Marshal waited. After a due interval he was graciously received. His life was passed between his embassy at San Sebastian and Franco's temporary capital under the lee of the cathedral spires at Burgos, with trips to Paris for instructions and tours all over Spain; and when business took him to Burgos, they used to find him lunching in a little wood outside the town.

That summer he stood watching in Madrid, as General Franco celebrated victory over his own countrymen with lifted arm, gay smile, and little tasselled cap at a long parade in the broad avenue. Pétain was dressed modestly as a civilian, though when they took him round the battlefields in June, he recalled his military past and was politely reminded of Verdun by Teruel. In August he was at Barcelona and crossed the frontier into France, where his eyes were gladdened by the spectacle of large numbers of Spaniards who preferred the sordid discomfort of French camps to their own country under General Franco. But France had little thought to spare for Spanish refugees that autumn, as the Germans screamed defiance at the waiting Poles and bombed their grounded aircraft in the grey September dawn. The first offensive of a highly unfamiliar pattern was opening; and as the Germans brought war to Europe for the third time in his life, Pétain looked on from the French embassy in Spain.

In October he put on his uniform to honour a military funeral at Pamplona, where they were burying General San-jurjo who had served with him in the Riff and died a martyr, because his plane had failed to keep a revolutionary ren-dezvous in Spain. The indomitable octogenarian toured Spain unweariedly. The Archbishop had been most gracious at Seville; and when he visited the north, his pilgrimage took him to the great cathedral of St. James of Compostella. Now his embassy was in Madrid; and a neutral capital in time of war was a most interesting place. He walked every morning in the Retiro; but he seemed very tired in the afternoons. His German colleague could not have been more polite; they shook hands warmly, when they met; and when Primo de Rivera was buried at the Escorial, von Stohrer and all the diplomats rose as the Marshal walked into the vast chapel, and all the banners of the Nazi youth were lowered as he left. Early in 1940 a trade agreement attested his care for Franco-Spanish harmony; and it was plain that his relations with the enemy had not been unduly impaired by war. Indeed, there were complaints; and that spring a minister in Paris was mildly startled by the Marshal, when his visitor rose to his feet and said, "They will need me in the second fortnight of May."

The war had dawdled through a stationary phase along the

frontier, in which it was conducted on the uneventful lines approved by General Chauvineau. In the monastic silence of his headquarters General Gamelin entertained a caller with his evocation of the stationary wars of the Eighteenth Century, when armies went into winter quarters and nothing happened until a brief, decisive action. That, Gamelin felt sure, was coming soon; and when it came, he believed that it would be swift and terrible, more terrible than people thought. It might come in March; but it was almost sure, he said, to come in May.

It was at the end of March that Pétain told de Monzie they would need him in the second fortnight of May. Was it more than an old man's vanity? He had already told an American journalist that he prayed "that the Germans try to break through the Maginot Line. It can be broken through at a cost. But let them infiltrate through. I'd like to be in command of the Allied army then." But then one did not always tell the truth to neutral journalists; and the Marshal's private views might be less cheerful. General Gamelin did not seem to encourage his interest in army matters; but Pétain was far from satisfied with what he heard about the troops' morale and that, he wrote, was going to be tested in the spring. Had he more reasons for believing that the testing time was coming in the second half of May? It scarcely needed private revelations by his German colleague in Madrid to tell him the season at which active operations would be in progress, although the date was slightly later than that sometimes selected in the last war and was, in fact, that actually chosen by the German high command this time.

But why should he be needed? He had already refused Daladier's request to join the Cabinet, because he had little faith in the Prime Minister. Yet more watchful eyes were turning towards the Marshal. For his old associate, Laval, had been thinking a good deal about him. Impressed with Pétain's decorative qualities in their encounters at home and abroad in

1931 and 1935, Laval had formed the notion of a government of which he would steer the course behind the Marshal's noble figure-head. He was speaking of it so early as
October, 1939, speculating about a war government with
Pétain—"I know his prestige. His name would rally the best
and most active people." When somebody objected that the
Marshal was old and tired, Laval waved him aside—"That
does not matter. What would be asked of him? To be an
ornament on a mantelpiece, a statue on a pedestal. His name,
his prestige—no more."

But Laval was still in the shadows; and here, on May 1,
a new Prime Minister was asking Pétain to leave Madrid and
join the government in Paris. For Daladier had succumbed
to Allied reverses in Norway; and the brisk Reynaud reigned
in his stead. The Marshal took his soundings, calling on de
Monzie once again, who found him "graver and gloomier
than usual. He knows more than I do. We exchanged depressing views." One day he turned up at the Ministry of Marine,
inspected it, and asked for Darlan. "Well," said the Marshal,
"something, at any rate, still works in this country. Can I
rely on you, Admiral?" It was not altogether clear in the first
week of May, 1940, why the French ambassador to Spain
needed to rely on the head of the French navy, even if he
was proposing to join M. Reynaud's administration. What was
coming in the second half of May? They knew before he
reached Madrid. For he left Paris on May 9; and in the night
the German armies launched their assault on Western Europe.

5

He was in Madrid for eight days more; and in those eight
days between May 10 and 17 the Germans changed the face
of Europe. Attacking at a pace and on lines with which their
adversaries were unfamiliar, they had submerged Holland and
were flooding Belgium fast; and their first assault on France,

launched with a nice sense of history and the inadequacy of
General Corap's Ninth Army at Sedan, had punched a hole
in the French line. German parachutists and air-borne troops
alighted on Dutch landing-grounds and Belgian forts; German bombers methodically massacred Rotterdam, while their
fighters machine-gunned refugees along the crowded roads;
and when their dive-bombers came screaming down, the
French gave way. The line which they were holding had
been fortified; but the Parisians, according to a British staff
officer, "stood the noise—there were hardly any casualties—
for only two hours, and then they bolted out with their hands
over their ears like a lot of frightened old ladies." The French
command was left lamenting the destruction of "what they
called 'their physical make-up.' They could stand no more,
they were finished, mentally vanquished, and finally we heard
a word constantly repeated. The armies, he said, were *épuisé*."
Their morale was never strong; and it had collapsed before
the terrifying novelty of the dive-bomber.

France had gone sombrely to war. This was not the mood
of 1914, when they mobilised with songs and flowers in their
hats. It was quite different this time; nobody sang the *Marseillaise* in 1939; and one British resident noted that "there was
no enthusiasm," though he discerned "determination and an
angry acquiescence, a firm courage and resignation." Wars
are not won by resignation; but how could they be blamed?
It was only twenty-five years since they had marched singing to the war; and 1,500,000 of them had not come back.
They had been mobilised three times in the last twelve
months; and this, they felt, must be the last time. People
heard them say '*Il faut en finir*' and were heartened by their
grim resolution to make an end of it. Of what? Of the unrestful Germans, whose intrusion interrupted all their lives
once or twice in each generation, or of the whole business
of war and soldiering? A watchful Englishman, who visited
them at the front, found "no hatred there, no desire to hurt,

no irreconcilable antagonism; but impatience . . ." Impatience has not won many battles; and the French mood was hardly calculated to command victory. But how many of their leaders believed in victory? The French reviews of 1938 and 1939 had made a brave display; but now the generals were silent, and the politicians were already muttering in corners. For French politicians believed in themselves, but not in one another; and their public was touched with a fatal scepticism, born of too much knowledge of French politics.

How could they believe in France, if they were ironically convinced, as one observer read their mood, "that politics were a racket . . . that all political ideals and 'isms' were a matter of salesmanship and that the only thing a sensible man could do was to follow the advice of Candide and cultivate one's little garden?" Profoundly disillusioned, Frenchmen took refuge in a devastating irony. Wit had always been more powerful in France than elsewhere; and perhaps the Germans were right to disapprove of it, since there were few moods less calculated to produce unquestioning patriotism. Besides, the ensuing moral was congenial to every Frenchman, since his primary concern had always been his own affairs. If the community was ceasing to command his loyalty, these would come first and then he would follow where they led him. That was the lesson of the peasant virtues in which France was rich; and as urban faith in politics was burning low, all of them, townsmen and countrymen alike, would go the same way home. French patriotism was exposed to the disintegrating power of these solvents. It was not long since Clemenceau had said, "*Il n'y a plus de pays. Des hommes juxtaposés, ce n'est pas un pays.*" Was France much more than that in 1939? If not, the war was starting with the mood of 1917; and this time there was no Clemenceau to stem the dark waters of disintegration. The old man once wrote that "Athens and Rome, the two greatest things of the past, were swept away on the day that the sentinel failed." Now France was in grave danger; and the sentinel was not in sight.

Pétain watched the swift unfolding of the tragedy beyond the Pyrenees; and everybody in Madrid was saying that he would soon be off to Paris to sign an armistice. If this was how he had felt in 1917 and 1918 (one bitter countryman of his said afterwards that he had always suffered from a suppressed capitulation), there was more excuse in 1940. Besides, he did not seem to share the unfavourable view of Nazi Germany common among his fellow-countrymen; and since his elevation to high military rank he had a touching faith in the International of generals. *"Au fond,"* he once said to a diplomat, *"il n'y a pas beaucoup de différence entre un général français et un général allemand. Ce sont deux généraux. Entre généraux, on s'entend toujours."* If that were so, all that was necessary was the intervention of a soldier of his own professional eminence, and then everything would be satisfactorily arranged. A telegram from the Prime Minister called him to Paris on May 18. He had said that they would need him in the second half of May; and he obeyed the summons. The Marshal travelled through the night; and when the unpleasant news from Belgium met him at the station, he remarked that the Allied advance had been a blunder, adding excusably: *"Nous sommes victimes des neutres."* On the next day France learnt that Pétain was Vice-Premier and Weygand had replaced Gamelin in supreme command.

That was on Sunday; and by Tuesday the Germans were on the Somme at Abbeville, heading for the coast and dangerously interposed between the Franco-British force in Belgium and the rest of the French army. This was the situation which they had all dreaded in March, 1918, when Haig and Foch fought desperately in front of Amiens; and it was enlightening for any readers of General Chauvineau who might be still in doubt as to what an armoured raid could really do. The front, ignoring Pétain's teaching, had obstinately ceased to be continuous; the Germans reached the Channel ports that week; and by May 28 the British and some French in Flanders were backed against the coast. King Leopold surrendered; and that day de Monzie saw the Marshal once again. He found him curiously calm—"Prodigious and noble serenity . . . He has no doubts as to how it will end. We must act as though something could still be done. We are no longer playing for victory, but for honour. 'How,' he asked, 'has *he* brought us to this?' He waved a hand in the direction of vague responsibilities and took mine in his own pair of lovely hands. I have been warned." It was a strange scene in Pétain's little office at the Invalides, as the French and British were falling back towards Dunkirk—the old man, and the anxious politician, and the vague intimation that someone was to blame. If so, it must be a civilian, since the Marshal had just scolded the Prime Minister for speaking irreverently in public of the high command:

"The army is the moral and material defence of the country. In peace, and above all in war, it stands for the best of the nation; it is its only safeguard . . .

"The army is *one*, because it is founded upon discipline. Attacks upon its officers, assaults upon the natural confidence of the French soldier in his leaders gravely compromise our essential strength and diminish it in the eyes of the public.

"The publicity given to dismissals of generals *when we are in actual danger* is, intentionally or unintentionally, derogatory to the army. We are not concerned to criticise steps that were fully justified and *always* occur on the transition from peace to war . . .

"The country naturally forgets the faults that it and all of us have been committing for the past twenty-two years—the taste for a quiet life and the disinclination to make efforts, which have done far more to put us where we are than any individual failures.

"That is the *mea culpa* that we owe, if we would be saved . . ."

This was a depressing document for a Prime Minister to receive from his leading colleague. For at a moment when it was becoming obvious that French military methods were entirely obsolete it breathed the old spirit of military infallibility, dear to French soldiers in the age of Dreyfus; and the sole remedy proposed appeared to be an act of public penance on the part of the entire community.

While Pétain seemed content to despair in Roman attitudes, the military situation was not yet past praying for. True, the campaign in Flanders had ended in the evacuation from Dunkirk of 224,585 British and 112,546 of their allies. But Weygand still commanded the bulk of the French army; and if they were prepared to fight, he was quite justified in telling the Prime Minister that he was "far from hopeless." But were they? General Georges had already declined to order a counter-attack on the ground that he "could not give orders so far in advance of the inclinations of the divisions." That was uncomfortably reminiscent of 1917; and this time there was no British army to take the weight off them. The bitter truth was that, if they ever had the heart to fight, they had lost it now. The spectacle of German air superiority over the battlefield, the crushing weight of German metal, the creeping fear of treachery, and the growing certainty that their own command was quite unequal to the pace and needs of modern warfare all unnerved them; and as mile after mile of France was left to the oncoming Germans, the shaken men confronted with diminishing resistance the contagion of long lines of sad-faced refugees. A fatal mood was growing on them. For an army that begins to wonder what is happening at home is lost.

Paris would soon be behind them. The Prime Minister might use brave words in the fearless old fashion of Foch and Clemenceau about fighting before Paris and behind Paris and then fighting on in the provinces and overseas. But one air-raid had been enough for Paris; and that fatal pride in its perfection, which reappeared in French reluctance to deface the countryside with demolitions, soon denied the unscarred city the more honourable marks of London. A few British troops still fought beside them, where Highland chivalry in Normandy declined to retreat at the pace of their own motor transport in order to conform to the slower movements of a French division, whose transport was horse-drawn. But the immediate course of operations depended on their own efforts; and they were flagging fast.

Pétain left Paris with his colleagues on June 9; and for a confused week the Government was in Touraine. Weygand could still assure the Prime Minister that they had "reached the last round. There is nothing to show that we cannot pull it off in the last round." But when he told the Cabinet that the war was lost and that they must ask for an armistice so that the army might keep order after the defeat, Pétain sat nodding gravely and agreed in a few sentences. That week the Prime Minister heard Mr. Churchill declining sadly to consent to a separate French armistice; and the tragic question was left for further consultation between the allies after a last appeal to President Roosevelt.

The Marshal's mind was quite made up; and as the quiet Loire flowed between the green hills of Touraine, he faced the grim alternatives. The army was receding southwards on a sagging front from the sea to the Eastern frontier, where the unbroken mass of the Maginot Line still waited for an invasion that refused to come where it had been expected. One notion, which General de Gaulle, the new Under-Secretary of War, was pressing upon Reynaud, was that they should withdraw into Brittany until better times and hold the western gate of France in the "*Réduit breton*" with the unconquered sea behind them. The Prime Minister's appeal to Roosevelt, with its statement of an intention to "shut ourselves up in one of our provinces," appeared to indicate that this was his choice. There were even tentative enquiries about

official accommodation at Quimper; and the next stage was
to be withdrawal to Algeria and later, if that were submerged,
to French territory in the New World. After all, this was
no more than the King of Norway and the Queen of Holland
had already done. Indeed, their exiled governments were
actually on foreign soil. But would it suit the French? Weygand preferred capitulation. They had been defeated; and the
French military mind could not escape a modest certainty
that what had happened to themselves must shortly happen
to the British. One soldier told Reynaud that in three weeks
England would have its neck wrung like a chicken; and Weygand, speaking to somebody at Tours that week, gave them
eight days. But he was disinclined to wait so long, since he
had informed his colleagues that the army was responsible
for keeping order; and if it was permitted to dissolve, who
could tell what might happen? This victim of strong political
delusions was haunted by alarming visions of the Communists
in charge of the deserted capital; and when his evocation of
the *Spectre rouge* was inconsiderately exorcised by Mandel,
who telephoned to Paris and found that all was quiet, Weygand refused to be comforted. For French Communism was
not quite so red as it was painted, although obedience to Moscow had imposed an equivocal attitude towards the war. But
Weygand and the high command were for immediate surrender; and when he announced their view, it was acceptable
to Pétain.

The Marshal's choice was stated lucidly in a document read
to his colleagues on June 13, of which the text was subsequently published under his authority:

> "We all recognise that the military situation is extremely
> grave. It is such that, unless the French Government asks for
> an armistice, it is to be feared that the troops will no longer
> obey orders and may be swept away by a panic, which would
> render the army incapable of the slightest manœuvre . . .
> "We must consider the consequences of a continuation of

the struggle. Assuming that we persist by forming a national fortress, its defence could not be entrusted to routed French troops, but only to fresh English divisions.

"Even if this fortress in a coastal area could be organised, in my view it would be no guarantee of safety and would leave the Government exposed to the temptation of abandoning this precarious shelter.

"Now the Government cannot leave French territory without emigrating and deserting. The duty of the Government, come what may, is to stay in the country on pain of ceasing to be recognised as a Government. To deprive France of her natural defenders in a time of general confusion is to abandon her to the enemy, to kill the soul of France—and thus to render impossible her revival.

"The rebirth of France is far more likely to come from the soul of our country, which we shall preserve by staying where we are, than from a reconquest of our soil by Allied guns in circumstances and after an interval which cannot be foreseen.

"I am therefore of opinion that we should not leave French soil, and that we should accept the suffering which will be laid upon the country and her sons. The French Revival will be the fruit of that suffering.

"Thus the present question is not whether the French Government should or should not ask for an armistice, but whether the French Government should ask for an armistice or leave Metropolitan France.

"I declare that, so far as I am concerned, outside the Government, if necessary, I shall refuse to leave France. I shall stay among the French people to share their grief and misery.

"An armistice is, in my view, the necessary condition of the survival of eternal France."

This could not be plainer. If he had to choose between surrender and withdrawal to a distant corner of the country, the Marshal chose surrender. Regarding the French army as incapable of defending Brittany, he was not prepared to contemplate withdrawal to French territories overseas. It seemed quite beyond his comprehension to fight on from North

PÉTAIN IN BAD COMPANY.
The Marshal meets Marshal Goering. St. Florentin in December, 1941.

(Photo: Keystone Press)

Africa behind the undefeated guns of the French fleet. There was a strong tradition in French history against public men who emigrated; and some peasant feeling seemed to bind him to the soil of France. He had not travelled much in a long life; and he did not propose to go abroad. Besides, a prolongation of the war to a victorious conclusion appeared to promise nothing better than the recovery of France *"par des canons alliés"*; and that was a solution for which he had no taste. He had never liked the British, and it would be unbearable to be indebted to them for the continued life of France. A muddled mysticism told him that this was only to be won through suffering; and the sooner they began to suffer, the better it would be.

This strange recital drew from Reynaud the harsh comment that it was inconsistent with the nation's honour. He might have added that Bazaine had been sentenced to death for a good deal less, since the capitulation of a starving garrison after two major defeats compared favourably with what was now proposed. But Weygand and Pétain were insistent; and a growing number of their civilian colleagues began to agree with them. The Marshal had indicated plainly that, if his view was not accepted, he intended to resign. This meant a crisis; and eager politicians scented the familiar atmosphere. The bitter farce was played out at Bordeaux in crowded restaurants and quiet rooms, where Laval saw the Marshal, and Reynaud, a tragic Pierrot, struggled with his dissolving Cabinet and his overwhelming Columbine. Bordeaux had not been permitted to decide the country's fate in 1914. But this time it was the decisive scene. The reply from Washington was inadequate; British consent to a French armistice was made conditional on the despatch of the French fleet to British ports; and a British offer of Anglo-French confederation was barely noticed, eliciting the scornful comment from Pétain that "they want to make us into another Dominion." The Cabinet met three times on June 16; Pétain forced the pace; and when the final meeting ended, Reynaud resigned and before midnight Marshal Pétain left the President of the Republic as his Prime Minister.

6

The first acts of the new Premier were a wireless message to the Germans asking for an armistice and a request to Señor Lequerica for the good offices of Spain. Then he addressed his people:

> "By request of the President of the Republic I assume to-day direction of the Government of France. Sure of the affection of our admirable army struggling with a heroism worthy of its long military tradition against an enemy superior in numbers and equipment; sure that its magnificent resistance has discharged our duty to our allies; sure of the support of those ex-Service men whom I have led; sure of the confidence of the whole people, I give myself to France to diminish her misfortune.
>
> "In these grievous hours my thoughts are with the unhappy refugees who crowd our roads in utter want. I express to them my compassion and my solicitude. With a heavy heart I tell you to-day that we must try to cease the fight.
>
> "Last night I communicated with the enemy to ask if he is ready to seek with us, as between soldiers, after the conflict and with Honour a way to end hostilities . . ."

The dismal voice dragged on until an ill-timed gramophone informed his hearers, on the lifting notes of the *Marsellaise*, that *"Le jour de gloire est arrivé!"*

Three days later, as the French armistice commission got under way to meet the Germans, the Marshal gave his countrymen a few more of his reflections:

> "Not so strong as twenty-two years ago, we had fewer friends. Too few children, too few arms, too few allies—these are the causes of our defeat . . .

"We shall learn the lesson of lost battles. After our victory the spirit of enjoyment prevailed over the spirit of sacrifice. Men demanded more than they gave in service. Men grudged their efforts. Now they have misfortune.

"I was with you in the glorious days. As head of the Government I am and shall stay with you in the dark days. Rally to me. The fight goes on for France, her soil, and her sons."

On the next day the watchers by the railway siding outside Compiègne, where Foch had signed the armistice in 1918, saw gloating Germans and dejected Frenchmen re-enact the ceremony with the parts reversed, outlined in dismal shadow-pantomine on the dusty windows of his railway carriage. The terms—complete surrender, demobilisation and disarmament of all French forces except a tiny remnant, and a German occupation of two-thirds of France (including Alsace-Lorraine)—were a strange comment on the Marshal's notion of good feeling between soldiers and the requirements of French honour, on which he still found a good deal to say. For on the day that the cease-fire was sounded he told his hearers that "Mr. Churchill is a good judge of the interests of his country, but not of ours, and still less of French honour," omitting to inform them that this had called for the liberation of 400 German airmen shot down by the R.A.F. to operate against Great Britain, as well as for a misleading silence on the fact that the scale of British aid to France had been settled by agreement before the war and exceeded in the course of it. Untroubled by the memory of more than 100,000 Frenchmen evacuated by the British from Dunkirk or of 6,000 Highlanders trapped on the coast of Normandy because they chose to travel at the rate of their less mobile allies, he proceeded to the regeneration of his country.

This was to be achieved by an administration of which the leading ornament was Laval. His part in the spiritual programme was still obscure; and there was a danger that, when France recovered from the shock, there might be some reluctance to seek salvation along the Marshal's lines. Even the President of the Republic was only narrowly restrained from leaving for Algeria in order to prolong French resistance; and a shipload of public men (including Daladier and the unmanageable Mandel, whom a long apprenticeship with Clemenceau disqualified for the higher defeatism) had already sailed for Casablanca. France was still the Third Republic; its constitution was still public law; and if that were left in force, there might be complications. For the Chamber, which had been elected in 1936, was due for re-election in 1940; and the inoffensive M. Lebrun would remain President of the Republic until 1946. Elections were distasteful to the Marshal-Premier. So, for that matter, was the Chamber. He had never been at ease there; and the best way out appeared to be a revolution which would relieve him from all further trouble with Presidents, electors, and their Deputies by destroying the Constitution of 1875. The Third Republic was, when all was said, a touching survival of the horse-and-buggy age; and France seemed to deserve something more up-to-date. Created in an era of defeat, it was no more than a Weimar Republic that had made good; but now the time had come to end it with an act of legislative violence.

That was the next stage of the Marshal's progress. His capitulation had already consummated a surrender far beyond the basest imputations of Bazaine's accusers. For Bazaine had been condemned for the surrender of a fortress before its starving garrison had been required to do all that (in the judgment of the court) was demanded by honour and duty. But Pétain's surrender demobilised whole armies in Syria and North Africa before they had been called upon to fire a single shot and disarmed an undefeated navy. Then he proceeded to a step Bazaine had never thought of. Since it was not enough for him to rule France as Prime Minister of the Third Republic, the intrepid octogenarian replaced it with a new form of government consisting of himself.

This revolution was effected in the second week of July by the promulgation of a Constitution Act with the regal opening, "We, Phillippe Pétain, Marshal of France, hereby declare . . .", which left its beneficiary Head of a new creation termed 'L'État Français' and modelled on the neighbouring dictatorships of Spain, Germany, and Italy. France was no longer a democracy, and all authority resided in the Marshal. Inaugurated by an old man at a health-resort, this organism coincided in extent with the shrunken limits of Unoccupied France; its foremost legislator was Laval; and its leading institution was a veteran of eighty-four, who had assumed the post of *Chef d'État*, as his dazed and shaken country peered uncertainly into an uninviting future.

7

An ignoble parenthesis in French history, the Vichy Government had an effective life of two years and four months between its institution in July, 1940, and its effacement by the German occupation of the whole of France in November, 1942. In form it was a monarchy in the modern manner. The Marshal's tone was less paternal now. "My ministers," he said, "are responsible to me and to me alone. I am the man on whom History will pass judgment. Hitherto I have spoken to you as a father. To-day I command you as your leader." France had not heard such language since Napoleon, although it was familiar in German and Italian ears. But Pétain's affinity was rather with the Spanish model. He had fraternised with Primo de Rivera and adorned Franco's triumph in Madrid. Like them, he was a soldier; and since dictators of their pattern were expected to be devout, he discovered unsuspected depths of piety. A simultaneus enthusiasm for the family illuminated this determined bachelor, who had postponed marriage until he reached the age of sixty-four and, one of a family of seven, was never seen with his own relations. But as it had set out to be the antithesis of the Third Republic, the new French monarchy must be nothing if not *bien-pensant*.

Pious, commanding, and severe, the sovereign of eighty-four began his reign without uncertainties except as to the succession; and since this problem was of some urgency, it was solved from time to time by palace revolutions. For the new French monarch had a nice, if fluctuating, taste in Dauphins. At first his affections rested on the unprepossessing head of Laval. But when his heir presumed too far, the Marshal promptly disinherited him, installing Darlan in his place. This idyll lasted for a year, until Laval's charms prevailed once more; and as the shameful months dragged by, his subjects (who were not consulted) watched a Lear, obstinate and tremulous, balancing uncomfortably between a parliamentary Goneril and a sea-faring Regan.

France responded to this strange autocracy with something more than dull acquiescence. For it had always been their way to desert defeated governments. Two Bonapartes had ended that way; and there was no reason why the Third Republic should be spared. Apart from the inherent vice that it had lost a war, it had other weaknesses, which politicians of the Right were eager to repair by drastic treatment. In the last war Charles Maurras and his friends had subordinated their convictions to the national emergency. But this time they gave full play to their views regardless of the country's situation; and large sections of the public were not unresponsive. Confronted with authority embodied in the Marshal's person, they learned to cheer his white head; and his countrymen were drawn to this living fragment of their past, because it was somehow comforting to remember Verdun out of the depth of their defeat. Besides, a latent craving for strong government had worked in them for years. One observer had already diagnosed their "*nostalgie du pouvoir fort*"; and after their cruel experiences they had little heart for resuming the swift, exciting game of politics. It was arguable that their failures had some connection with this form of sport, although it was not clear that salvation was to be found in a military caste which had proved itself totally inadequate for modern war. Indeed, there was some irony in turning to the Marshal, who had staked their future on the Maginot Line. But drowning men are rarely critical of planks; and they clung desperately to this fragment of the past, which seemed to promise that their problems would be solved without mental effort on their part. That was, to weary men, the supreme merit of strong government; and the inverted appeal of Pétain's military prestige to a nation in eclipse afforded the strange spectacle of the Bonapartism of defeat.

For victory was not the sole spring of military autocrats, since Primo de Rivera had come into power after the reverse at Anual, and a defeated nation had turned to a German Marshal after the failures of 1918. Europe had already seen the Cæsarism of defeat in Germany; and as Pétain followed suit, the young hopefuls of French Fascism (most of whom had started life as Communists) waited to play Hitler to his Hindenburg. But he had watched a better precedent in France, when the wounds of 1870 were healed by another Marshal and men sang songs in honour of

> *Notre Bayard couvert de gloire,*
> *Notre chef, illustre vaincu.*

Was Mac-Mahon in his mind, when Pétain came to power? He had watched the Marshal when he was a young man after the defeats of 1870; and now he was a Marshal too, and there had been still more defeats. Mac-Mahon had once proclaimed *"l'ordre moral"* and presided over a penitential mood in France. That was when Pétain was at St. Cyr, fresh from the Dominicans at Arcueil; and what seemed good to the cadet might still appeal to him at eighty-four, when Pétain was himself *'Notre chef, illustre vaincu.'*

His calls to penitence were uttered at brief intervals over the air in mournful tones, compared by one ecstatic follower to *"ce son de cloche grave et presque sévère,"* a comparison that irresistibly recalls Courteline's less appreciative rendering of *"ce timbre grave et lent propre aux horloges de province."* Now the old schoolmaster in him rose to heights of pedagogy on a national scale; and he did not refrain from dogmatic statements on the cause of all his country's evils, which he diagnosed pontifically as the consequences of too much individualism. His admirers produced a sickly literature of his praises, which occasionally soared into hagiography with such outpourings as *Quand le Maréchal Pétain prend son bâton de pélerin.* Strongly flavoured with the nostalgia of defeat (since its favourite personalities were Roland and St. Joan, and its favourite resort St. Helena), it was pervaded by a strange impression that he was engaged in saving France from the English. In a sense he was, since a strong aversion for his former allies appeared to guide his foreign policy. For his capitulation had been based upon the imminent collapse of Britain; and the longer it was postponed, the more inexcusable the armistice became.

Born of the armistice, the Vichy Government proceeded with the renovation of its truncated country, as this process was understood by Fascists. The forbidden note of *'Liberté, Egalité, Fraternité* was replaced by the anæmic substitute, *'Travail, Famille, Patrie.'* Youth received its due homage, since both Italy and Germany were understood to have been regenerated by excited adolescents. Clemenceau had once spoken harshly of *"des jeunes gens . . . avec des idées de vieux"*; and the aged Marshal found no difficulty in getting on with youth of this calibre, although he seemed to find Borotra's conversation at a Festival of Youth a shade exhausting. It was not easy to preside with dignity over a Round Table, of which the Galahad was Laval. But this difficulty was removed before the end of 1940; and the Marshal breathed his relief to an American reporter, to whom he spoke of the late heir in terms of physical repugnance. Darlan succeeded him as Dauphin; and though admirals are rarely strong in sociology, his dislike of the British (who embarrassed French sailors with the distasteful memory of Nelson and had shelled his precious warships at Oran) left nothing to be desired. But when his turn to go arrived in 1942, the mutable testator who ruled France at eighty-six informed the world that there was not a cloud between himself and Laval and that "he has given me his hand, and hand in hand we shall march forward."

The sombre truth was that, so long as the wheels went round, the old man was content. The war was over; and the clear French trumpets were only heard where de Gaulle's brave remnant still fought on. The abject philosophy of salvation by surrender had prevailed. France had denied her origins; and the politicians, whom Marshal Pétain had found such a burden, were put on trial at Riom. French soldiers had never been judicial; and since the Marshal had already announced that the prisoners were guilty, the trial somehow lacked conviction. But no doubt the Germans would be gratified, if a French tribunal had the good feeling to find Frenchmen guilty of having caused the war. (Germans were always sensitive about war-guilt.) But that was not the issue, since the prosecution only charged them with causing the defeat, omitting to say anything unduly harsh (for the honour of the army was now a primary consideration) about General Gamelin. This time a soldier was not to bear all the blame of their defeat. That might have satisfied Mac-Mahon; but it would never do for Pétain, whose doctrine of atonement called for national humiliation upon a wider scale. Bazaine had been his country's scapegoat; but his country was Pétain's.

If they were all to do penance, it would be a good beginning to condemn the Third Republic in the person of its last three Prime Ministers. This would be a salutary lesson for the voters who had supported them. But the grim charade of Riom was not played out, because the prisoners were braver men and better advocates than Vichy had anticipated; and the case was hurriedly adjourned. France, it seemed, was not to have a Reichstag trial. But there was no reason why it should not have Nuremberg laws; and the Marshal's legislative mechanism turned against the Jews. They were easy victims, although it was a little strange to see the torch of liberty that France had lifted to the stars lowered to light the faggots of a new Inquisition. But France must learn to stoop, if they were to move with the times. Besides, an old anti-Dreyfusard was now their ruler; and it would please the Germans.

That was his guiding star. The Germans tantalised him with the hope of recovering a million French prisoners of war on the day of final victory; and this hope drew him to strange meetings with the affable Goering and his incalculable master and down the dismal path of collaboration. A German victory was the one way to justify what he had done; and his policy did nothing to avert it. Indeed, as he walked slowly on his stick across the park at Vichy, where Laval sipped the waters and Darlan sucked his pipe, the Marshal could reflect with modest pride upon a handsome contribution to this agreeable result. The superfluous elimination of French fleets and armies overseas had created a formidable Second Front against the British in Egypt and the Mediterranean, when they seemed barely capable of holding their own island; the opening of French landing-grounds in Syria to German planes threatened to break their Empire's back, whilst a strenuous defence cost his late allies 1,500 casualties; and the master-stroke of yielding Indo-China to the Japanese betrayed them in the East. Few allies have lent nobler aid than Vichy gave the Axis; and the occupation of his little kingdom on Armistice Day, 1942, was a poor reward.

This was the end of Pétain's unhappy reign. For his kingdom

was divided and given to the Germans and Italians, while the Marshal was left uttering disregarded anathemas to his dissolving forces in North Africa. The play was over, with Laval in sole control (if any Frenchman was still in control) of France and an army that refused to listen to the sad, familiar voice ingeminating that he was still their guide and that their sole duty was obedience. Nobody obeyed him now; and they were far from the proud days of "We, Philippe Pétain, Marshal of France . . ."

It would soon be eighty-seven years since a child near St. Omer was named Henri Philippe Benoni Omer Joseph Pétain. "And it came to pass, as her soul was in departing (for she died) that she called his name Benoni." The first son of sorrow never knew his mother; for she died. But when Pétain was born, France, less fortunate, lived on.

8

The last word was with the Duke, surveying with a disillusioned eye the unedifying prospect of other Frenchmen changing sides. He had seen Marshal Marmont and Marshal Bernadotte betray their Emperor; and when the enquiring Mr. Creevey asked him at Brussels in the anxious summer days of 1815, whilst Europe held its breath, if he was counting on any deserters from the French army, Wellington's deep voice replied.

"Not upon a man," said the Duke, "from the colonel to the private in a regiment—both inclusive. We may pick up a Marshal or two; but not worth a damn."

AUTHORITIES

CHAPTER I

1

The world of February, 1811, may be reconstructed from vol. XXI of *Correspondance de Napoléon Ier* (1867), supplemented for routine matters by vol. IV of his *Correspondance Inédite* (1913), for the aspect of the French army by *L'Armée Française* (1885-9) by É. Detaille and J. Richard and *Nos Soldats du Siècle* by Caran d'Ache, and by vol. VII of Wellington's *Dispatches* (1838) and vol. VII of his *Supplementary Dispatches* (1860).

2

The facts of Bazaine's birth are in the *État des Services* exhibited in his trial, and its obscurities are discussed in vol. I of General Palat's *Bazaine et Nos Désastres en* 1870 (1913) and vol. IV of G. Bapst's *Le Maréchal Canrobert: Souvenirs d'un Siècle* (1909); his own comment is quoted from a letter of June 24, 1871, to his sister in the writer's possession. Details of Napoleon's activities in 1811 are in vols. XXI and XXII of his *Correspondance* and of his residence at the Grand Trianon in E. Cazes' *Le Château de Versailles et ses Dépendances* (1910).

3

Bazaine's enlistment and career in the 37th Infantry appear in his *État des Services*, supplemented by vol. I of General Palat's *Bazaine et Nos Désastres en* 1870 and *L'Armée Française* by É. Detaille and J. Richard.

4

The early history of the Foreign Legion in Algeria is to be found in General P. Azan's *L'Armée d'Afrique de* 1830 *à* 1852 (1936) and vol. I of C. Rousset's *L'Algérie de* 1830 *à* 1840 (1887), supplemented by *L'Armée Française* by É. Detaille and J. Richard, *La Légion Étrangère en Espagne*, 1835-1839 (1907), by P. Azan, and *Histoire de l'Afrique du Nord* (1931) by C. A. Julien; Bazaine's promotions, decoration, and wound in his *État des Services*.

5

The operations of the Foreign Legion in the Carlist War, including a number of letters from Bazaine, are recorded in General P. Azan's *La Légion Étrangère en Espagne*, 1835-1839, supplemented by Major F. Duncan's *The English in Spain; or the Story of the War of Succession between*

1834 *and* 1840 (1877), *The Bible in Spain* (1842) by George Borrow, *Isabelle II, Reine d'Espagne* (1934) by Pierre de Luz, *Carlistas de Antaño* by B. de Artagan (1910), and the present writer's *Palmerston* (1926). Bazaine's correspondence with Senilhes and notes on the officers of the Legion are printed by Azan.

6

Bazaine's activities between 1838 and 1842 may be reconstructed from his *État des Services,* supplemented for the siege of Miliana by General P. Azan's *L'Armée d'Afrique de 1830 à 1852* and vol. II of C. Rousset's *L'Algérie de 1830 à 1840;* for the camp of St. Omer and the *Chasseurs à pied* by vol. I of G. Bapst's *Le Maréchal Canrobert* (1904) and *L'Armée Française* by É. Detaille and J. Richard; and for soldiering in Algeria generally by vol. I of General du Barail's *Mes Souvenirs* (1897), Marshal de Saint-Arnaud's *Lettres* (1864), Marshal Franchet d'Espérey's *Bugeaud* (1938), and vol. I of C. Rousset's *La Conquête de l'Algérie, 1841–1857* (1889).

7

Bazaine's activities between 1842 and 1854 appear in his *État des Services.* Material on the *Bureaux arabes* is available in General Azan's *L'Armée d'Afrique de 1830 à 1852,* vol. I of C. Rousset's *La Conquête de l'Algérie, 1841–1857,* and G. Delayen's *Les Deux Affaires du Capitaine Doineau* (1924); military operations in Azan, Rousset, and Marshal Franchet d'Espérey's *Bugeaud,* supplemented by vol. I of General du Barail's *Mes Souvenirs;* personal details as to Bazaine in vol. IV of G. Bapst's *Le Maréchal Canrobert* and vol. I of General Palat's *Bazaine et Nos Désastres en* 1870; general politics in *The Second Empire* (1922) by the present writer.

Bazaine's controversy with Mac-Mahon on the subject of his marriage is placed by Bapst subsequent to his attainment of the rank of colonel in 1850. But du Barail (*Souvenirs,* III, 202) dates it prior to 1850 during Bazaine's tenure of the *Bureau arabe* at Tlemcen as a lieutenant-colonel; and I have preferred to follow the more contemporary witness. Bazaine's *État des Services,* as reproduced in *Procès Bazaine,* 3, dates his official leave to marry May 15, 1852. But General Palat corrects this to May 15, 1854, stating that the ceremony took place on June 12 of the same year; and I have adopted the later date, which is more easily reconciled with the fact that Madame Bazaine accompanied her husband to the seat of war in the same month.

Cavaignac's letter of April 20, 1848, and Mac-Mahon's letter of December 24, 1850, were quoted by Bazaine's counsel at his court-martial (*Procès Bazaine,* 742).

The writer visited Tlemcen in 1928.

AUTHORITIES

CHAPTER II

I

The growth and ingredients of Bonapartism are analysed by the present writer in *The Second Empire*.

2

The literature of the Crimean War is extensive; the French side may be studied in the two vols. of C. Rousset's *Histoire de la Guerre de Crimée* (1878); details in vols. II, III, and IV of G. Bapst's *Le Maréchal Canrobert, L'Armée Française* by É. Detaille and J. Richard, and vol. I of General Palat's *Bazaine et Nos Désastres en* 1870; general history in vol. I of P. de la Gorce's *Histoire du Second Empire* (1908) and the present writer's *Second Empire*.

Pélissier's letter of October 21, 1855, was quoted by Bazaine's counsel at his court-martial (*Procès Bazaine*, 742).

3

The world of April, 1856, may be reconstructed from vol. III of G. Bapst's *Le Maréchal Canrobert* and vol. V of Marshal de Castellane's *Journal* (1897).

Pétain's birth, which is erroneously dated May 24, 1856, by *Encyclopædia Britannica* and B. H. Liddell Hart in his *Reputations* (1928), was officially celebrated in France on April 24 (*The Times*, April 25, 1941) and is dated April 24, 1856 by General Laure in his *Pétain* (1941).

4

Bazaine's decorations and appointments in his *État des Services*, which dates his return from the East as June 24, 1857. This must be an error in the document or in its reproduction in *Procès Bazaine*, since the last French troops left the Crimea on July 5, 1856, and he was appointed Inspector-general of the 18th Infantry district on June 28, 1856. I have therefore followed General Palat in placing his return to France in 1856. Particulars of the Doineau case in G. Delayen's *Les Deux Affaires du Capitaine Doineau* and vol. II of General du Barail's *Mes Souvenirs;* Bazaine's experiences at Bourge in vol. IV of G. Bapst's *Le Maréchal Canrobert;* general history in vol. II of P. de la Gorce's *Histoire du Second Empire* and the present writer's *Second Empire*.

5

The war of 1859 is recorded in vol. III of G. Bapst's *Le Maréchal Canrobert*, vol. IV of Émile Ollivier's *l'Empire Libéral* (1899), vol. III of P. de la Gorce's *Histoire du Second Empire*, and the present writer's *Second Empire*, supplemented by vol. V of Marshal de Castellane's *Journal*.

Bazaine's letter of July 6, 1859, is in the writer's possession.

6

Bazaine's letter of March 24, 1860, is in the writer's possession.

CHAPTER III

1

The genesis of the Mexican expedition is summarised in the present writer's *Second Empire* and vol. IV of P. de la Gorce's *Histoire du Second Empire;* the Jecker claims are analysed in an appendix to G. Niox's *Expédition du Mexique,* 1861–1867 (1874).

2

The literature of the Mexican expedition is extensive and of uneven quality. Apart from summaries in vol. IV of P. de la Gorce's *Histoire du Second Empire,* the present writer's *Second Empire,* vols. VI and VII of É. Ollivier's *L'Empire Libéral* (1902–3), and vol. VII of E. Lavisse's *Histoire de France Contemporaine* (1921), the diplomatic preliminaries are fully analysed in *The Mexican Adventure* (1935) by D. Dawson; and *Expédition du Mexique,* 1861–1867 by G. Niox contains a full military narrative. The aspect and feeling of the campaign may be recovered in its early stages from G. Bibesco's *Combats et Retraite des Six Mille* (1887) and in its later stages from E. de Kératry's *La Contre-Guérrilla Française au Mexique* (1868) and General Brincourt's *Lettres* (1923).

Bazaine's activities are fully documented in vol. I of *La Intervencion Francesa en Mexico segun el Archivo del Mariscal Bazaine* (Mexico, 1907); comment in Bapst and Palat, and a few anecdotes (often unfriendly) in vol. II of *Mes Souvenirs* by General du Barail, who was Minister of War at the time of Bazaine's court-martial; Bazaine's appointment in 1862 in vol. II of Marshal Randon's *Mémoires* (1877).

The writer visited Mexico in 1933.

3

Bazaine's papers from his assumption of the Mexican command in October, 1863, to Maximilian's arrival in May, 1864, are available in vols. II, III, IV, and V of *La Intervencion Francesa* (Mexico, 1908), supplemented by P. Gaulot's *Rêve d'Empire* (1889); military operations in *Expédition du Mexique* by G. Niox, supplemented by vol. II of General du Barail's *Mes Souvenirs;* European diplomacy in D. Dawson's *Mexican Adventure.*

The writer has indicated G. Bapst's extremely circumstantial anecdote of the tragedy of Bazaine's first wife (followed by Palat), although it is rejected by R. Christophe in *Bazaine Innocent* (1938), because it is not easy to discern the motive for fabricating an episode in no way discreditable to Bazaine.

AUTHORITIES

4

Maximilian's reign has attracted a large, unequal literature from E. de Kératry's *L'Empereur Maximilien, son Élévation et sa Chute* (1867) to E. C. Corti's *Die Tragödie Eines Kaisers* (1933) and B. Harding's *Phantom Crown: the Story of Maximilian and Carlotta of Mexico* (1934); personal details in J. L. Blasio's *Maximiliano Intimo* (Mexico, 1905) and H. de Reinach Foussemagne's *Charlotte de Belgique, Impératrice du Mexique* (1925); Court etiquette in *Reglamento para el Servicio y Ceremonial de la Corte* (Mexico, 1865); Bazaine's correspondence in vols. V and VI of *La Intervencion Francesa* (Mexico, 1908-9).

5

The last phase of the Mexican adventure may be recovered from vol. V of P. de la Gorce's *Histoire du Second Empire*, G. Niox's *Expédition du Mexique*, and vols. VII and IX of É. Ollivier's *L'Empire Libéral* (1903-4); Bazaine's correspondence to November, 1865, in vols. VII, VIII, IX, and X of *La Intervencion Francesa* (Mexico, 1909-10); Charlotte's letter of February 14, 1865, quoted by Bazaine's counsel at his court-martial (*Procès Bazaine*, 742); comment and anecdote in G. Bapst and Palat; Maximilian's court-martial in *Causa de Fernando Maximiliano de Hapsburgo, que se ha titulado Emperador de Mexico, y sus llamados Generales Miguel Miramon y Tomas Mejia* (Mexico, 1868).

CHAPTER IV

I

European politics in the present writer's *Second Empire;* military conditions in vol. IV of G. Bapst's *Le Maréchal Canrobert*, vol. III of General du Barail's *Mes Souvenirs*, and Captain L. Le Guillou's *La Campagne d'Été de 1870* (1938).

2

Bazaine's appointments between his return from Mexico in 1867 and the outbreak of war in 1870 in his *État des Services;* his relations with Thiers and the Opposition in G. Bapst, Palat, and vol. IX of É. Ollivier's *L'Empire Libéral* (1904); details of his military activities and opinions in *Considérations Générales* prefaced to Bazaine's *Épisodes de la Guerre de 1870 et le Blocus de Metz* (Madrid, 1883); the possibility of Bazaine as Minister of War in 1869 in vol. III of General du Barail's *Mes Souvenirs;* Bazaine's opinion of Victor Noir riots in vol. XII of É. Ollivier's *L'Empire Libéral* (1905); Madame Bazaine's Court dress in *Chronique Parisienne des Six Derniers Mois d'Empire* (1912) by P. Ginisty and M. Quatrelles L'Épine.

3

The outbreak of war in 1870 is summarised in the present writer's *Second Empire;* fuller narrative in vols. XIII and XIV of É. Ollivier's *L'Empire Libéral* (1908–9).

4, 5, 6, & 7

The bibliography of the war of 1870 is extensive, Captain Le Guillou's *La Campagne d'Été de* 1870 (1938) being the most recent study. Bazaine's own account of his operations is to be found in his *L'Armée du Rhin depuis le* 12 *Août jusqu'au* 29 *Octobre* 1870 (1872), *Mémoire et Rapport sur les Opérations de l'Armée du Rhin et sur la Capitulation de Metz* (1873), and *Épisodes de la Guerre de* 1870 *et le Blocus de Metz* (1883), of which the first was published in Paris prior to his court-martial, the second exhibited in his defence (*Procès Bazaine*, 136–155), and the last published in Madrid after his condemnation and escape. Of other witnesses General Jarras is, in many ways, the most detailed and impartial in his *Souvenirs* (1892); Émile Ollivier in vols. XV, XVI, and XVII of *L'Empire Libéral* (1912–15) is generally favourable to Bazaine; the opposing view is invariably followed by G. Bapst's *Le Maréchal Canrobert* and (where possible) by General Palat's *Bazaine et Nos Désastres en* 1870. These may be supplemented by the detailed analysis of General H. Bonnal's *Le Manœuvre de Saint-Privat* (1904); additional material in General Montaudon's *Souvenirs Militaires* (1900).

8 & 9

The siege of Metz may be reconstructed in immense detail from Bazaine's court-martial. His own narratives are cited above; and General Jarras continues to be an honest, if hostile, witness. Other narratives are available in General Fay's *Journal d'un Officier de l'Armée du Rhin* (1889) and G. T. Robinson's *The Fall of Metz* (1871); Colonel d'Andlau's anonymous *Metz: Campagne et Négociations* (1872) states the case against Bazaine in an extreme form, which reappears in P. and V. Margueritte's novel *Le Désastre* (1899), a military counterblast to É Zola's *La Débâcle* (1892). Full commentaries, uniformly hostile to Bazaine, are available in vol. II of General Palat's *Bazaine et Nos Désastres en* 1870 and E. Bapst's *Le Siège de Metz en* 1870 (1926), a continuation of his brother's unfinished *Le Maréchal Canrobert*. Comte d'Hérisson's *La Légende de Metz* (1889) and *Les Responsabilités de l'Année Terrible* (1891) are favourable to Bazaine and contain much original material including the Marshal's annotations on Archibald Forbes' defence of his conduct.

The writer visited Metz in 1907.

AUTHORITIES

CHAPTER V

I

French reactions to the capitulation of Metz in vol. II of J. Favre's *Gouvernement de la Défense Nationale* (1872); Field-Marshal Sir J. Burgoyne's letter in *The Times*, November 21, 1870 (misdated 1873, two years after the writer's death, by Bazaine in his *Épisodes* and R. Christophe in *Bazaine Innocent*); Madame Bazaine's movements in D. Bazaine's letter of December 15, 1887, printed in Comte d'Hérisson's *La Légende de Metz*; Bazaine's captivity in his *Épisodes de la Guerre de 1870 et le Blocus de Metz*; financial charges in vol. II of General Palat's *Bazaine et Nos Désastres en 1870*, supplemented by Bazaine's letter of November 2, 1870, in the writer's possession.

2

Thiers' preference of Bazaine to command the Army of Versailles in vol. III of General du Barail's *Mes Souvenirs*; Cissey's opinion as to Bazaine's return in Comte d'Hérisson's *Les Responsabilités de l'Année Terrible*; Bazaine's letter of June 24, 1871, in the writer's possession; preliminaries of the court-martial in *Procès Bazaine*, vol. III of General du Barail's *Mes Souvenirs*, and Bazaine's *Épisodes*; d'Andlau's narrative in his *Metz, Campagne et Négociations*, and his subsequent career in U. Gohier's *L'Armée contre la Nation* (1899); Aumale in vol. V of *Journal des Goncourt* (1891).

3

Verbatim reports of the court-martial are available in *Procès Bazaine* (1873) published by *Moniteur Universel* and *Le Maréchal Bazaine* (1874) published by H. Lebrun in *Causes Célèbres de Tous les Peuples*, supplemented by *The Times*, October, November, and December, 1873; paternity of Aumale's "*La France existait toujours*" traced to Bugeaud's "*La France reste*" in G. Bapst's *Le Maréchal Canrobert*, I, 397; Mac-Mahon's decision to commute the sentence in vol. III of General du Barail's *Mes Souvenirs*.

4

Tributes after the sentence in Bazaine's *Épisodes* and E. Peyron's *Bazaine devant ses Juges*; prison life and escape in Bazaine's *Épisodes*, G. Delayen's *Les Deux Affaires du Capitaine Doineau*, vol. III of General du Barail's *Souvenirs*, and Comte d'Hérisson's *La Légende de Metz*.

CHAPTER VI

Bazaine's movements between his escape on August 9, 1874, and arrival in Madrid, June, 1875, in *The Times*; letter of September 6, 1874, to J. Gordon Bennett in *The Times;* address in London stated in his letter of March 9, 1876, to A. Hayter; letters of March 9, 1876, to A. Hayter and March 11, 1879, to Comte de la Chapelle, in the writer's possession; letters to Alfonso Bazaine in E. Peyron's *Bazaine devant ses Juges;* letter of January 6, 1888 (possibly to Comte d'Hérisson), in the writer's possession; death and funeral in *The Times,* September 24, 1888, and Comte d'Hérisson's *Les Responsabilités de l'Année Terrible.*

CHAPTER VII

Post-war politics in G. Hanotaux's *Histoire de la France Contemporaine, 1871–1900* (1903–8), vol. VII of E. Lavisse's *Histoire de France Contemporaine* (1921), J. Bainville's *La Troisième Republique, 1870–1935* (1935), J. E. C. Bodley's *France* (1899), D. Halévy's *La Fin des Notables* (1930), and *La République des Ducs* (1937), D. W. Brogan's *The Development of Modern France, 1870–1939* (1940), and C. de B.'s *Letters from Paris, 1870–1875* (1942); post-war military art in J. Richard's *En Campagne: Tableaux et Dessins de A. de Neuville* and *En Campagne (Nouvelle Série): Tableaux et Dessins de Meissonier, E. Detaille, A. de Neuville, etc.*

Pétain's career to 1914 in General Laure's *Pétain* (1941); army organisation in General Weygand's *Histoire de l'Armée Française* (1938), *L'Armée Française* by É. Detaille and J. Richard, vol. III of General du Barail's *Mes Souvenirs,* and G. Voulquin's *Frontières Françaises;* Boulanger episode in A. Barbou's *Le Général Boulanger: sa Vie Militaire et Politique* (1887) and M. Duplay's *Le Général Boulanger* (1936); Dreyfus case in *Le Procès Dreyfus devant le Conseil de Guerre de Rennes* (1900), *Les Lettres de M. Émile Zola et les Poursuites* (1898), É. Zola's *La Vérité en Marche* (1901), U. Gohier's *L'Armée contre la Nation* (1899), and *Psst . . .!* (1898–9) by Forain and Caran d'Ache; French military thought in Lieut.-Col. de Thomasson's *Les Revers de 1914 et ses Causes* (1919), F. Engerand's *Le Secret de la Frontière* (1918), and E. L. Spears' *Liaison, 1914* (1930); Pétain's choice of a house at St. Omer in General Laure's *Pétain* and *Images du Maréchal Pétain* (1941) by H. Bordeaux.

CHAPTER VIII

I

Pétain's career from the outbreak of war to the end of 1914 in General Laure's *Pétain,* supplemented by B. H. Liddell Hart's *Reputations* (1928) s.v. *Pétain,* E. L. Spears' *Liaison, 1914,* General Lanrezac's *Le Plan de Campagne Français et le Premier Mois de la Guerre* (1920), vol. I of C. E. Call-

AUTHORITIES

well's *Field-Marshal Sir Henry Wilson* (1927), vol. I of *Official History of the Great War: Military Operations, France and Belgium, 1914* (1933), and *Joffre ou l'Art de Commander* (1933) by H. Bordeaux.

2

Pétain's career from his command of XXXIII Corps to that of Second Army in General Laure's *Pétain*, supplemented by vol. II of *Official History of the Great War: Military Operations, France and Belgium, 1915* (1928) and B. H. Liddell Hart's *Reputations*. Personal details in vols. VI and VII of R. Poincaré's *Au Service de la France* (1926-33), E. L. Spears' *Liaison, 1914*, and C. à C. Repington's *The First World War* (1920), I. 84; French religious despair, 1914-15, in R. Poincaré's *Au Service de la France*, V. 205, VII. 194; Bordeaux, 1914, *Ibid.*, V. 260, 293; Maurras, 1915, *Ibid.*, VII. 82.

3

Pétain's account of Verdun is available in *La Bataille de Verdun* (1929), published in English as *Verdun* (1930). This is supplemented by General Laure's *Pétain;* personal details in vol. I of *The First World War* by C. à C. Repington, vol. VIII of R. Poincaré's *Au Service de la France*, and *Mémoires du Maréchal Joffre* (1932); comment in vol. III of W. Churchill's *The World Crisis* (1927), B. H. Liddell Hart's *Reputations* and *A History of the World War* (1930), and vol. I of *Official History of the Great War: Military Operations, France and Belgium, 1916* (1932); and local photographs and maps in Michelin's *La Bataille de Verdun* (1919).

4

Lord Bertie's comment on Pétain in D. Cooper's *Haig* (1935), I. 282; Pétain's religion in C. à C. Repington's *First World War*, I. 549; Pétain's tongue, *Ibid.*, I. 549-50; military discipline, 1917, in General Laure's *Pétain;* politics and Laval, 1917, in H. Torrès' *La France Trahie: Pierre Laval* (1941); antecedents of Nivelle's offensive in C. Bugnet's *Rue St. Dominique et G.Q.G.* (1937); Pétain's views and appointment in vol. IX of R. Poincaré's *Au Service de la France*, vol. I of C. à C. Repington's *First World War*, vol. I of C. E. Callwell's *Field-Marshal Sir Henry Wilson*, and vol. II of D. Cooper's *Haig;* general narrative in vol. III of W. Churchill's *World Crisis* and vol. III of D. Lloyd George's *War Memoirs* (1934); British attitude to Pétain's appointment in C. à C. Repington's *First World War*, II, 68, 72; French mutinies in D. Cooper's *Haig* (1936), II, 118, 134, General Laure's *Pétain*, vol. IV of D. Lloyd George's *War Memoirs* (1934), E. L. Spears' *Liaison, 1914*, 536-7, and C. Bugnet's *Rue St. Dominique et G.Q.G.*

5

Lloyd George interview in his *War Memoirs*, IV, 2129; Lloyd George's judgment on Pétain, *Ibid.*, V, 2929; details in vol. II of C. à C. Repington's *First World War*, vol. II of D. Cooper's *Haig*, and vol. IX of R. Poincaré's

Au Service de la France; Pétain's methods in General Laure's *Pétain;* Clemenceau in his *Grandeurs et Misères d'une Victoire* (1930) and *Les Plus Belles Pages de Clemenceau,* G. Lecomte's *Clemenceau* (1918), J. Martet's *Le Silence de M. Clemenceau* (1929), *M. Clemenceau peint par lui-même* (1929), and L. Treich's *Vie et Mort de Clemenceau* (1929), and *The Liberators* (1942) by the present writer s.v. *Clemenceau;* Clemenceau's judgment on Pétain in R. Poincaré's *Au Service de la France,* IX, 367, 420; Pétain in 1918, *Ibid.,* vol. X.

6

March offensive in vol. I of *Official History of the Great War: Military Operations, France and Belgium,* 1918 (1935); Poincaré's account in vol. X of his *Au Service de la France;* Haig's account in vol. II of D. Cooper's *Haig;* Lloyd George's account in vol. V of his *War Memoirs;* Churchill's account in vol. IV of his *World Crisis;* defence of Pétain in General Laure's *Pétain.*

Doullens conference in same authorities, supplemented by vol. II of C. E. Callwell's *Field-Marshal Sir Henry Wilson,* B. H. Liddell Hart's *Foch* (1931), and L. Treich's *Vie et Mort de Clemenceau.*

Beauvais conference in same authorities, supplemented by vol. II of *Official History of the Great War: Military Operations, France and Belgium,* 1918 (1937).

7

Events between May and December, 1918, in General Laure's *Pétain,* vol. X of R. Poincaré's *Au Service de la France,* vol. II of D. Cooper's *Haig,* vol. VI of D. Lloyd George's *War Memoirs,* B. H. Liddell Hart's *Foch,* and General H. Mordacq's *L'Armistice du 11 Novembre 1918* (1937).

CHAPTER IX

1

Pétain in 1919 in C. E. Callwell's *Field-Marshal Sir Henry Wilson,* II. 189, C. à C. Repington's *First World War,* II. 539–41, and H. Bordeaux's *Images du Maréchal Pétain* (1941); marriage in *The Times,* September 15 and 16, 1920; work as Inspector-General of the Army in General Laure's *Pétain;* Pétain in Morocco, *Ibid.,* supplemented by H. Celarié's *L'Épopée Marocaine* (1928), A. Maurois' *Lyautey* (1931), and V. Blasco-Ibañez's *Alphonse XIII démasqué; la terreur militariste en Espagne* (1924); Pétain and Maginot Line in General Laure's *Pétain,* supplemented by his own *Verdun;* politics in D. W. Brogan's *Development of Modern France* and H. Torrès' *La France Trahie: Pierre Laval.*

2

Pétain as Inspector-General of Air Defence and Minister of War in General Laure's *Pétain,* supplemented by D. W. Brogan's *Development of*

AUTHORITIES

Modern France and C. de Gaulle's *Vers l'Armée de Métier* (1934), published in English as *The Army of the Future* (1940).

3

Pétain's opinions and political activities in *Images du Maréchal Pétain* by H. Bordeaux, *L'Affaire Frogé* (1934) by R. Christian-Frogé, *The Twilight of France, 1933-1940* (1942) by A. Werth, and *Pétain-Laval: The Conspiracy* (1942) translated by M. Sadleir, supplemented by General Laure's *Pétain;* military opinions in Pétain's preface to General Chauvineau's *Une Invasion est-elle encore possible?* (1939).

4

Pétain's embassy to Spain in General Laure's *Pétain,* supplemented by *The Twilight of France* by A. Werth, *Pétain-Laval: The Conspiracy,* W. Shirer's *Berlin Dairy* (1941), E. J. Bois' *Truth on the Tragedy of France* (1940), and news-reel material kindly made available by British Movietonews Ltd.; Gamelin's views in J. Romains' *Sept Mystères du Destin de l'Europe* (1941).

5

Outline of military operations in Lord Gort's Dispatches, *London Gazette,* October 10, 1941, I. Hay's *The Battle of Flanders, 1940* (1941), *The Diary of a Staff Officer at Advanced Headquarters, North B.A.A.F.,* 1940 (1941), and E. Linklater's *The Highland Division* (1942); French morale in W. S. Maugham's *France at War* (1940), A. Koestler's *Scum of the Earth* (1941), and R. Balbaud's *Cette "Drôle de Guerre"* (1941); Pétain's activities and opinions in General Laure's *Pétain, Pétain-Laval: The Conspiracy,* M. Dejean's *Le Complot Pétain* in *France,* April 11, 1942, P. Reynaud's letter of April 5, 1941, to Pétain in *France,* March 12, 1942, supplemented by E. J. Bois' *Truth on the Tragedy of France* and P. Barrès' *Charles de Gaulle* (1941); Pétain's memorandum of June 13, 1940, in General Laure's *Pétain,* 432-3.

6

Pétain's Premiership in General Laure's *Pétain,* supplemented by E. J. Bois' *Truth on the Tragedy of France;* armistice and Vichy revolution in *The Government of Vichy* (1942) by P. Tissier and *Pétain-Laval: The Conspiracy.*

7

Vichy Government in *The Government of Vichy* by P. Tissier, supplemented by *Pétain-Laval: The Conspiracy,* T. Kernan's *Report on France* (1941), G. Winter's *This is not the end of France* (1942), A. Arenstam's *Tapestry of a Debacle* (1942), and newsreel material kindly made available by British Movietonews Ltd.

8

Wellington's judgment on French Marshals in *The Creevey Papers,* 228.

INDEX

INDEX

INDEX

INDEX